HARVARD STUDIES
IN COMPARATIVE LITERATURE

FOUNDED BY THE GENERAL EDITOR

WILLIAM HENRY SCHOFIELD

PROFESSOR OF COMPARATIVE LITERATURE
IN HARVARD UNIVERSITY

IV

MEDIAEVAL SPANISH ALLEGORY

TOMB OF ALFONSO TOSTADO DE MADRIGAL
CATHEDRAL OF AVILA

HARVARD STUDIES IN COMPARATIVE LITERATURE
VOLUME IV

MEDIAEVAL SPANISH ALLEGORY

BY

CHANDLER RATHFON POST

ASSISTANT PROFESSOR OF GREEK AND OF FINE ARTS
IN HARVARD UNIVERSITY

GREENWOOD PRESS, PUBLISHERS
WESTPORT, CONNECTICUT

Library of Congress Cataloging in Publication Data

Post, Chandler Rathfon, 1881-1959.
   Mediaeval Spanish allegory.

      Reprint of the 1915 ed. published by Harvard Univer-
   sity Press, Cambridge, which was issued as v. 4 of
   Harvard studies in comparative literature.
      Includes bibliographical references.
      1. Spanish literature--Early to 1500--History and
   criticism. 2. Allegory. I. Title. II. Series:
   Harvard studies in comparative literature, v. 4.
   PQ6060.P7 1974   860'.9'15   73-137072
   ISBN 0-8371-5535-5

Originally published in 1915 by Harvard University Press,
Cambridge, Massachusetts

Reprinted in 1974 by Greenwood Press,
a division of Williamhouse-Regency Inc.

Library of Congress Catalog Card Number 73-137072

ISBN 0-8371-5535-5

Printed in the United States of America

TO MY MOTHER

PREFACE

IT is my purpose in this volume to trace the development of Castilian allegory from its first appearance in the vernacular during the thirteenth to its culmination in the fifteenth century; but the history of the type may be better followed by some reference to precedents in the Latin literature of the peninsula. The Middle Ages, to which I have restricted myself, may be regarded as extending in Spain to the accession of Isabella the Catholic in 1474, although forewarnings of the Renaissance begin to intrude themselves somewhat before that date. Since, however, allegory does not suddenly cease with the death of Isabella's predecessor, Henry IV, I have added a brief examination of its subsequent vicissitudes, during the late fifteenth and early sixteenth centuries. I do not pretend to have included every example that falls within the period, inasmuch as a mediaeval writer was so to the manner born that he could seldom complete an otherwise unadorned production without lapsing here and there into allegory; but I trust that I have excluded no integral part of Spanish allegorical history.*

* An asterisk or similar mark in the text indicates a note at the end of the volume.

The book falls into two main divisions, the first treating the general aspects of the subject, the second the chronological evolution of the type.

To Professors J. D. M. Ford and W. H. Schofield I am deeply indebted for reading the proofs and for many other services. Professor Ford suggested to me the idea of the work, and both he and Professor Schofield have aided me constantly with the kindest, readiest, and most valuable advice.

Cambridge, Mass., December, 1914.

CONTENTS

PART I

THE NATURE OF MEDIAEVAL SPANISH ALLEGORY

PART II

THE EVOLUTION OF MEDIAEVAL SPANISH ALLEGORY

PART I

THE NATURE OF MEDIAEVAL SPANISH ALLEGORY

CHAPTER I

INTRODUCTION

THE word "allegory" is now employed as a convenient pigeon-hole for such a hodge-podge of writings that the difficult task of definition at once imposes itself upon anyone who is audacious enough to meddle with the subject. I do not presume to offer a definition that will satisfy the conceptions of every investigator, nor am I concerned to establish my own conception against all others. My desire is to discuss a certain type of Spanish literature, for which I must find a name. Since in common parlance most compositions of this kind are dubbed allegories, I adopt the term as a *modus operandi*, waiving any argument with the learned pundits as to its propriety.

I mean by allegory that literary type which crystallizes a more or less abstract idea by presenting it in the concrete form of a fictitious person, thing, or event. Under such a definition would be included the ordinary divisions of mediaeval allegory, of which Spain affords abundant examples. The crystallization of abstractions into fictitious persons is illustrated by the tediously common figures of the Virtues and Vices ; the concrete pres-

entation of an idea through an imaginary thing
appears in a passage of the *Libro de Buen Amor*
by Juan Ruiz, the truest Spanish poet of the fourteenth century, where he advises as a defence
against the Vices the ghostly weapons of the Sacraments and the Virtues; the crystallization of
abstractions into events is found in the descriptions
of the vicissitudes of love as occurrences in a
fantastic garden or forest, and in the eulogies of
potentates by depicting them as the recipients of
honours at pretended courts. Strictly speaking,
those cases in which one concrete thing is figured
under the guise of another are metaphorical rather
than allegorical; but we need not consider separately the few examples produced in Spain, for
instance, the compositions in which Fray Diego de
Valencia depicts human beings under the forms of
inanimate objects, his mistress in the semblance of
a garden of delights, laden with luscious fruit and
melodious with sirens' songs,* and the seven children of Don Fernando of Aragon as so many
plants watered by two perennial springs from Paradise.† Emphasis should be laid in the definition
upon the adjective "fictitious." Allegory starts
with an idea and creates an imaginary object as its
exponent. If one starts with an actual object and
from it receives the suggestion of an idea, one
is a symbolist. The primary difference between

symbolism and allegory is that the former sees "sermons in stones"; the latter from phantom stones builds sermons.

Certain Spanish poems, resembling the French *pastourelle* and the Provençal *pastorela*, describe with picturesque detail the encounter of the author with a maiden in the country under varying attendant circumstances. When these meetings are regarded as ideal, setting forth in concrete form some abstract relationship, such as the perfect union between the lovers, they constitute a species of allegory or symbolism. If occasionally they chance to have a basis in reality, they would fall under the latter heading; but since in the majority of instances they are palpably inventions, I have not sought to distinguish the two types. Characteristic illustrations are afforded by Francisco Imperial, the Sevillan poet of the beginning of the fifteenth century. In one instance he pictures a lady hunting by the banks of the Guadalquivir.* He hurries to dismount at her feet, but she forestalls him, takes the garland from her head, and humbles herself before him. When he beseeches her to desist, she addresses him a whole strophe in French thanking him for the honour that he has bestowed upon her through his verses. The idyll concludes with the writer's offer of his services. The episode is an exquisite allegory of the poet's devotion to his lady and of her gratitude. If such an event actually occurred, similar in all details or merely in the underlying idea, it is still conceived as typical of the harmony existing between the pair.

In all probability, however, these incidents are imaginary, for they readily pass into the realm of fancy. In another poem* of this very sequence to the lady whose identity he conceals under the title *Estrella Diana*, he represents himself as about to do battle for her before the Court of Love, encased in armour forged out of her different charms, and in a third † he apostrophizes Poetry and Rhetoric, who have enthroned themselves in her. Again, within the limits of a single piece, ‡ the author, who is probably Imperial, begins as if recounting a real meeting, and then soars serenely off into the domain of pure invention. Floating in a boat upon the Guadalquivir, he espies his lady upon the island of Sancho Afán, bow and arrow in hand, amidst "laurels of fresh verdure." Heedless of her warning not to disembark, he leaps upon the shore, only to receive a wound from her poisoned shaft. She has stricken him down for an offence against her, but upon his denial of serious guilt she bids him extract the arrow and pardons him. The delicate narrative crystallizes a strained relationship, but contains such obviously fictitious

elements as the envenomed dart. It is plain, by
the ease with which the author makes the transition from the descriptions of such encounters to
the ordinary sort of erotic allegory and to the
common personifications, that he deems them all
members of the same category.

If allegory be thus understood, what is its connection with that favourite mediaeval type, the
vision?* As by constant manipulation allegorical
composition acquired greater artistic excellence,
the custom became more general of adorning it
with a visionary framework. The reason is not
far to seek. The imaginary events were of so extravagant an order as to distress even the mediaeval man, fond though he was of the weird and
bizarre. No mind can long find food in the utterly unreal. Those who catered to the taste of
the times perhaps unconsciously sensed the difficulty, and discovered a remedy ready at hand. If
they could veil their material in the haze of a
dream, which was the natural atmosphere of chi-
merical happenings, it would seem less remote
from the sphere of human experience and hence
less incredible. Anything might occur in a vision;
the reader could accept, and even relish, allegorical
eccentricities thus enhanced. Since the vision itself was as popular as the allegory for which it came
to be used as an ornament, such a combination

possessed the additional advantage of a double interest. The writer killed two, nay three, birds with one stone : he satisfied the craving for the supernatural, he maintained a pseudo-realistic *milieu*, and he appealed the more strongly to the approbation of his fellows by uniting the two objects of their literary admiration, allegory and the vision.

Inasmuch, then, as any discussion of mediaeval allegory involves reference to the vision, it is not necessary to apologize for tracing its evolution in Spain. The early ecstasies of holy personages, relating visitations of angels or demons, journeys to the other world, or the like, of which the Iberian peninsula produced even many Latin examples, were sincerely thought to be objectively real, and not the imaginative dressing of some spiritual truth. When literature, however, became more and more a conscious art, though there still persisted the description of saintly visions conceived as actual experiences in a comatose state, the visionary form was appropriated as a mere device. During the initiatory stages of the appropriation, it is often impossible to determine, if the subject is religious, whether the writer believed in the events that he unfolded. The best instance in Spain is Gonzalo de Berceo, the monastic poet of the thirteenth century. In his work may be distinguished two, and possibly three, different attitudes towards a purely artificial use of the vision. The *Vida de Santa Oria* is virtually a long series of visions, experienced by the holy nun and her mother, Amuña, the chief of which, constituting the pivot of the whole composition, is Oria's dream of an assumption into heaven and the sight of the throne prepared for her in paradise. The maid's confessor, who wrote the lost Latin biography that Berceo paraphrased, probably had implicit faith in all that he recorded. One can only guess whether Berceo himself put any credence in such decorative details as the column of steps leading into heaven, the mysterious tree in the kind of earthly paradise at the top, and the curious figure of Voxmea beside the vacant throne of Oria ; but it is almost certain that he regarded as true in general outline the saint's journey beyond the veil and the mother's glimpses of her dead husband and of her daughter's glory, and that he bestowed an objective existence upon the various guides and other personages who appear in the world beyond. From elaborate and highly coloured visions like this, however real to the mind of the writer, it is but a step to the purely fictitious journeys of the fifteenth and sixteenth centuries, such as Juan de Mena's experience in the mansion of Fortune

in the *Laberinto*, Santillana's encounter with the
stricken ladies in the *Comedieta de Ponza*, or Juan
de Padilla's circuit through the *Twelve Triumphs
of the Apostles*. If Berceo had not believed Oria's
raptures, he might still have utilized them as an
innocent subterfuge for setting forth concretely and
more effectively the saint's spiritual ascendency and
certainty of bliss.

The *Vida de Santo Domingo de Silos* is nearer the
artificial use of the form. In the one vision that
Berceo relates, Domingo, coming in the midst of
a gloomy region to a river whence issue two
streams, one white, the other crimson, crosses a
glass bridge fraught with terrors, and is rewarded
by two heavenly messengers with three crowns
of unearthly brilliancy, one for holiness in the religious life, one for his devotion to the Virgin, one
for his services to the monastery. Here again,
with Grimaldus, whom Berceo translates freely,
the story probably went for its face value. But to
Berceo the setting itself must have been more or
less imaginary, and the presentation of the crowns
may or may not have been understood as upon a
plane of partial truth. In any case the vision is an
attractive device for making concrete the holy
man's success in the three forms of his activity,
and is thus not so remote an ancestor of that
peculiar Spanish type of allegory popularized by

Santillana and Juan de Mena, the Coronation, in which the author purports to dream that the person whom he wishes to extol is crowned by the Muses, the Liberal Arts, or the Virtues.

If Berceo could with surety be declared the author of the *Libro de Alexandre*, he would then illustrate still better the adaptation of the vision to allegory. In one section of the epic, Nature, afraid lest Alexander steal her secrets and hold her in subjection, is represented as descending through all the accumulated horrors of hell, graphically retailed at length, to seek aid of Satan, and as finally prevailing upon him to convoke an infernal council, in which Treachery proffers herself to stir up Antipater against his sovereign. Although these episodes are not actually a vision of the author or of anyone else in the composition, for the present purpose they may be considered as such, since they are like the details of the ordinary vision of the infernal regions. How much of the story the author or his Latin source, Gautier de Châtillon, accepted, is again difficult to determine; obviously certain details must have been discredited, such as the personification of Treachery and of the Vices who beset the entrance to hell. The participation of Treachery in the council is a concrete presentation of the motive that actuated Antipater. Within certain limits, then, the writer employs this descent into hell as a picturesque device to indicate more vividly the reasons for the rebellion against Alexander. Whether or no Berceo be responsible for the poem, it gives us that point in the evolution of allegory where the vision is partially fictitious and is utilized as a literary artifice.

There is only a short road to travel to the allegorical use of a whole vision. In the fifteenth century the Marquis of Santillana, Juan de Mena, and their successors freely employ a pretended dream for erotic, eulogistic, and all ordinary fantasies, and in some cases even invent a heavenly vision to increase the interest of religious material. For the purpose of setting forth the propriety of canonizing the Dominican, Vincent Ferrer, and the Franciscan, Pedro de Villacreces, the Marquis conceives that, transported to the celestial realms and to the presence of the saints and angels, he hears St. Dominic praying for the double honour and beholds an angel, descending to announce the divine compliance. In a similar fashion, to impress more deeply on his readers the glory of the Apostles, Juan de Padilla indulges in the same sort of vision as is granted to Berceo's saints. The difference is that Berceo more or less believed in these raptures; Santillana and Padilla practised them unblushingly as tricks of the trade.

CHAPTER II

THE CONTINUITY OF SPANISH ALLEGORY

PREVALENT misconceptions of the evolution of Spanish allegory require that from the first we stress its essential continuity. Beginning some fifty years ago with the critical writings of Amador de los Ríos, the accepted view has been that at the opening of the fifteenth century there took place a sharp break with the old literary tradition; that hitherto allegory had not enjoyed wide popularity, or that at least its use in any specified work had not been extensive or elaborate; and that at the dawn of this century, through a widespread imitation of Dante, for which Francisco Imperial was largely responsible, its vogue was vastly increased, but in a form differing widely from the precedent set by the few examples already existing in the peninsula. Amador de los Ríos emphasized rather the newness of the allegorical type that was derived from the *Divine Comedy* and began in the fifteenth century.* Puymaigre went so far as to stress the importance of Dante in actually introducing allegorical expression into Spain, contrasting the continuous allegories after Imperial's time with the earlier short, scattered, and

isolated episodes.* Baist distinguished between
the playfulness and superficiality of previous allegory in the vernacular and its serious and pro-
tracted employment by Imperial for a definite
purpose.† His theory is only another aspect of
Puymaigre's opinion. Reactionary in tendency,
the three articles of Savi-Lopez were valuable for
their analysis, however slight, of Spanish allegory
in the preceding centuries.‡ Of more recent scholars, Sanvisenti investigates the earlier allegory in
the peninsula no further than to remark that it prepared the soil for the reception of the Dantesque
seed.§ Farinelli, in a comprehensive recension of
Sanvisenti's book, enumerates the elements that
he believes were brought into vogue by Imperial's
compositions : the discussion of the Virtues, appearing later in the works of Fernán Pérez de
Guzmán, Santillana, Gómez Manrique, Diego de
Burgos, Juan de Padilla, and Álvarez Guerrero ;
the conception of Fortune from the seventh canto
of the *Inferno;* the *selva selvaggia;* and the old
man as guardian of purgatory.||

On general principles, however, the sudden introduction, interruption, or alteration of the allegorical tradition is unlikely. If there is one thing
above all others that modern methods of study
have taught, if there is one thing that persistent
delving after origins has revealed, it is this : artis-

tic and literary movements do not leap forth into history unheralded and full-grown, but are the result of the ordinary process of generation. The principle of evolution applies with particular emphasis to Spanish allegory, the history of which was graced by no supreme genius who by sheer force of personality could materially change its character. It is not a sudden and isolated phenomenon, but a gradual development. The mature examples of the fifteenth century are produced by a long growth, the transitional stages of which can be clearly discerned.

The continuity of Spanish allegory I shall hope to demonstrate in the course of the later discussion. We shall find that the tendency to allegorize is as deep-rooted in the Iberian peninsula as in any other district of Europe, nay, more so, if priority in time is of any significance, for the first Christian manipulation of allegory as the setting of a whole composition is the achievement of Prudentius. It is like carrying coals to Newcastle to ascribe the allegorical inclination to foreign influences when the very tradition of its Christian use has a foundation in Spain. There was no need of extraneous stimulus to expression in this *genre* for a race that could produce a Villena, who, just as Landini read into the *Æneid* an intricate Neo-Platonic allegory, discerned in Virgil's poem a veil for the ages of man, the Virtues and Vices, as well as the brevity of human life, and who created an allegorical setting for a treatise on leprosy! The chief elements of allegory written in Spanish are present in the older Latin literature of the country. The first attempts in the vulgar tongue stand in such close relation to those in Latin that they are sometimes mere translations, and the connection between the early Christian centuries and the Middle Ages is unbroken. The first Spanish examples are in all essentials similar to those of the fifteenth century, the heyday of Spanish allegory. The products of the later period cannot be divorced from those of the thirteenth or fourteenth centuries. The greater interest in the type evinced about 1400 is not to be assigned to the influence of Dante, but to natural laws of development; it is the culmination of a gradually unfolding movement. The step from the attitude of Juan Ruiz towards allegory in the fourteenth century to that of Imperial in the fifteenth is no broader than the step from Berceo in the thirteenth to Juan Ruiz. The advance is constant. Not only is the proportion of allegory greater in the extant works of the latter than in those of any of his predecessors, and equal to the proportion in Santillana himself, but in nature it resembles the allegorical products of John II's court. The works

of Berceo, Juan Ruiz, and the anonymous writers
of the elder days are not to be regarded as preparation for the reception of exotic elements, but
rather as the primitive stages of fully matured
native productions, say, sometimes themselves at
an identical degree of development. Nor is there
any sudden change within the fifteenth century
itself. The old types are improved by Imperial
and receive still higher artistic expression in Santillana and Juan de Mena, whose followers simply
elaborate upon their models.

With Don Enrique de Villena and Juan Rodríguez de la Cámara, beside the still persisting
classes appears a slightly different type, derived,
not from Dante, but from the antiquarianism that
had been slowly overspreading the peninsula; so
that, as far as the Renaissance in Spain is traceable to native and not to Italian sources, this new
kind of allegory may be called indigenous. If,
however, Villena was conversant with the Spaniard Theodulfus, who employed the type in the
ninth century, he would afford another instance
of continuity, merely resuscitating a form that for
the nonce had fallen into desuetude.* It varies
in no determinative manner from the traditional
classes, for the innovation consists chiefly in the
bestowal of classic titles upon the old allegorical
objects. Thus, in Theodulfus, Proteus signifies

truth and Hercules valor; in Villena's *Doce Trabajos de Hércules*, the old figure of Humility is baptized as Atalanta, the old tree of knowledge gives place to the apple of the Hesperides; in the *Siervo Libre de Amor* of Juan Rodríguez de la Cámara the vicissitudes of passion are set forth by the time-honoured method of a journey through a fantastic landscape, but there are such elements in the landscape as the tree of Venus, which betokens amorous success, or the olive of Minerva, which stands for prudent indifference to love. The attitude in these compositions is similar to that of paintings like Botticelli's *Pallas and the Centaur*, the interpretation of which is that the arts of peace, under the Medici, triumph over the excesses of war. This humanistic allegory or symbolism is but a more luxuriant offshoot from the same old trunk, the roots of which stretch far back into the past of Spain.

CHAPTER III

THE FRENCH INFLUENCE

THE best proof of the continuity of Spanish allegory is its dependence, throughout its history, upon France. The taste for allegory is innate in the people, a large amount of the material is of native origin, and its treatment always bears the impress of the racial characteristics. Yet French prototypes modify greatly the Spanish tradition, and, from the earliest appearance of composition in the vernacular, Gallic influence combines itself inextricably with the native elements and becomes an inseparable part of the fabric. It is the woof woven across the indigenous warp. The general assumption has been that Imperial inaugurated a new habit of foreign borrowing, transferring his affections from France to Italy. He is supposed to have founded a new school based upon the prototypes of Dante. The truth lies in exactly the opposite direction. Since Imperial reverts more than before to French models, his poems form an important stage in a tradition already firmly established in the Iberian peninsula. Sanvisenti's belief in a preponderance of the Dantesque over the Gallic influence is untenable, and Farinelli's stress upon northern sources is needed as a corrective. The body of Imperial's poems is French; certain of the decorative details alone are Dantesque. Inasmuch as northern characteristics strongly colour Spanish allegory with the same tone from first to last, they afford an incontrovertible proof of the essential unity of the evolution through the different centuries.

Only a slight acquaintance with the European Middle Ages is necessary to realize that the French influence upon allegory in Spain was a foregone conclusion. It is an axiom that France was the great radiating centre of mediaeval letters. Allegory in its English, German, and (to some extent) its Italian manifestations, was derived from France; and Spain, so closely connected historically with that country, was not likely to constitute an exception.

The relationship is confirmed by borrowings in other fields. I review the most significant examples.* The whole question of the epic is too much in dispute to justify any categorical statement. National prejudice has played a large part in the discussion. The tendency of Puymaigre †\nhas been to emphasize the predominance of France in all forms of Spanish letters; while Amador de los Ríos and Menéndez y Pelayo patriotically champion Spanish originality. Even Menéndez y Pelayo,* however, though he tries to prove that the *Poema del Cid* and the *Crónica Rimada* are French neither in general spirit nor in incidents, and that French and Castilian epics are branches of the same stem, cannot deny northern influence upon certain details. There surely was a stage of translation or close imitation of French epics, represented in the *Crónica General* by the prose paraphrases of a Spanish *Mainet* or *Karlot*, a poem relating the heroic deeds of the young Charlemagne.† The epic on Bernardo del Carpio, so far as its construction can be gleaned from the *Crónica General*, was indubitably a direct imitation of the *Chanson de Roland*, but in its use of French methods to present a truly Spanish hero, it must have embodied a stage one point in advance of mere translation.‡ The evolution is thus far parallel to the naturalization of the French epic in Italy, but there is no certain trace in Spain of composition in a garbled conglomeration of the two tongues. Ushered in by such a history, the purely Spanish type that appears in the *Poema del Cid* surely retains more French elements than Menéndez y Pelayo would admit; the very name, *cantar de gesta*, is of some significance. The later *Poema de Fernán González* still exhibits traces of Gallicism in the author's allusion to Roncesvalles, expressing sorrow that the prowess of Bernardo del Carpio had not changed it into a victory over the Moors.* With regard to the cultured epic, it is possible that the *Libro de Apolonio* was not derived, as is usually assumed, from the *Gesta Romanorum*, but from the French *Jourdain de Blaie*.† Fitzmaurice-Kelly,‡ although clinging to the source in the *Gesta Romanorum*, acknowledges that the new monorhymed quatrain of verses of fourteen syllables, the so-called Alexandrines, points to French or Provençal influence. The *Libro de Alexandre* is a somewhat free translation of the Latin *Alexandreis* of a Frenchman, Gautier de Châtillon, with additions from the *Roman d'Alexandre* of Lambert le Tort and Alexandre de Paris, from the version in lines of ten syllables by the "clerc Simon," § and from other sources. The lost epic mentioned by Santillana in his *Proemio*, the *Votos del Pavón*, was a translation or adaptation of Jacques de Longuyon's *Voeux du Paon*.||

Religious verse is not less imitative. The relation of Berceo's visionary and allegorical passages to the north is corroborated by the derivation of the *Signos que Aparescerán ante del Juicio* from the *Quinze Signes* ¶ and the possibility that the *Duelo de la Virgen María* is translated from a fragment of a lost Latin mystery written in France. Of a somewhat earlier period, the anonymous *Vida de*

Santa María Egipciaca is an adaptation of the *Vie de Sainte Marie l'Egyptienne*, and the *Libro de los Tres Reyes de Oriente* is certainly based upon a French model.* The Spanish mystery on the three wise men is also evolved from the Benedictine liturgy of Orléans.

Prose composition is saturated with French elements. In the reign of Sancho IV (1284–95) a translation was made of Brunetto Latini's *Livres dou Trésor* by the King's surgeon, Alfonso de Paredes, and his secretary, Pero Gómez; † and upon it were based encyclopaedic compilations such as the *Castigos y Documentos*. A more pretentious literary effort, begun perhaps under Alfonso X, continued under Sancho, and possibly not finished until the reign of Alfonso XI,‡ was the *Gran Conquista de Ultramar*, dealing with the period from the beginning of the Crusades down to the death of St. Louis, and comprising translations from several French sources.§ Chief among these was Guillaume de Tyr's *Historia* (or a French translation of it); less important were the French *Chanson de Jérusalem* and the Provençal *Cansó d'Antiocha*, and for subordinate incidents, *Berthe au Grand Pied* and *Le Chevalier au Cigne*. Shorter prose fiction, also, has its roots partly in France, as is witnessed by the translations in the Escorial manuscript: *Un noble cuento del emperador Carlos*

Maynes de Roma from the fragmentary *Sébile*; *El cuento muy fermoso del emperador Otas de Roma* from the *Florence de Rome*; *Un muy fermoso cuento de una santa emperatriz* from a *dit* of Gautier de Coincy; the *Estoria del Rey Guillelme* from a redaction of Chrétien's *Guillaume d'Angleterre*;* and another *Santa María Egipciaca* and the *Santa Catalina*, based on French prose versions.† At the instance of Alfonso XI was undertaken a translation of the *Roman de Troie* of Benoît de Sainte-More.

In the Archpriest of Hita the case for the Gallic provenience of much of the allegory, to which I shall return presently, is strengthened by other northern borrowings in the poem. Possibly he drew the inspiration for his *serranillas*, or mountain-songs, from the widely prevalent type of French *pastourelle*.‡ Even Menéndez y Pelayo,§ whose patriotism here again leads him to deny any essential French influence, admits northern derivation in the case of satirical tendencies. The French provenience of some of his *enxemplos* is generally conceded.‖ The tale of the drunken hermit was taken from two *fabliaux*, *L'Eremite qui s'enyvra* and *L'Ermyte que le Deable conchia du coc et de la geline*.¶ The poet himself in another instance states his source:

Esta fabla conquesta, de ysopete, sacada,**

that is, one of the collections of Aesopic fables, called *Isopet*, whether written by Marie de France or by some *trouvère* of the thirteenth or fourteenth century.*

During the first centuries of composition in the vernacular, therefore, the whole stream of Spanish letters felt a vigorous impulse from the great flood of production across the Pyrenees. In the fifteenth century the habit of French imitation still persisted. At the beginning of the period, the reign of John II, its most pronounced manifestation, as I shall seek to prove, was to be found in the allegorical poets, who were the principal literary figures of the time. The epic, which in the preceding period yielded clear instances of northern leanings, was dead; but in pseudo-historical prose, the *Mar de Historias* of Fernán Pérez de Guzmán is largely an adaptation from a French version of Guido delle Colonne's *Mare Historiarum.*† That the "matter of Britain" was still popular is indicated by several allusions in the poets of the *Cancionero de Baena*, most interesting among which are those to some version of that best of late chivalrous romances, the *Amadís de Gaula*. Whether this unpreserved version was Portuguese or Castilian, the references at least reveal a continued admiration for the French romances, since even though the *Amadís* can as yet be traced to no particular original, it was greatly indebted to the Breton cycle.*

With the reigns of Henry IV and of the Catholic Kings, the energy begins to die out of allegory, and although the number of allegorical compositions is still legion, their authors usually imitate or elaborate upon their great predecessors of the former generation. Gómez Manrique, Diego del Castillo, Juan de Andújar, receive the French influence through Santillana and Juan de Mena rather than directly. The mediaeval types of literature are waning, and with them the Gallic inspiration that has been dominant throughout the Middle Ages. An interest in Italy is substituted, yet not in the Italy of Dante but in that of the Renaissance. The Spaniards are becoming more original, and are no longer under such obligations to foreigners. The native drama takes a vast stride forward under the guidance of Juan del Encina and the author of the *Celestina;* the satire of the *Coplas del Provincial* and the *Mingo Revulgo* is essentially Spanish in tone; Jorge Manrique's sepulchral ode, even if some Arabic or other platitudes flitted through his mind, is a product, in all that matters, of his own genius. Just as French elements, however, are reflected in the late manipulators of allegory, so the publication of the first extant version of the *Amadís de Gaula,* in

1508, betrays a lingering fondness for the chivalrous romance. The important fact is that northern
influence continues potent in other types of literature during the period when allegory reaches its
height, the reign of John II.

CHAPTER IV

THE ITALIAN INFLUENCE

THE study of the nature and genesis of Spanish allegory, as we have had occasion to note, has hitherto been beclouded by the dependence of scholars upon the statements of a critic whose general achievement was so considerable as to gain credence for certain mistakes in detail that were the results, partly of the defective knowledge and methods of his time, partly of a too readily synthetic mind. Amador de los Ríos, in his desire to reduce the complexity of literary factors to a few simple formulae, ascribed every form of allegorical manifestation in the fifteenth century to the influence of the *Divine Comedy*. Having once made this assumption, *a priori*, it was easy enough for him, since Dante's poem includes so many different aspects of mediaevalism, to discern more or less exact analogies to Spanish productions. Amador's theory has prevailed from the middle of the last century, when he wrote, down to our own day. Sanvisenti, though he assumes the attitude of an independent investigator, really makes no advance. Farinelli stresses more than any previous writer the French elements in Span-

ish allegory, yet fails to shake himself absolutely
free of the time-hallowed tradition.

My conviction is that we must break completely
with this long line of criticism. I shall seek to demonstrate that in those few instances in which the
influence of Dante in Castile is distinguishable it
is inorganic and, for all practical purposes, infinites-
imal, not determining to any appreciable degree the
nature of the compositions wherein it occurs. The
sporadic borrowing is restricted almost entirely
to the *Inferno* and *Purgatorio*, the *Paradiso* being
usually found too abstruse. The assertions regarding imitations of the *Vita Nuova* and the *Canzoniere*
may be denied absolutely ; no one has claimed that
Dante's other works made any impression in Spain.
The occasional use of Benvenuto da Imola's commentary is evidence of the tendency that led
Spaniards to prefer later Italian treatments of
Dantesque material to the *Divine Comedy* itself.
Imperial began the petty thieving ; and, on antecedent probability, it was not likely that his successors could learn from him the habit of robbery
on a large scale. The Marquis of Santillana goes
no farther in his pilferings ; and Juan de Mena
almost completely abandons the practice. In Diego
de Burgos, imitation of the *Divine Comedy*, though
more extensive than in anyone else during the
century, is restricted almost wholly to a number

of scattered stylistic reminiscences, and does not affect the general allegorical content. The determinative personalities who impart the tone to the literature of the period, the Marquis of Santillana and Juan de Mena, do not model themselves upon Dante. Juan de Padilla, at the beginning of the sixteenth century, forms an isolated instance of a more vital study of the Italian poem.

The chief reason for the unimportance of Dantesque influence in Spain is that an allegorical tradition existed already, largely dependent upon France and so securely founded that it could not be altered. The *Divine Comedy* could not affect its structure organically, but could only supply decorative elements. The difficulty of Dante's allegory discouraged real imitation. He employed the ordinary device of a journey to the other world, but its architecture was so elaborate and the interpretation of the allegory so complicated that the Spaniards hesitated to copy any considerable section. Their appreciation was restricted to certain parts of the machinery that Dante shared with other mediaeval writers, and since these did not differ from the forms that they were already employing, they merely adorned their compositions occasionally with slight details purloined from the Italian epic.

Educated in the mediocrities of French and

Provençal erotic verse, they perhaps found Dante's lyrics of the *dolce stil nuovo*, when not too obscure, at least too lofty and intangible in conception, and they were overawed by the *Divine Comedy*. Dante, as a mediaevalist, might be expected to appeal to Imperial and even to Santillana and Juan de Mena, who, though forerunners of the Renaissance, belonged still largely to the old dispensation ; but he elevates the ideas of the Middle Ages to so high a pinnacle, and so transfigures them with his own personality, that the pupil could seize only upon fragments of the poem and found anything that approached a repetition impossible, for even the best Spanish poets of the fifteenth century were blessed with no more than distinctly secondary talent. When, at the end of the fifteenth, and through the sixteenth century, Renaissance enthusiasm increased, it militated against an appreciation of the poet whose work was at once the type and the apotheosis of mediaevalism. In humanism Spain and France were a hundred years behind Italy, where the interest in the antique was stimulated earlier by proximity to the civilization of Rome. The literature of Castile in the fifteenth century was closely allied to that of the Trecento in Italy. The men of letters at the court of John II thus turned more naturally to Petrarch and Boccaccio,

in whom they found much the same incongruous fusion of mediaevalism and inklings of the
Renaissance.

Of the former it was, of course, the *Trionfi* that
affected Spanish allegory, providing, especially,
both the example and the material for the long
lists of historical votaries of Love, Chastity, Fame,
and similar personifications.* Santillana himself
composed a *Triunphete de Amor* in emulation of
the great Italian, and was assisted in evolving the
type that I have called the Erotic Hell by recollections of the *Trionfi*. Of Boccaccio's works,
the *Amorosa Visione* exercised an influence in
Spain that has never been properly appreciated.
The scene there described as painted upon one
wall of the hall of Glory perhaps led Santillana to
bestow definite form upon that other great allegorical type, the Panegyric, and the pictures in the
hall of Fortune were present to Juan de Mena's
mind when he wrote the *Laberinto*. The *Corbaccio*,
again, is one of the foundation stones for the Erotic
Hell, and the forbidding wilderness where the author finds himself astray is certainly as effective
as the *selva oscura* of the *Divine Comedy* in fur-
nishing a background to the many allegories of
sinister content. Other Italian compositions by
Boccaccio played a less significant rôle. Of the
Latin works, the *De Casibus* performed an encyclo-

paedic office similar to that of Petrarch's *Trionfi*, supplying a list of famous downfalls that was utilized by such rhymesters as Gonzalo Martínez de Medina. It was also one of the numerous sources from which the Spaniards drew their conceptions of Fortune, and, as Santillana himself acknowledges, it suggested to him the idea of the *Comedieta de Ponza.*

Outside of the great Tuscan triumvirate, little Italian influence is perceptible. Upon such sporadic cases as that of Brunetto Latini it is not necessary here to dwell. Possibly the Italian adaptations of the Dantesque matter, Federigo Frezzi's *Quadriregio*, and Zenone da Pistoia's *Pietosa Fonte*, were known to the Spaniards of the fifteenth century and helped to produce the various allegorical types. Fazio degli Uberti's wearisome personifications of Poverty and other abstractions may have found favour in the Iberian peninsula. When the Spaniards did look towards Italy, they were attracted rather by the allegory of Petrarch, Boccaccio, and the other successors of Dante, because its prettiness and playfulness were more in accord with the tradition of their own country and with their own attitude, trained in the school of France, than the severity and intricacy of the "sublime Florentine."

CHAPTER V

UNDER this caption I purpose to mention those subjects for which the Spaniards revealed a special predilection, omitting reference to topics which, receiving but a single or occasional treatment, are not an earnest of the national taste. The origins and evolution of each type I shall analyze more minutely in tracing the historical development of allegory.

The temperament of the race and the reliance upon French prototypes ensured the good fortune of the erotic motive. Various aspects of love are figuratively set forth: the struggle within the soul between chastity and passion, as in the *Libro de Buen Amor* of Juan Ruiz and the *Sueño* of Santillana; the triumph of love, as in the same work by Juan Ruiz and the *Triunphete* of the Marquis;* the amorous wound, as in two of Imperial's poems; the relation between lovers, symbolized by the ideal meeting of a *pastourelle*. The torment of love was voiced in a peculiarly Spanish form of allegory, the development of which will be discussed separately, the Erotic Hell.

Another subject for which the Spaniards evolved

a particular allegorical expression was the eulogy of some famous personage. Compositions of this nature may be described as Panegyrics, an important subdivision of which is the still more essentially Spanish form, the Coronation. Inasmuch as the Panegyric was treated as often as the Erotic Hell, it is likewise reserved for separate discussion.

Thirdly, it became a custom, for which there was some precedent in France, to deck out political matter in an allegorical dress. Imperial thus describes the birth of John II, and Ruy Páez de Ribera the establishment of the regency. The latter even causes a heavenly messenger to outline in a vision the tactics that his compatriots should pursue.* His distinguished contemporary, Villa-sandino, sets the death of Henry III in a figurative framework. Santillana continues the practice by treating political corruption in the *Visión* and the disastrous naval battle of Ponza in the *Comedieta*.

Because of her extravagant passion for didacticism, Spain naturally gave birth to many examples of the common allegorical type by which an abstract quality, such as Justice, Poverty, or Fortune, is analyzed through presentation under a more concrete form, usually personification. The Virtues and Vices, as popular as elsewhere, were honoured with continuous treatment, from the

Psychomachia of Prudentius to Imperial's *Decir de las Siete Virtudes*, Juan de Mena's *Debate de la Razón contra la Voluntad*, and the *Gracia Dei* of Jerónimo de Artés. Their vogue was accentuated by the publication about 1279 of a work that enjoyed wide favour, the *Somme des Vices et Vertus* by the French Dominican, Laurentius, or Frère Lorens.* The figurative explanation of other abstractions, such as Age, Sorrow, and Poverty, became very fashionable at the opening of the fifteenth century in the hands of Ruy Páez de Ribera and Villasandino.

Of allegorical settings, the visionary journey to supernatural or imaginary realms was the most widely employed. The gloomy Spanish nature found satisfaction in visions of hell. In the beginning, they were believed actual occurrences, for example, in the writings of St. Valerius ; finally, the infernal regions were forced into service only as a suitable background for sinister topics, — in the *Alexandre* for depicting the conspiracy against the prince, or, more usually, for amorous despair, when the word " prison " was often used instead of hell. The fondness for such dread experiences was so pronounced that Juan de Mena introduced one gratuitously into his Coronation without giving it a place in the logical scheme and was followed in this inartistic innovation by Diego de Burgos and Diego

Guillén de Ávila, both of whom dwell upon the details of hell more than upon those of purgatory. Thanks to the same gruesome proclivity, the Dance of Death was early naturalized in the peninsula. Fictitious journeys to the supernal regions were almost as frequent. One recalls readily Santillana's *Canonización* and the works of Juan de Padilla. It was most commonly at the end of Panegyrics that heaven or a terrestrial paradise was depicted as the spot where the person eulogized received the glorious fruition of his merits. Juan de Mena and his followers indulge in the common French fiction of a journey to the palace of Fortune, Fame, or a similar goddess; the later exponents of the Panegyric, Diego de Burgos and Diego Guillén de Ávila, seem to have had the Temple of Fame vaguely in mind. In general, a vernal garden or a grove, whether seen in a vision or not, was the approved setting for a pleasant subject, especially for the Court or the Procession of Love; a dismal vale, forest, or desert for an unpleasant subject, as in Santillana for the proclamation of Villena's death, or in Ribera for the debate of Grief, Old Age, Exile, and Poverty.

There is some reference in Imperial and his contemporaries to the Court of Love, the conception of which had been gradually evolved in France.* They imagine it rather under its legal phase. In

one poem Imperial seeks to protect himself against
the darting charms of Isabel González by requir-
ing that she and Venus register their oaths before
the god of Love as judge not to take the poet
prisoner and that they dispatch the signed and
sealed document to him as surety.* In an interchange of verses between Imperial and other poets,
the Court of Love is still regarded in its judicial
aspect, but as the lists in which the decision is
made by an appeal to arms. Fernán Pérez de Guzmán and Diego Martínez de Medina rebuke him
for his insolent praise of Estrella Diana, and the
former cites him before the Court.† Imperial responds, swearing in the hands of his lady, with
Venus again as witness, that he will defend her
honour before the God of Love.‡ Santillana in his
Triunphete de Amor has in mind a Court of Love
of the usual French type, where the god is not so
much a judge as a general monarch, for, though
the Marquis does not transport us to the actual
Court, he causes to defile before us Cupid and
Venus with their retainers.

The most important instances of this fiction, both,
curiously enough, by men named Escrivá, carry
us somewhat beyond our period. In the work of
the Comendador Juan Escrivá,§ in prose and verse,
from the end of the fifteenth century, Love visits
the amorously desperate author, and, on listening

to his complaints, offers to summon his lady to
trial. Escrivá is then borne in a cloud to a kind
of terrestrial paradise, in the midst of which, on
an orange-grown hill surrounded by a stream, is
the god's domain. He is ferried across by Care in
the bark of suffering, and guided by the maiden
Hope to the dwelling. The appearance of his
mistress occasions a debate between the pair upon
the placing of blame for his intolerable condition, and she is finally adjudged guilty by Cupid
and sentenced to a loveless life. This dictum, which
is as severe a condemnation for himself, the writer
refuses to accept, and abandoned by Hope, he is
whisked away in the cloud again and left to his
sinister cogitations. The Italianate Ludovico Escrivá, writing about 1537, in hopelessly precious
and tautological prose, the *Veneris Tribunal*,* represents himself, in the same amorous despair, as dis-
puting with two friends a common quibble of the
Court of Love: "Which is greater delight to the
lover, to see the beloved object, or without seeing
her to think of her?" The discussion being cut
short by nightfall, he dreams that he is transported
to the abode and tribunal of Love, all the elements in which he carefully describes. Before the
enthroned Venus and Cupid, surrounded by their
attendants, the old question is subtly and tediously debated by a matron championing the second

alternative for an aged courtier and by her daughter championing the first for a younger gallant, and it is in favour of the youthful pair that the goddess finally gives sentence.

In a poem of the Comendador Ludueña, who flourished under Ferdinand and Isabella, the suggestion is given by an ecclesiastical tribunal: Cupid, with Sorrow as clerk, excommunicates the lady, who has robbed the author of his sense and liberty, condemning her to loss of beauty, graces, and reputation, and cursing her with a terrible interdict, but at the end the lover lodges a petition for her pardon in case she shall repent and alter her cruel fashion.* Closely allied to the idea of the Court of Love are the erotic Testaments, as of Alonso Enríquez, Pedro de Urrea,† and Juan del Encina, in which the author, succumbing to the tender passion, makes suitable allegorical bequests.‡

Certain kinds of allegorical machinery were particularly attractive to Spaniards. The vogue of the figurative Battle was established by Prudentius in the *Psychomachia*. Examples from the fourteenth and fifteenth centuries respectively are the struggle between Flesh and Lent in the *Libro de Buen Amor* of Juan Ruiz and the conflict between the forces of Love and those of Chastity in the *Sueño* of Santillana. The same state of mind produces the allegorical symbol of armour, of which there is a whole arsenal, as varied in material as the collection of actual specimens in the Real Armería at Madrid: Juan Ruiz constructs his protection against the deadly Sins from the Virtues and Sacraments; Imperial defends himself against his literary enemies by vesting himself with the charms and merits of his lady. Possibly the starting-point with the pious Spaniards for such allegory was St. Paul's splendid exhortation to the Ephesians to take unto themselves the "whole armour of God," where the different metaphorical pieces are all defined.*

Hand in hand with the device of the Battle goes the Debate, in which various personifications maintain their respective theses. Spanish literature presents a formidable array of this somewhat tedious form, arguments between Body and Soul, Heart and Mind, Age and Poverty, Reason and Will, between any abstractions the characteristics of which the author wishes to bring into relief.

Beginning with Villasandino, another peculiarly national mode of treating personifications was evolved: a group of them appear stricken with grief and are usually consoled in one way or another. In a very simple *Decir* of this sort, Villasandino hears Moderation, Generosity, and Goodness complaining that wickedness has the upper hand.† In another and more important poem, he is visited by three female figures, Queen Catherine, Justice, and the Church of Toledo, all of whom bewail their loneliness at the death of Henry III, and are in turn comforted with exhortations to attach themselves respectively to the young King, the Infante Don Ferdinand, and the Archbishop Pedro de Luna.* The most artistic use of the motive is Santillana's *Visión*, wherein he discovers by a fountain the three figures of Fortitude, Loyalty, and Chastity in great distress, and, on learning that they can find no resting-place in Spain, sends them for consolation to dwell with his lady.

Finally, as humanism gains in force, amidst this machinery appears the type already mentioned, which substitutes for the old symbols classical personages, objects, or myths.

There are three ways of handling the allegorical material. The first is somewhat crude: the allegorical fiction is relegated to a short introduction, and the later and principal part of the composition is an exegesis of this fiction. Thus in Berceo's *Miracles of Our Lady*, the allegory is a setting for the various miracles that constitute the body of the work. The author as a pilgrim chances upon a garden which corresponds in every detail to the countless bowers of contemporaneous French literature and to the almost equal number in Spanish literature of the fifteenth century. Hav-

ing described the conventional constituents of the
garden, he immediately starts to elucidate, in the
most painstaking fashion, but in a somewhat
haphazard order, their figurative meanings. The
length of the exegesis, twice as great as that of
the description of the garden, betrays the desperate didacticism of the age and the race. " Sirs
and friends, since what we have said is obscure, it
is our wish to expound it : let us remove the shell,
let us go to the kernel of the matter, let us seize
upon the inner sense and abandon the outer."
The pilgrimage is the weary journey of mankind
through the world :

> Todos somos romeos que camino andamos;

and one thinks of Dante's similar allegory, though,
of course, the *Divine Comedy* was not yet written :

> Nel mezzo del camin di nostra vita.

The Blessed Virgin is the garden, " in whom each
weary pilgrim finds repose," green with the freshness of her maidenhood. The four clear foun-
tains are the Gospels, which emanated from her
supervision. The shade is her mediation, the trees
her miracles. The birds are the saints who have
sung and the choirs who sing her praises : " these
are nightingales of great delight." The flowers are
her mystic titles, which are all duly explained.
Berceo then begins upon his real subject, an ac-

count of twenty-five of Our Lady's miracles. The allegory is merely a pretty device to enhance the appeal of the whole composition. Likewise, in the *Alexandre*, which is possibly by Berceo, the Vices appear as malignant figures besetting the entrance to hell, and are afterward minutely analyzed.

Because of the Spaniards' didactic propensity, which here expresses itself in a fondness for meticulous exposition, this manner of presentation, despite its clumsiness, is continued through the fourteenth and fifteenth centuries. Juan Ruiz, with more artistic sensibility, usually preserves the fiction throughout; but in one instance he brings the Vices upon the stage as retainers of Love, and then, unable to resist the mediaeval velleity for analysis of these personifications, lapses into a lengthy dissertation upon their nature. The plan is not essentially different in the principal verses of Imperial and his contemporaries. They resort to the allegory only at the first as an attractive frame to the bulk of the composition, which is really a homily. An apt example is Imperial's poem upon the seven Virtues, the longest, the most pretentious, and, because of a hypothetical Dantesque influence, the most famous of his productions. In a dream, amidst the beauties of a garden similar to that of Berceo, the writer beholds seven stars, each containing a

feminine form and surrounded by rays in which
shine semblances of maidens. The rest of the
Decir is occupied entirely, first with the identifi-
cation of the astronomical ladies as the seven
Virtues and the attendant Virgins as subordinate
phases of each Virtue, and second, with an elucidation of their various qualities. The description
of the garden occupies a comparatively larger
space than in Berceo, but only because the exposition of the Virgin's numerous miracles requires
more verses than the commentary upon the seven
Virtues. As the earlier poet explains the trees in
his narrative of the miracles, so the later, although he does not himself interrupt the illusion,
yet causes the guide to explain in several stanzas
the significance of the stars. In his other long
poem, on the birth of John II, Imperial does not
step out of the fiction and explain; but the purpose is still half didactic, an analysis of the respective influences of the planets, which are here
brought into the scheme as the personified bene-
factors of the Prince.

In the other poets of the dawning century the
allegorical introduction does not occupy even so
much space as in the *Miracles of Our Lady*. Ruy
Páez de Ribera sets his debate about the crowning sorrows of Poverty * in a gruesome valley,
to which he assigns but four lines, and having

sketched the appearance and actions of the four figures of Grief, Age, Exile, and Poverty, in the next three stanzas he proceeds to the main purpose of the composition, the argument between the four upon the respective disadvantages of these evils. His debate between Pride and Moderation * is marked by the same characteristics. The general form known as the Debate, indeed, developed partly in response to this conception of allegory; the body of the composition is didactic, and the personifications in question and the setting, if there be one, are briefly outlined at first. The Debate is superior artistically to the type illustrated by the *Milagros* of Berceo because the author does not intrude his own personality to expound the characteristics of the personifications, but allows them to be their own mouthpieces. In Ribera's stanzas upon the regency † the description of the garden covers only two lines; the description of the three thrones of the king and the two regents is longer, but, beginning with the eighth stanza, the poem consists of the people's outcries in adulation of the new King and in the explanations by the allegorical lady of the significance and the occupants of the thrones. Since in all these compositions, and generally in this coterie, allegory is employed as a setting to didactic matter in the same manner as in Berceo's poem, Imperial

and his contemporaries cannot be regarded as having by their treatment of allegory instituted a new
school.

Even later in the century, writers revert to this
method. In the *Cárcel de Amor*, Diego de San
Pedro employs allegory after the fashion of Berceo
as an attractive introduction to narrative. Sub-
stantially the work is a romantic novel treating
the sad passion of Leriano and Laureola, but the
author first shows the hero to the reader as a captive of Love recounting his metaphorical torments. The exegesis of these is much longer than
the similar passage in Berceo, placed more artistically, however, in the mouth of Leriano himself.
The fiery seat, for example, is his "just afflic-
tion"; the two women who press down upon his
head crowns of iron spikes are his anxiety and
passion; the negro who seeks to take away his
life is Despair. Likewise, Juan Rodríguez de la
Cámara gives an imaginative introduction to his
work upon the virtues of women and true nobility.

In the second manner of presentation, the allegory is maintained throughout with little or no
interpretation. There had been instances of this
attitude in the earlier period, notably in the works
of Juan Ruiz and Imperial; but with the keener
aesthetic sensibility of the oncoming Renaissance,
the best poets of the fifteenth century in general

refuse to violate congruity by destroying the illusion. The change, of course, is partly due to a
higher respect for allegory. They no longer consider it merely a sugar coating for didacticism, and
therefore do not debase it to an introductory device. The movement of the narrative does not
come to a standstill through a lapse into exegesis.
Entranced by the fantasies of the allegorical realm,
they seem almost to think first of the form and
then to search for some subject to suit it. Except
in the case of the Debate, where, as we have seen,
the lack of harmony is less flagrant, they do not
employ allegory merely as a setting to erudition,
but choose subjects in which the fiction hardly
needs elucidation and therefore can be maintained
until the end. Whereas the profounder mind of
Dante introduces no detail into the *Divine Comedy*
to which he does not lend a vital significance,
they are so interested in the imaginative tissue
that they go on to weave in other connecting elements which have no figurative meaning.

A good example is Santillana's *Sueño.** After an
invocation to Mars, he dreams, as he dwells in
the city of Tranquillity, that a lovely garden is
forthwith changed to a hideous wood; and the
harp to whose notes he has listened is transformed
into a serpent that bites his left side and awakens
him. Then follows a conventional debate of Mind

and Heart upon the reality of dreams, in which
the latter proves that they are trustworthy omens.
After traversing wild forests in great tribulation
of spirit, on the eighth day the Marquis encounters an old man, the classical seer Tiresias, who,
on learning of his threatening dream, bids him
seek the aid of Diana against Love. In a flower-
ing meadow along a river he finds the goddess
and her nymphs hunting and obtains her protection. The battle is set against Venus, Laziness and
Understanding fighting for him against Beauty,
Prudence, Dexterity, Nobility, Grace, and Youth.
Repulsed, Diana rallies her forces and succeeds in
driving back Cupid; but Venus, Jupiter, and Juno
hurry to his succour and capture the author, who
lies mortally wounded upon the field. The fundamental episode of the battle explains itself, and
such elements as the guide Tiresias and the background of the meadow are added merely to fill out
and decorate the story. Santillana even neglects
the opportunity for a minute analysis of the dream
in which Berceo would have exulted. It was the
transparent veil of erotic allegories such as this
that ensured their popularity.

In the same way, partly because no elucidation
is required, the Marquis sets forth allegorically, in
the *Defunción*, the mourning for the great literary
noble, Villena.* Having climbed a darkly wooded

mountain which is beset by many wild beasts and classical prodigies stricken with grief, he discovers on the summit, in the midst of a sorrowing company, the nine Muses bewailing Villena's death; and joining in the lament he wakes from his dream. It is again significant that, although in general the meaning is clear enough, in the case of the different monsters, where others with less feeling for consistency would surely have thought an explanation necessary, Santillana is unwilling to sacrifice the illusion. This second mode of presentation, because of the instinctive artistic endowment of the race, was adopted by the greatest Italians, such as Dante, Petrarch, and Boccaccio.

A third and less frequent mode of presentation, used particularly by composers of the second type of Erotic Hell, is to define the symbol as soon as it is mentioned. I quote a typical passage from the *Siervo Libre de Amor* of Juan Rodríguez de la Cámara, describing his descent along the road of unrequited love: "And my free will, watcher of the roads, which are all thoughts, parting from the company, did not delay in following the descending way, which is desperation, indicated by the poplar, which is a tree of paradise consecrated to Hercules." * Imperial's employment of the other two modes has been mentioned, and he uses this juxtaposition of the literal and allegorical

senses in the poem that describes an amorous
wound received from the bow of his lady, the
cord of which is various thoughts, the arrow-point
torment with sweet odours, the feather delight
and vain pleasures.* The method of labelling the
object with its significance is the most unsatisfac-
tory of all, since it at once destroys the illusion,
whereas the first method preserves it at least for
a while. The three methods, of course, are not
sharply differentiated, and each more or less en-
croaches upon the others. In Imperial's *Decir* on
the birth of John II, the fiction is continued, and
there is a good deal of allegory setting forth this
event without exegesis ; but the didactic matter
on the planets is so extensive as almost to turn
the allegory into an introduction. In the poem
on Love's wound, the illusion is broken only for
the one stanza to expound the constituents of
the bow.

CHAPTER VI

THE PANEGYRIC

ONE of the two peculiarly Spanish types of allegory is the Panegyric, in which the Virtues, the Liberal Arts, or the Muses are usually represented as honouring some famous man who has distinguished himself in any of the activities of life symbolized by these personifications. The most characteristic form is the coronation at the hands of the allegorical figures, and such a composition is then given the title of *Coronación*. The homage, however, may be expressed in other ways, as by a spoken encomium, a lament, an enthronement, or an apotheosis. The type appears in other countries, as in the Italian Zenone da Pistoia's *Pietosa Fonte*; but the Spaniards, with their predilection for stately and pompous court spectacles, employed it very often and developed it to its most characteristic expression.

The evolution is gradual. The earliest hint is afforded by those clerical compositions, half imagined, half believed, in which a saint is depicted as the recipient of concrete compensation for a virtuous life. Gonzalo de Berceo has two examples. Oria in her *Vida* dreams of an ascent into heaven and the sight of the throne prepared for her in paradise. Of the many visions that the author ascribes to Santo Domingo de Silos, he relates only one, but this most apposite, — the crossing of a dreadful bridge, at the end of which two angels bestow upon Domingo three brilliant crowns, one for pious observation of the monastic vows, one for devotion to the Virgin, one for his rehabilitation of a monastery.* A significant influence in the production of the type was the mystical scene from the life of the Virgin, the Coronation, a common subject for painting and for church portals; and there exists at least one example of a literary treatment from the fourteenth or early fifteenth century, composed in the usual visionary framework, *Una Coronación de Nuestra Señora fecha por el Bachiller Fernán Ruiz de Sevilla.*† In the middle of the night, as he calls upon Our Lady, the author hears the trumpets of four heralds and also voices from the four quarters of the universe, summoning to heaven's high festival; and then, in the midst of the celestial host, which consists of the nine orders of angels hymning their Queen and of all the saints bringing their tribute of worship, he witnesses the ceremony of the Coronation. Inasmuch as this culmination of the Virgin's glory, taking place in the supernatural realm, is incased in the same machinery as so many contemporary poems, the transition to the purely allegorical use of the motive was rendered all the easier; and in the later developments of the Panegyric the praises of the angels and saints are paralleled by the eulogies of the Muses and Virtues.

It is not until the middle of the great allegorical century, the fifteenth, that the form assumes definite outlines. The poems of Francisco Imperial and Ruy Páez de Ribera, however, at the beginning of the century, must have suggested some of the main elements. In the former's *Decir* on the birth of John II,* he is awakened, amidst an allegorical bower, by the polyglot cries of a woman in travail, to behold advancing a lioness ensconced upon a bull, signifying the confinement of the Queen, mistress of the province of Leon, at the town of Toro, and in the air above, eight stars glittering in eight feminine countenances, eight more faces of handmaidens, and also twelve other brilliant visages, all singing canticles to God. The eight stars are the seven planets and Fortune. The planets in turn bestow their beneficent influences upon the nascent prince, each granting him for his service one of the maidens, who are the Virtues; and Fortune, as the universal mistress, sanctions and completes their gifts by her own indulgence, presents him with the eighth Virtue, Prudence, and endows him with the graces of the

twelve other faces, which are the signs of the
zodiac. Pushing through the jasmin, the writer
sees the royal child in the hands of the lioness, with
angel's features, lion's breast, and horse's body,
having in his hands a crown and a sword and on his
shoulders a pennant with the arms of Spain. At
Discretion's suggestion he hurries forward to kiss
the infant's hand, but is ejected from the precincts
by the gardener. The only significant variations
from the ordinary *Coronación* is that it is a child
rather than a successful adult who is glorified, that
he is blessed rather than crowned, and that personifications of stars act the rôle of the customary Virtues or Muses. The mediaeval theory of planetary
influence may perhaps have assisted to suggest the
idea of benediction by allegorical figures in the
later form.

Imperial himself, however, is indebted for the
underlying conception, to an earlier composition,
the *Anticlaudianus* of Alanus de Insulis,* which
was another of the sources from which the *Coronación* was built. In this rich treasure-house and
unceasing delight of the Middle Ages, Nature
summons a council of the different Virtues, Concordia, Copia, Favor, Iuventus, Risus, Decus, Pu-
dor, Modestia, Ratio, Prudentia, Honestas, Pietas,
Fides, Largitas, and Nobilitas, that they may produce a perfect man. Prudentia is dispatched in an

allegorical chariot to ask the soul of God; and when once they have received this gift they vie in endowing it with every favour. The participation of Fortune is especially remarkable as an analogue to the *Decir* of Imperial: Nobilitas, considered as the daughter of Fortune and unable to bestow her presents without the maternal advice, seeks her mother's mansion and obtains her coöperation in the Utopian scheme. As in Imperial's garden, the council and the benediction of the Virtues take place in the ever verdant bower of Nature, which is described at greater length than in the Spanish work as miraculously fertile without the efforts of man.

The poem of Ruy Páez de Ribera upon the regency for John II furnishes a precedent similar to that created by Imperial. In the conventional garden, Ruy Páez beholds in the midst of a vast concourse of people, the Queen-mother giving signs of joy for the promises incarnate in the infant King but still bearing the traces of recent grief for her husband, Henry III.* A fair damsel then guides him into the garden and shows him upon three thrones the infant sovereign, and the two regents, the Queen and Ferdinand of Aragon. The subjects intone several stanzas of eulogy to the King, and the damsel identifies and praises the two regents.

At this period, in his verses upon the death of Henry III, Villasandino devotes a whole composition to the grief of Queen Catherine and of two allegorical figures, Justice and the Church of Toledo, a subject which is to constitute the body of some of the later Panegyrics.

The type awaited the master hand of the Marquis of Santillana to receive its artistic form and its vogue. He based himself first upon the prototypes to which I have referred, especially the sacred visions. Other suggestions were not lacking. An ineradicable impression must have been left upon the sensitive imagination of the sixteen-year-old lad by the splendours of the actual coronation of the regent Ferdinand as King of Aragon, especially the dramatic spectacle attending the festivities and described by the chronicler Álvar García de Santa María, for which Don Enrique de Villena may have composed the dialogue. A child enthroned in kingly state upon a tower, symbolizing the monarch, was eulogized in turn by the four Virtues, Justice, Truth, Peace, and Mercy, enacted by four maidens seated on four pinnacles of the tower. This is probably only one among numerous other similar theatrical pageants of the period, and to compose the ordinary *Coronación*, it would be necessary merely to expand the stage directions of such a piece into narrative form and to add a visionary introduction. Since it was ordinarily a literary person that was so honoured, the Marquis was doubtless affected also by the great literary courts known as *puys*, at which successful competitors were crowned.* The coronation of Petrarch at Rome for his humanistic achievements was one of the famous events of the previous century and set the poets of the Renaissance to dreaming of, and not seldom to attaining, this token.

With such ideas flitting before his mind Santillana wrote the *Coronación de Mossén Jordí.*† The love motive is combined with that of the Coronation. At dawn, in the usual meadow of amorous allegory, the author beholds a Triumph of Venus, who, in the midst of her women, is borne in a kind of howdah upon a huge elephant. When she has been enthroned, at the request of Homer, Virgil, and Lucan she orders the coronation of the Catalan poet Jordí de Sant Jordí. After the ceremony, the piece ends abruptly, like most of Santillana's works, with the departure of the four poets.

In its essence the composition is plainly connected with the Court of Love. The coronation of the poet who has defended Cupid with the pen corresponds in the allegorical sphere to the knighting of the warrior who has defended his sovereign with the sword. French literature offers

many analogies. In the *Lay Amoureux*, Eustache
Deschamps witnesses a procession of Love and
his attendants, and is presented to the god on
account of the honour he had done him in his
writings.* Jean Froissart, in his *Paradys d'Amour*,
is conducted to the pavilion of Love, kneels before his lady, and is crowned by her in reward for
a *ballade*.† In his *Joli Buisson de Jonece*, Plaisance,
Desir, Humilité, Jonece, Maniere, Pité, Doulç
Semblant, and Franchise, after a literary contest
in which each expresses a wish in verse, with the
poet as secretary and a wreath for a prize, set out
to seek Love as judge ; but the vision comes to a
sudden conclusion. ‡ In the anonymous *Echecs
Amoureux*, a damsel, after defeating the author at
a game of chess, is awarded a chaplet by Déduit.§
In Jean de Condé's *Messe des Oisiaus*,|| Venus
herself, as in the Spanish poem, is the person who
takes her seat to dispense justice.

Upon familiarity with French sources, Santillana
superimposed a knowledge of Italian analogues.
Although in the fundamental idea nothing at all
is to be discerned of Dante's encounter with the
great poets of Limbo, there may be a slight recollection of the *valle fiorita* in the seventh canto
of the *Purgatorio*, which in his annotations to the
Divine Comedy the Marquis interpreted as the
valley of fame, following the commentator, Ben-

venuto da Imola, from whom he drew more than has generally been known. A more likely Italian prototype is the *Amorosa Visione*. In the hall of Glory Boccaccio sees depicted upon one wall the great writers of antiquity; and whereas in the *Inferno* Dante is simply received by the other poets, here, as in the usual form of the Panegyric, he is actually crowned. The officiant in the ceremony is Philosophy, who, like Venus in Santillana's verses, is surrounded by her maidens, the seven Sciences, and her votaries, the sages and famous writers of Greece and Rome. Homer, Virgil, and Lucan appear in the passage of the *Amorosa Visione* as well as in the *Inferno*. The *Coronación de Mossén Jordi* is thus only another important proof of the Spanish inclination towards Italian manipulations of Dante in the Trecento rather than towards Dante himself.

For another sort of Panegyric, the centre of which is a lament by allegorical personifications for the deceased, Santillana establishes the precedent in the *Defunción de Don Enrique de Villena*, the substance of which I have already given.* In Spain itself he had as a precedent Villasandino's verses on the death of Henry III, and in France Watriquet de Couvin's *Dit du Connestable de France*, in which Prouesse, in her own name and in the name of her three sisters, Largesse, Cour-

toisie, and Loyauté, bemoans the death of the
Constable Gautier de Châtillon.* The central idea
is enshrined by the Marquis in an imaginary journey through the realms of inanimate and animate
nature, both exhibiting signs of mourning, until,
attaining the summit of a mountain, he finally witnesses the manifestation of grief by reasonable
beings, the Muses. In another less familiar piece,
El Planto de la Reina Doña Margarida,† he en-
grafts the amorous motive upon the threnody, as
upon the coronation in the eulogy of Jordí. At
night the author beholds by his bedside the goddess of love summoning her followers to bewail
one who has just died, *la mejor de las mejores*.
With great anxiety he inquires whether it be his
mistress or Queen Margaret and is told that the
former still survives. As from the tombs at the
last trump, hosts of classic lovers pass before his
sight, lamenting the Queen in divers fashions, according to the mandate of Venus; and when the
falling stars proclaim the dawn, the vision van-
ishes.

The work of Santillana contains tangible evidence that in his development of the Coronation
form he was influenced by the visions of honour
paid to saints to which I have before alluded. The
verses on the canonization of Vincent Ferrer and
Pedro de Villacreces,‡ a species of religious Pane-

gyric, afforded a transition to the purely secular type. Caught up to heaven, the author beholds the various categories of saints, the nine orders of angels in resplendent glory, and especially two processions of Dominicans and Franciscans. St. Dominic makes his supplication for the canonization of the great Dominican preacher and the Franciscan friar, and is gratified by the descent of an angel proclaiming God's consent. Santillana here enhances by an allegorical setting the same petition for the canonization of Vincent Ferrer that he embodied in one of his religious sonnets.*

With the *Coronación* or *Calamicleos* of Juan de Mena,† the form becomes much more elaborate. On an April day, with the intent of attaining the summit of Parnassus, the poet finds himself astray in a dark valley, by the bank of a deep river, where at nightfall he beholds, under the direction of the three judges, Minos, Rhadamanthus, and Aeacus, and before the three Furies, the punishment of the condemned, those who, as Tisiphone tells him, suffer

por mal uso
del espiritu confuso.

Warned by the Fury, he escapes in a bark across Acheron, where he encounters the seven marine perils, *siete peligros marinos*, which consist of dangerous parts of the sea, such as the Syrtes, and sea

monsters, such as Scylla and Charybdis. When he
awakes from the sleep in which his frightful journey has plunged him, he takes his way through a
wood, inhabited only by the wise, until he attains
the grove upon the summit of Parnassus, rich in
every kind of tree and watered by the conventional
fountain. Here are the seats of the classic worthies,
and hither come the nine Muses escorting the
Marquis of Santillana beneath a canopy. He is
ensconced upon a throne and crowned by the four
Cardinal Virtues. After an apostrophe to the goddess of Fame, the writer is abruptly transported to
the earth.

Juan de Mena is the first to endow the Coronation with a definite literary aspect. In Santillana's
Coronación, the erotic aspect is still important; in
the *Calamicleos*, it is lost altogether. Whereas the
Marquis imagines Homer, Virgil, and Lucan as the
presenters, and Venus as the ruler of the ceremony,
Juan de Mena grafts upon the form the nine
Muses as presenters, combining the matter of Santillana's *Coronación* and *Defunción*, and employs the
four Virtues for the act of coronation, honouring
the Marquis not as the servitor of Love, but as
a model of literary achievement and moral excellence. He may have been somewhat influenced
to compose a literary coronation also by the dream
related of Dante's mother in pregnancy by Ben-

venuto da Imola, in the introduction to whose comment we have certain evidence that Mena was much interested. Dante is brought forth beneath a laurel, and in his childhood seeks to climb the tree to pick its berries. Mena may have recollected the following sentences in Benvenuto's exegesis of the dream : " Laurus significat ipsam scientiam poeticam infusam a coelo ipsi autori. . . . Quod conabatur capere frondes significat ingens desiderium, quod habebat, laurae obtinendae." *

Whether he had read while in Italy the *Pietosa Fonte* of Zenone da Pistoia,† I cannot determine. At least, it was not generally known in Spain, for I have been able to find no record of it in catalogues of libraries nor any exact reminiscence of it in the literature. Surely if it had come at all into the hands of fifteenth-century Spaniards, it would have obtained wide popularity, since its substance was so closely related to the very themes of which they were so fond, and there would be some mention of Zenone's name. The composition is in essence a Panegyric for Petrarch. The author is led into the conventional garden, where before the throne of Jove appear in turn the personifications of the World and of Florence, mourning the death of Petrarch, the latter adding a wail for five other sons of hers. The Liberal Arts and the Muses then present to Jove the different works

of the poet, Apollo and Minerva, with seventy
philosophers and many writers of ancient days,
escort him to the throne, the former crowns him
with three wreaths of palm, olive, and laurel, and
four angels descend to transport him to the highest
heaven, to which Jove has assigned him. As in
certain later Spanish examples of the Panegyric,
Zenone introduces the coronation with an allegorical lament. But the absence of any verbal identity
between the Spanish and Italian poems makes it
possible that each is a separate growth from the
same mediaeval stem.

A mere Coronation, however, does not satisfy
Mena's ambitious temperament and luxuriant the-
ories of poetry. Since the presence of a kind of
heaven offered the opportunity, he must needs
involve this purpose by depicting, like Virgil, like
Dante, like many mediaeval writers, the pains of
the damned and the joys of the blessed. So in the
first of the four preambles,* which happily leave no
room for critics to dispute over the poet's conception, he defines the title : "Many times, nay the
majority of times, it happeneth that the names of
things declare and show to us the character of the
things of which they are the names, and therefore
it is not reasonable to neglect understanding a
name that I have given to this brief compend-
ium : which name is *Calamicleo(s)*, and this name

is composed of two words, one Latin and the other Greek : *calamitas*, which in Latin meaneth ' wretchedness,' and *cleos*, which in Greek meaneth 'glory.' . . . And this name suggesteth that in the present treatise the desire of the author was to write of those two ends, that is of the misery of the evil and the glory of the good : because one opposite placed by the side of another is brought into clearer relief, according to the philosopher : so that in this place glory will appear greater glory placed near wretchedness : and the contrary." Having once conceived the idea of a Panegyric, he may have been influenced to add the description of hell also by a Renaissance dread that a mere Coronation did not conform to any of the three acknowledged classical types, tragedy, satire, and comedy. In the second preamble he defines these types according to the conventional ideas, and is careful to show that the *Calamicleos* is both satire and comedy.

Another consideration that led him thus to round out his vision was doubtless the great number of mediaeval poems in which both a place of sorrow and of joy were represented. Virgil had passed from Hades to the Elysian fields, and in many of the monkish journeys to the other world, as in the Spanish ecstasies of Maximus and of Bonellus by S. Valerius, both heaven and hell were seen. A certain class of French *dits* are often of this nature. Raoul de Houdan in his *Voie d'Enfer et de Paradis* passes through both supernatural realms.* Jehan de la Mote composed an unpublished *Treatise* of the same kind.† Rutebeuf transforms this type somewhat when in his *Voie de Paradis* ‡ he depicts himself as avoiding the broad way and continuing on the narrow way to the town of Penitence; here he finds Pity, who shows him first the dwellings of the Vices and then those of the Virtues, until he finds a haven with Confession. Martin le Franc's *Livre du Champion des Dames,* of about 1442, is analogous to the *Calamicleos* in its use of this old material for another purpose.§ As the title reveals, its substance is a *débat* between Franc Vouloir and Malebouche on that favourite mediaeval question, the character of woman. The author in the castle of Love sees first a cemetery of unhappy lovers and the torment of condemned souls by devils, and at the end of the contest Franc Vouloir crowned as victor.

Under the weight of all this tradition, Juan de Mena felt it a duty to expand his Coronation into a double vision. That he distinctly intended a journey to hell and heaven becomes clearer from the commentary that he himself wrote. The grove on the summit of Parnassus is not only a Paradise of literary achievement but also a definite heaven, the dwelling place of God conceived under His attribute of wisdom. Parnassus represents God, and the Castalian spring His omniscience. Santillana is considered not only a literary genius, but also a universal man, presented by the Muses, crowned by the Virtues, and distinguished from others by an oak wreath for his fortitude and military prowess. Hell, by contrast, is the abode of ignorance, which, after the fashion of Socrates, Mena takes to be the root of evil ; but he is so strongly influenced by his models that he cannot refrain from expanding it into the ordinary mediaeval place of torment.

Gómez Manrique in the Panegyric for his dead uncle, Santillana,* stresses rather the element of mourning that had appeared in the *Defunción*. On his way to a vacation in a monastery, the author finds himself astray in the accustomed valley, passes there a troubled night, and pushes on to a sombre castle, in which he discovers the seven Virtues bewailing the death of the Marquis. After their long laments, Poetry appears, deplores the loss of Juan de Mena and of Juan de Ijar, and, more than all, of Santillana, then requests Manrique to write his encomium. In modest distrust of his own attainments, he suggests Fernán Pérez de Guzmán as a worthier panegyrist ; and the vision

fades away. The forms defined by Santillana are
being transmitted to the succeeding generation.
The chief point of Manrique's verses, the lament
of the Virtues and Poetry, is derived from the
lament of the Muses in the *Defunción*. The imitation becomes in places very exact, as when, like
the Muses cataloguing their former deprivations,
Justice speaks first of the deaths of the Bishops
of Avila and Burgos, Poetry of Juan de Mena and
Juan de Ijar, and Prudence even uses the Marquis's diction. The inorganic allegorical machinery
at the opening — the wandering, the disturbed
repose for the night in the valley, the advance the
next morning, the gloomy keep itself as the dwelling of the Virtues — is a reflection of those visits
to the infernal regions which, beginning with Juan
de Mena, are often combined with the other matter ; the details themselves are an obvious reminis-
cense of the weary journey to the Prison of Love in
Santillana's *Infierno de los Enamorados*. The idea
underlying the actual coronation here is expressed
in the command to compose a eulogy.

A third Panegyric called forth by the death of
the literary patriarch was the *Triunfo del Marqués*
by his secretary, Diego de Burgos.* Just before the
dawn of a spring morning, the author in a vision
learns the sad news from the new Marquis. No
sooner has the latter disappeared than Diego finds

at his side Dante himself, who, in the rôle of the conventional guide, conducts him for a whole tiresome day through the ordinary sinister desert, allows him to rest a night, the next morning shows him the yawning mouth of hell with some of its occupants, and after passing by purgatory, fetches him up in a terrestrial paradise. Here he enjoys the sight of the blessed ensconced in an amphitheatre, among them, in supernatural radiance, the old Marquis himself, the theological Virtues at his right, the cardinal at his left, the Muses and Arts upon the grade below. Forthwith a vast number of sages and warriors of ancient and modern days, both of Italy and Spain, each in a separate *copla*, eulogize Santillana from the literary and military standpoints. Finally, the Marquis advances in triumphal procession, until, having arrived at a Temple, which is the vestibule of heaven, he is enthroned, saluted with still greater honour, and caught up into felicity.

In this lengthy composition Diego de Burgos has developed the most pretentious Panegyric of the century. He has sought to crowd into one composition all the substance of his predecessors' simpler poems. From the *Calamicleos* he derives the idea of welding together the journey to the three realms of the other world and the central theme of the poet's glorification. Whereas Juan de Mena attempts to harmonize the two themes, however ineffectually, by giving the places of punishment and reward at least something of a literary savour, Diego de Burgos tries to attain congruity by laying the stress rather upon the religious phase, adding heaven to complete the three realms and regarding the Marquis not only as a poetic, philosophic, and military genius, but also as a beatified soul. The concepts of a day spent in the fatiguing journey, the repose at night, and the advance the next day, are not to be traced to Santillana's *Infierno* so much as to the *Calamicleos*, which constitutes the most potent formative influence. The deceased's immortal renown, as in the *Calamicleos*, rather than grief for his death, as in the *Defunción*, is the chief theme. Diego de Burgos is not satisfied with giving expression in his own introductory laments to the sorrow-motive of the latter composition; he adds and makes principal the motive of festive honour. It is not sufficient that the Marquis, like Villena in the *Defunción*, be lauded only by the Muses: Juan de Mena had progressed one step by importing the seven Virtues; and Diego de Burgos outdoes them both by including the plaudits of the world's famous men. The glory of a single occasion is not enough; with Petrarch's models before his eye* he depicts a triumph of the Marquis, the importance of which in the author's mind is indicated by the name that he gives to his piece. Still not content, he augments the impression by a second more splendid enthronement in a Temple of Fame. The *Triunfo del Marqués* affords the closest parallel in Spain to Zenone's *Pietosa Fonte*, especially in the detail of a translation to heaven; but analogies in language are still lacking. With Diego de Burgos and Gómez Manrique its influence is even more unlikely than with Juan de Mena, who by the test of approximation in time might be expected to imitate it, for the two former had definite Spanish prototypes to copy.

Towards the end of the century, in 1483, the long composition of Diego Guillén de Ávila upon the death of the great archbishop of Toledo, Alonso Carrillo,* is closely modelled in general scheme upon the poem of Diego de Burgos. The journey through the three realms of the other world is once more united to the enthronement of the hero in heaven. The work is divided into four parts. The first consists of such introductory details as the invocation, the time of the vision, and a tirade against Fortune for depriving mankind of the Bishop. In the second part, the description of hell, the variations from Diego de Burgos are comprised in a more extended and accurate analysis of its constituents and in the entrance of the guide

Dante not at the outset but in the midst of the
infernal terrors. In the third part, the description
of purgatory and the Elysian fields, Diego Guillén
is careful to imitate his predecessor in declaring
that his hero has already passed from the former
into the latter, but he differs in representing the
Bishop as appearing, then vanishing, then reap-
pearing at the throne of Fame, with his famous
deeds embroidered upon his garments, next as-
cending his own throne amidst the acclamations
of the crowd, and finally vanishing again.* The
fourth part is quite unlike the *Triunfo del Marqués*.
Dante takes his departure; and, whereas in the
Triunfo the assumption of the Marquis is merely
intimated at the very end, an extensive division of
Diego Guillén's poem is devoted to the vicissitudes
of Alonso Carrillo in heaven, whither the author is
quickly transported through the celestial spheres
by Divine Grace. An original turn is given to the
customary coronation by a new treatment of the
Virtues. The Bishop is admitted to the heavenly
palace through one door, representing religious
honour, by the allegorical figure of the Love of
God, and ascends higher and higher, received by
various Christian Virtues; he is then removed by
Grace, enters again through the door of civil and
military honour, and is welcomed on different steps
by other Virtues. Finally, he is conducted in tri-

umph to his throne and is clothed in a regal mantle by Felicity.

As a final example of the Panegyric, we may take the *Triunfo de la Fama y Glorias de Castilla* by the dramatic poet, Juan del Encina,* celebrating the achievements of Ferdinand and Isabella, especially the capture of Granada. Transported to the Castalian Spring, he beholds his literary predecessors slaking their thirst, and names, be it noted, with one exception, only those who have distinguished themselves in allegory. Juan de Mena, who is partly Encina's model, appears to act as guide, allows the writer himself to drink, and then leads him forward to the Temple of Fame. Sculptured in the several halls are, first, the great deeds of antiquity, then the glories of Spain, and finally those of the royal twain, the exaltation of whom is the purpose of the poem.

CHAPTER VII

THE EROTIC HELL

THE other type, which, through a still persisting admiration for French models and, more immediately, through the example of the Marquis, obtained a wide vogue, was the journey to an amorous purgatory or hell. The compositions that fall under this heading may be subdivided into two classes according to their allegorical attitude. To the first belong those in which, as in Santillana's *Infierno de los Enamorados* itself, the author ideates a real abyss of retribution for ill-starred lovers; to the second those in which, as in the *Desert d'Amours* of Eustache Deschamps and the *Prison d'Amours* of Baudouin de Condé, he conceives more fancifully the torment of the visionary world simply as a crystallization of the lover's woes in the actual world. The first class merges into the second, because the punishment of lovers is imagined, to a certain degree, as consisting in the pangs that the passion of love involves, allegorically set forth in biting wounds or consuming flames, but in the poems of the first class the reality of the nether regions is strongly emphasized. That the place of the vision is thought to be an actual penal institu-

tion appears in the inscriptions over the gates, as
in Santillana's prototype:

> El que por Venus se guía,
> Entre á penar su peccado.

In the first group, the author is more of a spec-
tator; in the second, he participates in the erotic
agonies. The distinction between the two types is
tangibly exemplified in the conspicuous absence
of contemporaries from the places of punishment
in the former class and their abundance in the
latter. Dantesque elements would be unnatural in
compositions of the more fanciful sort; but they
might be expected in the realistic class of allegories, to which, indeed, the *Divine Comedy* itself belongs. That they do not crop forth in poems of
this category, which are all more or less imitations
of Santillana's *Infierno de los Enamorados*, is signal
proof that their authors did not deem imitation
of Dante one of the Marquis's essential characteristics or the kind of verse that they were producing
dependent in any way upon the *Divine Comedy*.

As in the case of the Panegyric, the Marquis
here again establishes the precedent for the Erotic Hell, in the *Infierno de los Enamorados*.* Seized
and transported by Fortune to a dense and lofty
mountain forest, he falls asleep, and in the morning, while proceeding upon his journey, encounters a fierce boar. Hippolytus, in the guise of a

mediaeval knight, comes to his succour, and then leads him through a gloomy valley into a forbidding castle, where he beholds the torment of unhappy lovers, especially of the famous Spanish minnesinger Macías, who addresses him. His guide has vanished, and, as Ganymede by the eagle, he himself is whisked away to his natural state.

The poem belongs to the first of the two classes that I have indicated, but in mentioning the prototypes upon which he modelled himself, I shall not attempt to discriminate, since each class influenced the other. The French element is of much greater import than the Dantesque title and the general scheme at first sight would imply. The basic conception was derived, not from the *Inferno*, but from northern tradition. Dante's first *cantica* presents the suffering of every kind of evil-doer; certain French *dits* concern themselves, like the *Infierno de los Enamorados*, only with the sufferings of lovers, as a kind of antithesis to the delights of the Courts of Love. The germs of such composition are to be discerned in the Deserts of Love outlined by Eustache Deschamps. In the long *Lay du Desert d'Amours,** the lady describes first the time of her youth and popularity, expressing the joy of love directly under the figure of paradise. It is an easy step from the paradise to the hell of Love, and this is what Deschamps signifies by the less offensive phrase *Desert d'Amours*, under which is symbolized the desperation of the lady, past the bloom of youth and deserted by her single choice. It is to be noted that the desolate plain is as concrete as Santillana's hell or the opening scene of the *Divine Comedy*; though no individuals are named, it is inhabited by distraught lovers. The vogue of this sort of allegory is demonstrated by the existence of another composition by Deschamps upon the same topic, a *ballade* condensing the matter of the longer poem.*

A second kind of preparation is made by the specialized hells for offenders against the precepts of love. Here may be catalogued the popular type that has been called the *Purgatory of Cruel Beauties*, in which those are represented as punished who refuse to accept the amorous yoke.† To take one example from many, in the *De Amore* of Andreas Capellanus, the arid outer circle of the three that constitute the meadow of the Court of Love is assigned to refractory ladies, *quae amoris compati militibus noluerunt*, tormented on revolving beds of thorns. The author shows that he conceives this circle as a species of hell or purgatory by the language that he applies to it: *Coeperunt per siccitatis circumfluere partes, quia ille sibi erat locus ab antiquo paratus. . . . Tantus quidem dolor tantaque ibi erat afflictio, quantam vix crederem inter ipsas Tartareas potestates adesse.* In the anonymous *Apologia Mulierum* or *Le Mors pour les Mal Embouchiez* † is represented another kind of specialized hell, in contrast to that of Andreas Capellanus, for calumniators and maltreaters of women, whither, in a vision, the author is guided by Mercury and instructed in much the same way as in the *Infierno de los Enamorados*

With Baudouin de Condé's *Prison d'Amours* we come to a definite realm of amorous unfortunates with specific punishments. ‡ The writer describes the different parts of Love's tower, all of which he explains carefully in their allegorical significance after the fashion of the *Roman de la Rose*, until he comes to the great room where upon her wheel Fortune transports some to the heights of bliss, others to the depths of despair. Santillana's place of torment is also *en un castillo espantoso*, and he has been brought to the spot by the operation of Fortune. The analogy now becomes more exact. Both places are deadly dark; and the condemned are wounded to the heart, in Baudouin by small serpents, in the Marquis by some unmentioned means.

The *Hospital d'Amours*, § ascribed to Alain Chartier, presents the significant coincidence of a work mentioned by Santillana in his *Proemio* ‖ and closely analogous to one of his own compositions. In both, the author finds himself astray in a gruesome waste, from which the Spaniard is taken by Hippolytus to behold the hell of Love, and the Frenchman the pleasanter hospital of Love, in the midst of which, however, there is a region corresponding to the Spanish *Infierno*. The preliminary valley in the French, moreover, — itself resembling somewhat an amorous hell and especially the already mentioned Deserts of Despair, — exhibits some analogies to Santillana. It is full of loving suicides: those who, like Phyllis, have hanged themselves swing from trees; beneath, in streams of water, are drowned unfortunates, among whom, of course, he discovers Hero and Leander; at another side appear the bloody swords of those who, with Pyramus and Thisbe, have stabbed themselves; and lastly those who, like Dido, have burned themselves are consumed by a great fire. All these ancient worthies are seen by Santillana. After the Frenchman has been cured at the hospital, he chances upon the cemetery of Love, where he beholds the graves of Tristan and Lancelot, of *maint Roy, maint Duc, aussi maint Conte . . . Cheualiers, Clercz, et Escuyers,* and especially of Alain Chartier. He then strays into a hideous valley and encounters the corpses of false lovers, — *tous ceulx qu'amours excommunie,* where the verbal parallelism is so marked

as to suggest a direct imitation. He mentions by
name the bodies of Jason, Demophon, Æneas, Narcissus, Chartier's mistress, " La Belle Dame sans
Mercy," and Briseis. In the *Hospital d'Amours*,
then, the reference by name to many renowned lovers, seen in the Valley of Despair, the cemetery,
and the ditch of the excommunicate, affords the last
step of transition to Santillana's poem. The delight that the fifteenth century took in the *Hospital* is attested by a much more slavish imitation
than Santillana's in the *Livre du Cuer d'Amours
Espris* (1457) of the versatile King René of Anjou.* Heart, accompanied by Desire and Liberality, journeys to the chapel of the hospital of
Love, to the cemetery behind, over the gate of
which are hung the escutcheons of the many famous
personages who have been in the hospital, and to
the unburied heap of excommunicated lovers without. As René mentions the tombs of Boccaccio
and Petrarch, but not of Dante, one might sur-
mise that he found the lightness of the two later
writers' allegory more similar to that of his own
country than the profundity of the earlier.†

Fundamentally, indeed, the *Infierno de los Enamorados* is more nearly related to works of Boccaccio and Petrarch than to the *Divine Comedy*.
The general scheme is very similar in the *Corbaccio*, an Italian *Prison d'Amour*, in which the

torments of the prisoners symbolize the misery
of the amorous state. As Santillana is shown the
hell of Love that he may realize the desperate-
ness of that passion, so Boccaccio is shown a hell
which he calls a labyrinth of Love, and is informed of his mistress's foulness that he may re-
linquish his amorous purpose. The details are
significantly parallel. Each loses his way in a dire
valley, and is encountered by frightful beasts,
which, however, in the Italian are afterward declared to be transformed mortals; and as the Marquis is hindered in his path by the boar, so Boccaccio cannot advance for fear of the monsters.
Both are rescued from their plight by the persons
who are to be their guides, and are questioned in
similar language. In both compositions lovers suffer, in the Spanish from burning wounds, in the
Italian by metamorphosis into beasts. The purpose of each guide is accomplished, for both Boccaccio and Santillana renounce love at the end.

Although in general plan the hell of Love described by Petrarch in the *Triumphs* does not correspond so exactly as the *Corbaccio* to the poem of
Santillana, the naming of its occupants and certain
details seem to have influenced the Spanish piece.
After being transported with the rest of Love's
captives to the island of Cyprus, Petrarch passes
through the triumphal arch into a prison (*carcere*),

where he is confined for many years, finding his only solace in contemplating famous mortals, who like him are victims of the god. They are bound in ice and flame, and some are identical with those mentioned in the *Infierno*. The colloquy with Macías and his mistress is modelled rather upon the Francesca episode in the fifth canto of the *Inferno*, but it is noteworthy that Petrarch also encounters Paolo and Francesca and converses, furthermore, with another pair of famous lovers, the two that charmed so much his fancy throughout his literary career, Masinissa and Sophonisba. The dependence upon Petrarch is corroborated by the close connection of this passage in the *Trionfi* with another composition of Santillana's, the *Triunphete de Amor*, in which, like the Italian poet, he witnesses a triumph of Love before he enters into the prison of the *Infierno*.

This solid edifice of French and later Italian architecture is decorated with a few Dantesque motives, of no structural significance, however, and not transmitted to those who subsequently employ the form. The impressive opening scenes of the *Divine Comedy* always mingled somewhat in Santillana's mind with the more potent recollections of France and Boccaccio, producing here a slight reminiscence in phraseology of Dante's forest and an approximation in the episode of the boar to the appearance of the symbolic animals. Since pictorial representations are more likely to fix themselves in the consciousness than verbal, he was more attracted, doubtless, to this latter detail than to others, by the miniature in one of his manuscripts of the Italian poem depicting Dante at the foot of the hill confronted by the three wild beasts.* At the actual entrance to the castle of confinement the language again was bound to reflect the striking expressions of the third canto of the *Inferno;* and once within the pale the Marquis adds from the circle of the lustful certain touches that would suggest themselves in a Prison of Love, such as the introduction of the ill-starred lovers of Rimini and an unusually close imitation of the whole Francesca episode in the meeting with Macías. Vague memories of the ledge of Luxury in the *Purgatorio* also hover in Santillana's mind. Since, however, these slight pilferings are inorganic, the form of the Erotic Hell lies under **no** debt whatsoever to the *Divine Comedy.*

The popularity of the Erotic Hell is now assured. To the realistic category belongs the *Visión de Amor* of Juan de Andújar.† By the caprice of Fortune the author is carried away, like the holy men in monastic raptures, to a narrow, wooded vale, through which courses a river surmounted by a bridge of a single plank. In the midst of a central

meadow to which the bridge leads rises the ornate
throne of Justice. Before her, for sentence, defile
the accustomed throng of famous but suffering
lovers, drawn with one or two exceptions from
antiquity. Calling upon the poet to report her
action to mortals, she transfers the power of judgment to a vague *Conde Camarluengo*.* A cloud
obscures the vision from his sight, and he is transported to his starting point in the same mysterious
fashion. That the composition belongs to the realistic class is revealed especially in the judgment
passed upon offenders.

The machinery described in the first stanza is
very plainly derived from the *Infierno de los Enamorados*. In each instance Fortune is the operat-
ing genius, and strong emphasis is laid upon her
wilfulness in contrast to the author's helplessness
in her clutches. Despite the close textual analogy,
he does not extend his imitation to utilization of
any Dantesque details. The wailing couples resem-
ble rather the subject train of triumphant Love in
Petrarch; and instead of reproducing the reference
to Francesca da Rimini, Andújar mentions of moderns, besides the usual Macías, only Fiammetta
and Boccaccio.

The *Purgatorio de Amor* of the Bachiller Jiménez †
lies on the border line between the two classes.
Lovelorn and avoiding human habitation, the au-

thor in the wilderness sinks into the accustomed. vision. Cupid appears to him, and although met by a storm of recrimination, offers to show him the punishments of lovers in order to heal him of his passion. Furnished by the god with wings, he is borne to the entrance of purgatory, upon the iron doors of which he discerns a threatening inscription. He is now informed by Cupid that he too will have to suffer here, but is comforted by a legend on a banner above the doors :

> Nadie por amar se pierde
> Sino aquel que desespera.

The place is thronged with famous contemporaries, suffering physical pangs, which figure their mental torture, and bewailing their plight in amorous verse. Jiménez beseeches his guide to liberate him from the place of torment, for his passionate condition in the actual world is prison enough and he cannot be cured even by the sight of these agonies ; he obtains his petition by promising that he at least will make a strenuous effort to stifle the emotions of his heart.

The realistic element of the composition is the definiteness of purgatory, approached by a flight on wings, shut in by iron gates, and guarded by an inscription that specifically proclaims it a place of retribution ; more fanciful are the participation of the author himself in the torments and the consignment to the gloomy precincts of those who are still alive. In begging off from a longer sojourn in such regions, he declares his erotic condition in the actual world to be identical with that of the visionary sufferers. Greater prominence is given throughout to the idea that love is its own retribution, and in the two instances of Don Alonso de Cardona and Juan Hernández de Heredia, Cupid is so far from imposing the penalty that he seeks to alleviate the pain. It is not a far cry from these conceptions to the shadowy realm that is merely a veil for the grim realities of passion.

In the *Purgatorio de Amor* Dantesque imitation would be more unusual than in Juan de Andújar's poem. Despite such obvious recollections of the Marquis as a journey through a sinister desert before the actual material of the vision begins and an inscription above the forbidding doors, Jiménez nowhere imports the goods stolen from the *Divine Comedy*. His allegory is of quite a different nature from Dante's. The long parleyings with Cupid, in which the author refers to the conventional bow and arrows, brands, and poisons of the god, the allusion to Love's enemies, Chastity, Honesty, Shame, and Goodness, and the equipment of Jiménez with wings, show that the piece is an offshoot from the French school. Of

the same category is his other composition preserved in the *Cancionero General*,* wherein Cupid
himself is borne through a valley sick of love for
the author's own lady.

In novelistic fiction, the *Cárcel de Amor* of Diego
de San Pedro † (1492) again stands on the transitional line between the two types of amorous *In-
fiernos*. The framework into which is built the dis-
tressing tale of the unhappy lovers, Leriano and
Laureola, alone concerns our purpose. The author,
journeying through the usual *valles hondos y escuros*,
encounters a knight of ferocious aspect, dragging
after him in captivity a wretched mortal. On in-
quiry he learns that the former is Desire, chief
officer of the House of Cupid, transporting a victim to the Prison of Love. After the jailer and
the prisoner have vanished from his sight, he
lies down for the night on the summit of a high
mountain, but wakes in the morning to see before
him the Prison, which he takes great pains to
describe. Within, he finds the poor unfortunate,
fettered by three chains, stretching from three
images on the top of the castle tower, and suffering many gruesome torments. The prisoner forthwith explains that he is Leriano, the unhappy
captive of Laureola's charms, elucidates to the
author at length the allegorical significance of the
many tortures that he is enduring, and solicits his

aid. The rest of the *novela* treats of the understanding brought about between Leriano and Laureola through the efforts of the author and of the sad tragedy of their end. When San Pedro brings succour to Leriano, he again employs the allegorical form, imagining that he captures the prison with the assistance of Gratification, Hope, Repose, Pleasure, Joy, and Diversion.

The *Cárcel de Amor* conforms to the first type in that a fantastic vision is described as if it were an actual experience and in that, with two or three exceptions, the tale is not interrupted by exegesis of the allegory. An atmosphere of reality is created by recounting the journey with many details, for instance, as in Santillana's *Infierno*, a delay of a night before the principal episode. Additional realism is obtained by the close dependence of the two lovers' history upon the introductory vision, which, since the other incidents are made possible only because the author is filled with pity at the wretched plight of Leriano, becomes an integral and important section. The piece for the moment approximates the second type, when Leriano steps out of the story and vouchsafes a more than usually generous explanation of the allegory. The explanation itself reaches the height of fantasy, for Understanding, Reason, Memory, and Will are first considered as the pillars of the prison and then as persons, asked by Love whether they are willing to participate in Leriano's torture.

The connecting stream between the expanses of French and Spanish allegory, which hitherto, for the Erotic Hell, has run a more or less underground course, so that we have been obliged to discover by careful delving its existence and nature, now comes plainly to the surface. The *Cárcel de Amor* is unmistakably derived from northern sources; the inflowing current is apparent at every turn. The title itself demonstrates the relation to the French class of *Prisons d'Amour*. The analogy to Baudouin de Condé's long poem is very exact, for in both the several parts of the prison are interpreted allegorically. In the Spanish the foundation is Leriano's faith; in the French it is more complicated:

> Car je vous di par varité
> K'il est de pieres prescieuses . . .
> Car c'est biautés, sens et proëce,
> Honors, cortoizie et larguece,
> Douce raizons, parole estable,
> Simples regars et amiable,
> Nobilités sans felonnie,
> Acointance sans vilonnie ; *

and so on with Baudouin's usual intolerable prolixity. Leriano figures his anguish by a dark stairway, the Frenchman by the blackness of the prison. Or, again, Leriano is ensconced in a fiery

chair, and Baudouin's victim is the prey of a fiery
serpent. The notable similarity between the two
compositions is further proof of French derivation
for the general class to which the *Cárcel de Amor*
belongs.

Guevara's *Infierno de Amores* * is cast completely
in the more fanciful mould. Without the ordinary
machinery of a vision, he describes his amorous woes
directly under the image of hell. His lady's dis-
favour is equal to infernal agony. The customary
physical torments of parts of the body are applied
figuratively to his various faculties and emotions:
his thoughts are consumed with fire, his hope is
upset, his pleasures boil in cauldrons of grief, he
is the prey of dogs, his well-being is rent to pieces,
and he is blinded by his complaints. He encounters no other mortals in his *Infierno* and visualizes
no realities; hell is merely the fictitious picture of
his own sad plight. Here Dantesque reminiscence
was not to be expected; the type comes, rather,
from France and from Petrarch. The description
of mental states in physical terms is highly characteristic of the Italian sonneteer, and an extravagant Petrarchism is echoed in the verbal conceits
at the end.

The genesis of this kind of allegory is not far
to seek; the whole poem is but an expanded metaphor. The germ of the form may be discerned in

such other short passages from Guevara's verse as his declarations that the love of his lady has cast him into prison * and that infernal torture compared with that which emanates from her cruelty is pleasure.† In his *Sepoltura* ‡ he gives expression to exactly the opposite idea, imagining the chastisement, not of Cupid's captives, but of Cupid himself. After a long *débat* with Love upon his misdeeds, the author as judge condemns the god to death at the hands of the personified Sorrows that he has caused. He is to be buried in a tomb the details of which symbolize his various cruelties and upon the top of which are carved the names of those who died of affection. The latter part is plainly a reversal of the amorous interment which we shall soon see to be an offshoot of the Erotic Hell.

The *Infierno de Amor* of Garcí Sánchez de Badajoz,§ modelled, according to the author's explicit statement, directly upon that of Guevara, reveals its metaphorical nature in the very first *copla:*

> Caminando en las honduras
> de mis tristes pensamientos,
> tanto anduue en mis tristuras,
> que me hallé en los tormentos
> de las tinieblas escuras :
> víme entre los amadores
> en el Infierno d' amores,
> de quien escriue Gueuara.

There is no semblance of reality. He does not pass into the allegorical realm by means of a vision, but applies the language of the material world bluntly to the spiritual. He journeys in the depths of his thoughts; he advances in his sadness until he finds himself in the torments of hell. The abyss, to be sure, is full of other fellow-sufferers, but it has few characteristics of a real place of retribution, for Love holds spellbound both dead and living poets, each repeating lines of his own erotic verse, and the amorous deities show favour to a pair of their victims, Álvar and Alonso Pérez.*

Suggestions for such allegory are to be found, as in the case of Guevara, also in the other compositions of Garcí Sánchez de Badajoz. Adapting the verses of Job to his erotic despair,† he cries out against his mistress for hiding his soul in hell, and at the end he describes through several lines the infernal terrors in which his death from love will plunge him. Another composition entitled, *Otras Coplas de Garcí Sánchez, Fantaseando las Cosas de Amor,* ‡ approximates very closely the type of the Erotic Hell. The essence of the piece is an attempt on the part of Cupid to cure the author of his passion. The god first seeks to arouse fright by an elucidation of the meaning and the use of the terrible attributes with which he has appeared.

Failing in this method, he reveals to the poet the horror of his amorous state by commanding the superimposed suffering to disassociate itself from his original mental condition and to issue forth from his body. The passion materializes in the form of a smoking forge, the fire of which is his love, the coal his reason, the water tears, the bellows sighs, the anvil faith, the hammers anxieties, the tongs the fortune that he holds and by which he is held. But the poet remains obdurate to the end. This fiction and the *Infierno de Amor* are only different concrete expositions of the same psychic condition.

A most signal example of the Erotic Hell without illusion is Juan Rodríguez de la Cámara's allegorical *novela*, the *Siervo Libre de Amor* (about 1440), written in prose interspersed with verse.* It is divided into three parts which depict the three stages of his passion, each symbolized by a corresponding kind of road and by a tree of appropriate heraldic significance. With a delight in the analysis of his amorous depression akin to that of Boccaccio's in the *Fiammetta*, he recounts the conception of his love, the doubts raised by Discretion, the kindly attitude assumed by the coquettish lady, his epistle suing for something more than a smile, and his betrayal and loss of favour through the actions of a disloyal friend. Resorting to the temple of

Solitude, in company with its priestess, Bitterness, he resigns himself to dolorous meditation, which he figures under the above-mentioned allegory. As he wanders in the dark forest of his thoughts and in the desert of solitary contemplation, he comes upon the crossing of the three roads in the garden of Fortune. He beholds the highroad of reciprocated love, over which he has journeyed, with the green myrtle standing in the way. But the tree of Venus is withered over his head; the olive of Minerva in the third road, despoiled of its foliage, is no more inviting; and the birds change their joyful songs into sad dirges. Overcome by the heavy gloom of Nature, his Free Will takes the road of unrequited love, which is Desperation, betokened by the poplar. He begs Understanding, who for a long time past has walked apart in wrath, to accompany him along the sinister way to the Elysian fields, where he will wash away his desire in the forgetfulness of the Lethean stream, but Understanding refuses, depicting to him the terrors of the Virgilian Hades through which he must first pass. He then turns to his Heart, but having lost its liberty, the Heart cannot come to his succour. Lapsing into vituperation of his senses, he desires a death like that of Ardanlier and Liesa, whose story he proceeds to recount at length. He is aroused from his lethargy by the recollection of the tragic end of these lovers and seeks to retrace his steps to the crossroads that he may take the difficult path of indifference to love, but having lost his Free Will, he cannot find the way. The appearance of Discretion brings the composition to a sudden conclusion. Paz y Mélia is right in supposing it incomplete.* The part is missing which the author, in outlining the structure, has promised, the guidance back over the third road by Discretion.

The allegorical attitude is still more decidedly unrealistic than in the verses of Guevara or Garcí Sánchez. Each detail is labelled with its significance. The second part begins as follows: "As I . . . wandered through the dark forest of my thoughts, at the moment when the Crimean (?) mountains, consecrated to high Apollo, who is the sun, await his splendour, roaming through deserted and solitary contemplation, I arrived with great fortune at the three roads, which are three different thoughts." The sentence describing his descent along the second road has already been quoted in the general discussion of this placarded type of allegory. Understanding elucidates the myth of Cerberus: "The passage to the Elysian Fields is dangerous because of the frightful dog Cerberus, with the heads which are the three times, present, past, and future." He thus interprets his search for the third road: " Passing the great Alps of my thoughts, descending to the sombre valleys of my first impulses, arriving at the slopes of my timid contemplation, when the traces of footsteps failed, I inquired from the mountaineers, and they mocked me." Juan Rodríguez is not content even with this immediate exegesis, but he must needs explain his general plan and meaning once more in a kind of preface. In the *Siervo Libre de Amor*, upon the Erotic Hell has been superimposed the influence of those French compositions called *Voies de Paradis*, which describe not only the heavenly path but also the broad way "that leadeth to destruction." As a descent to the infernal regions is added to the later specimens of the Panegyric in order to satisfy the craving for novelty in a stereotyped form, so the Erotic Hell is complicated by fusion with another popular allegorical *genre*.

A second improvisation upon the theme of the Erotic Hell, combined with a journey to a terrestrial paradise, is the *Sátira de Felice è Infelice Vida*,* composed by the Constable, Dom Pedro of Portugal, likewise in Spanish prose and verse, between 1449 and 1455, during his sojourn in Castile.† He vaguely ideates an *Infierno* to symbolize his amorous distress, so decidedly unreal, however, that he experiences no restraint in leav-

ing it when, counselled by Discretion, he seeks
greater liberty for reflection. Having travelled all
night, he reaches at dawn a solitary mountain with
a grove, from which emerge the seven Virtues
with their handmaidens. Prudence, speaking for
the others, defends his mistress with great prolixity, asserting that they find their most welcome
abode in her, and comparing her, in the popular
pedantic fashion, to a vast number of ancient and
Biblical heroines. Her cruelty still remains without
an apology, and to this task the fair maiden Pity
now girds herself, but is refuted by the author.
Thus repulsed and convicted of sophistry, the
Virtues retire, and the lover, now breaking into
verse, is left in his suffering to direct a last desperate appeal to the lady. As the sun sets and
the moon rises, he brings the tale to an end, grasping his bared sword, in an agony of doubt as to
whether he shall commit suicide or await her response.

The whole composition, suggested perhaps by
the *Siervo Libre de Amor*, is written in the manner
of Boccaccio's amorous sentiment and untutored
humanism. It is hard to detect, with Menéndez y
Pelayo, the influence of the *Vita Nuova*, or with
Amador de los Ríos, that of the *Divine Comedy*.
The idea of the lady attaining the Empyrean
through the exercise of faith, hope, and charity is

certainly not sufficient to suggest a Dantesque imitation. The curious explanation of the title in the dedicatory letter to Queen Isabella of Portugal is quite in the style of Boccaccio: discerning in the word "satire," by an extraordinary derivation, the ideas of both blame and praise, he regards the work as an exaltation of his mistress's "happiness" in life and a condemnation of his own "unhappiness."

The idea underlying the Erotic Hell often appears in metaphorical passages from the amorous verse of the fifteenth century. It persists intact, or in but slightly different dress, as a basis for complete poems, during the immediately succeeding period. The *Fiestas de Amor* * of Pedro Manuel de Urrea (1486?–1530) is an excellent example of the more realistic category, strongly coloured by Petrarch's *Triumph of Love*. Opening with one of the common mythological periphrases for the hour of the day, here adapted from the first lines of the *Triumphs*, he represents himself, a captive of the amorous deity, as visited by Death. Despite his long arraignment of her, she offers to conduct him through the infernal regions, in order that by inspection of lovers' torments he may recover from his passion. The peculiarities of Urrea's system, for which he apologizes in his interesting Prologue to Don Jaime de Luna, are that all the victims of Cupid, who are partly drawn from Petrarch, belong to the gentler sex and that he has felt it necessary to swell the inmates with a long list of ancient sages who have no place in the scheme of the Erotic Hell.

The *Sepoltura de Amor** by the same writer is a modified form of the type. The language plainly reveals the place of punishment to be a mere rhetorical figure : the turnkey, for instance, is " the thought of him who enters there." There is so much pleasure mingled with the pain of the state that the prison symbolizes, and liberty is so exquisitely interwoven with captivity, that Urrea regrets the obligation to depart. Setting out on his journey, however, he comes to the thick and rocky forest of despair, which he expressly likens to that described by Juan de Mena in the *Coronación ;* and beside a spring of cold water, in the spirit of the Petrarchan contrasts and paradoxes that litter the whole work, " with sad tears of happy agony" he creates another fountain of burning fire! While he meditates upon his woes, he beholds a tomb approaching, accompanied by two men, one in white, his Thought, and the other in black, his Heart. By them he is covered with the black mantle of sorrow and the white of charity, placed in the sepulchre, carried to a mountain, and handed over to three other men, who convey him back over the same road to the old prison, in which he is glad to be interred.

The *Metáfora en Metros* by Quirós in the *Cancionero General* is really another Sepulture of Love.* The tomb is a cart drawn by twenty savages, who symbolize the different afflictions of passion, such as Envy, Despair, and Suspicion, and guided by the blind figure of Desire. The withered corpse of a youth lies upon it, his soul fluttering above him in the air and his lost life walking behind him in the form of a *dueña anciana*.

Another variation upon the same theme is the anonymous *Hospital de Amor* published in the *Cancionero de Amberes*, dated 1557,† and probably inspired by the *Hospital d'Amours*, ascribed to Alain Chartier, and the *Livre du Cuer d'Amours Espris* of René d'Anjou. After a fruitless attempt to dissuade him from further subjection to his lady, Hope causes the author to be transported in a cloud to a desert, where the hermit Care exhibits to him the Hospital. The physician, "ancient Time," conducts him on visits to several invalids, prescribing allegorical remedies, conversation and amusement for the malady of desire and sirups of patience and fortitude for jealousy. It is indeed a cheerless lazaretto, where the diseases are really incurable and whence all women are banished to a separate institution. Fatally stricken, the writer

himself is laid on a restless bed, and finally despatches the almoner, Thoughtfulness, with a letter
to his mistress, beseeching her, in a spirit of resignation, to undertake the burial of his body. The
conception of love as a fatal disease, here and elsewhere in European allegory, may have been suggested by Ovid.*

PART II

THE EVOLUTION OF MEDIAEVAL SPANISH ALLEGORY

CHAPTER VIII

PRECEDENTS IN THE LATIN LITERATURE OF SPAIN

PRUDENTIUS

PRUDENTIUS in the fourth century has the honour of being the first Christian to use allegory as the setting of a whole composition. In the *Psychomachia* he depicts the battle of the Virtues and Vices in the field of the human soul. After a preface and an invocation to Christ, Fides struggles with Cultura Deorum, Pudicitia with Sodomita Libido, Patientia with Ira, Humilitas with Superbia, Sobrietas with Luxuria, Largitas with Avaritia, and Concordia with Discordia, the Virtue in each instance triumphing. To be the inventor of a *genre*, and one the popularity of which was to run riot in the succeeding centuries, was no mean achievement.

The classical poets had often turned to allegory; but Prudentius was the first to employ it as the substance of an entire and extended composition for a serious didactic and Christian purpose, and he thus established the precedent for one of the favourite mediaeval forms. The result of all our modern delving after sources is, of course, to demonstrate that all literary types are bottomless pits; there is no beginning to the Renaissance; there is no beginning to romanticism; there is no beginning to allegory. One gets into a state of mind in which he almost doubts whether any quality is characteristic of any age; and then, in a reaction to sanity, he realizes that, although the origin of a quality may stretch back even to the dawn of civilization, the quality at some time comes to dominate a period or a work of literature, and may then properly be described as characteristic. So allegory dominates many mediaeval compositions and is typical of the Middle Ages in a sense that is true of no previous era. Towards this consummation Prudentius took the first broad stride.

One must beware, on the other hand, of belittling the debt of Prudentius to the past. Puech, in his admirable study,* points out possible suggestions for the *Psychomachia* in Claudian and Tertullian. The pagan allegories were ready at hand, from the personification of the Virtues in the Roman religion to the literary personification of the Vices at the entrance to Hades by Virgil, and waited only to be transfigured for Christian service. Much of the poem, indeed, springs from the familiarity of Prudentius with the pagan poets,† for example, those incidents of the battle that are modelled entirely upon the episodes of the *Æneid*, as

when Pride decries Humility after the manner in
which Turnus upbraids Æneas.* He reveals allegorical leanings in another work, the *Hamartigenia*,
where he enumerates the different Vices as the cohort
of Satan.† All these *motifs*, however, required careful transposition into another key, the addition of
fresh and transitional themes, and scrupulous elaboration, that they might be harmonized into such an
original and consistent whole as the *Psychomachia*.

The effect of this composition, as one of the
chief starting points for the legion of personified
Virtues and Vices in early Christian and mediaeval
literature, is well-nigh incalculable. Germane to
our purpose, in Spain itself, Prudentius is forthwith imitated by another Spaniard, Theodulfus,
and the current of his influence may be traced
down through the early centuries of Spanish literature even to the *autos* of Lope and Calderón.‡
The first pretentious allegorical production of the
fifteenth century, Imperial's *Decir de las Siete Virtudes*, is concerned with this very topic of the opposition between the Virtues and Vices.

PAULUS EMERITANUS

Not only do the germs of allegorical substance
manifest themselves in the *Psychomachia* of Prudentius, but the setting to much later allegory is
foreshadowed in Spain itself by the ecstatic visions

of the other world related in the seventh century by Paulus Emeritanus and St. Valerius. In the first chapter of his *De Vita Patrum Emeritensium,** Paulus recounts the dream of Augustus, a young acolyte of the church of St. Eulalia at Merida. The lad finds himself in a luxuriant meadow, the constituents of which may be paralleled in many a French and Spanish allegory : " I was in a pleasant place, where there were many fragrant flowers, greenest grass, roses, lilies, many crowns of gems and gold, innumerable silken veils, and a light zephyr, cooling all with a breezy freshness." It is the earthly paradise, where the saints banquet with Christ enthroned as master of the feast. The boy is presented and partakes of the ambrosial food. As the guests are dismissed, some evildoers are brought before the judgment seat and excluded. It is gratifying to discover thus early in Spain an interest in the fate of contemporaries beyond the grave ; Paulus, to whom Augustus tells his vision, on asking if he recognized anyone in paradise, receives the delicately sarcastic reply that the heavenly throng are of a different form and dress from those of the present day. Finally, Christ, who here acts the same rôle as the guide in later examples, leads the youth into His garden, which again contains the flowers, the sweet odours, and even the crystalline water of French allegory.

ST. VALERIUS

In his writings to Donadeus, St. Valerius relates three visions that are of even greater significance as creating precedents for future allegorical
machinery. The first he sets down from the report
of the monk Maximus,* with the avowedly didactic purpose of captivating the reader by the beauties of heaven and frightening him by the horrors
of hell. To the former the recluse is led by an
angel as guide to find the conventional material
delights of the mediaeval bower, and specific allusion is made to the spring, which is to become
the prescribed season for joyful allegory. The
description of the flowers and their all-pervading
perfumes is particularly sensuous. The stress upon
the refulgent light affords an earlier prototype for
that illumination of Imperial's visionary realms
which has been heedlessly ascribed to the influence of Dante's *Paradiso*. Maximus is next
conducted to a precipice over the abyss of hell,
whence rise a darkening mist, the traditional
stench, and sounds as hideous and as varied as
those that issue from the mouth of the *Inferno*.
With a warning to practice righteousness in order
to avoid the terror of this region and to attain the
felicity of the other, the soul is dismissed to rejoin
the body.

The same didactic purpose exists in the vision of Bonellus.* The monk is first taken by an angel to a celestial chamber, constructed of gold and precious stones, and having some affinity with the magnificence of countless mediaeval palaces of Fortune or Love. Here he is promised an abode, if he will but persevere. He is then plunged into the cavern of hell. His fall is interrupted by a first ledge, but a voice cries "Vadat." Precipitated again, he is caught on a second ledge, where a beggar whom he has befriended prays for him. The voice, however, cries once more, and he drops to the lowest depths. Hell thus seems to be, somewhat as in Dante, a conical excavation with several circles. Satan sits in the midst, enchained, wearing upon his head an iron bird in the likeness of a crow, to which are attached the ends of his fetters. There is even some account of specific punishments. A fire is burning like a huge torch, and a broad stream of pitch overflows the plain. A pair of gigantic demons torment two sinners, while a third demon, reaching only to the waist of the first, spurs on the executioners. After he has been shown a nether pit like the Virgilian Tartarus, he is attacked by archers, but repelling their shafts with the sign of the cross, he is finally spirited back to this life.

The third vision,† like that of Augustus in

Paulus Emeritanus, is experienced by a young servant of St. Fructuosus Baldarius. The guides are doves, as in Berceo's *Santa Oria*. The boy is presented at the throne of glory, which in this case is situated upon an oriental mountain. St. Valerius adds an original touch when he represents God as bidding him wait to return until the rising sun has passed, so as to escape scorching. In a passage remarkable for the splendour and stateliness of its prose, the sun is pictured as rolling by beneath them, preceded by a monstrous red bird, which, fanning the air with the flapping of its wings, cools the seething heat. As he descends, the youth enjoys one of those geographical surveys, which are the commonplaces of allegorical journeys in later times, appearing in Spanish, for instance, in Juan de Mena's *Laberinto*. The fertile imagination of St. Valerius, finding expression in such details as the bird-helmeted Devil and the demons of varying stature, or the passage of the sun and the grotesque bird that accompanies it, supplies a fitting precedent for the fantasy of fifteenth-century allegory.

THEODULFUS

If Theodulfus of Orléans was a native Spaniard (and of this there can be little doubt),* we have at the beginning of the ninth century an example of an ardent admiration for allegory, not only in this case implicit in the author's literary production, but explicitly acknowledged, and inherited, surely, from the writer whom he chose as his youthful model, Prudentius. Being one in the long line of sages who have sought to uncover the secrets of heaven and hell,* he helped to create an interest in the supernatural realms as settings. The first three *Carmina* of his fourth *Liber* and the second of the fifth demonstrate his fondness for allegory. In the first, *De libris quos legere solebam*,† declaring that he reads pagan works because under the poet's fiction verities are often hidden, he goes on to particularize. Proteus signifies truth, which, when disguised, assumes the forms of a thousand different lies, but when firmly grasped, resumes its pristine shape; the immaculate Virgo or Astrea symbolizes justice; Hercules represents valour, and Cacus theft. The main section of the poem is an exegesis of Cupid's different attributes: the wings bespeak his lightness; nudity, the bareness of his crimes; the quiver, the depravity of love; the bow, treachery; the torch, the ardour of passion. The conclusion consists of so intricate an explanation of the portals of sleep, the horn gate telling of truth entering by the eyes, the ivory of falsity issuing by the mouth, that the fifteenth century itself could not have dissected allegory with more meticulous delight. The discernment of a latent meaning in classic myths looks forward to the peculiar kind of allegory or symbolism for which the Marquis of Santillana praises the Italians.

The next two *Carmina* are inspired by the sight of two pictures. The first concerns itself with the seven Liberal Arts, which are disposed upon the semblance of a tree against the background of a disk representing the world. Grammar sits at the root of the tree; Rhetoric and Dialectic are upon branches at the right; opposite these, the four cardinal Virtues. Arithmetic is ensconced above with her feet on different branches; still higher on either side are Music and Geometry; and at the summit is Astronomy. The characteristics and attributes of these personifications are minutely explained. Thus Grammar is the origin or support of the tree because all other Arts without her are nothing worth; in her left hand she grasps a scourge to drive on the indolent and in her right a knife to remove the vices. Because wisdom exercises everywhere the primacy, Grammar's head is decked with a diadem, and Good Sense and Renown stand by, since she originates in either one of them. The Virtues are distinguished by the same attributes as in later centuries. Prudence holds a book, which is to be the possession of her devotees; Fortitude is clad in full armour that she may conquer Vice and establish Liberty; Justice wields the scales, the sword, the palm, and crown, in order to weigh the deeds and works of mortals and to punish or reward; Temperance bears the reins of restraint and a scourge for the slothful. The higher seat and the greater number of lines allotted to Astronomy provide an early instance of that allegorical interest in the heavens which is to be so prominent in the works of Imperial and Juan de Mena.

The other poem is marked by the same didacticism, and like much of the allegory of Theodulfus, is based upon St. Isidore. The feminine personification of the Earth as the mother of all created things nurses an infant and fills a basket with fruit. On her head are towers to denote cities; and she carries a snake to figure the wily nature of the husbandman, a key to open and close the year, cymbals to suggest the clatter of the workman's tools, and arms to inspire to patriotic strife. The domestic and savage animals are placed in submission to her, and close at hand is a saddle to signify that all things are moved while she herself is still. She is borne upon a chariot because the world is suspended in the air and upon wheels because it whirls in a swift course.

In the fifth book is preserved an important counterpart to the analysis of the Virtues in the poem upon the Arts,—a fragmentary description of what appears to have been a procession of the Vices, written when as a youth Theodulfus was still greatly under the influence of Prudentius.* Since he first depicts each personification and then states the performances of her victims, the poem is a prototype, in the realm of the Vices, of the Triumph as evolved by Petrarch and naturalized in Spain, in which Love, Chastity, Fame, and the like are escorted in procession by their historical exemplars; but since also he suggests as armour against the Vices the contrary Virtues, the fragment may be called a kind of *Psychomachia*. The fashion in which Theodulfus here employs personification or hovers upon its borders, forming a kind of Limbo between abstraction and personification and applying indiscriminately personal and impersonal words to the Virtues and Vices, demonstrates how natural and deep-seated in mankind is the allegorical instinct.

PETRUS COMPOSTELANUS

In the middle of the century preceding allegorical composition in the vulgar tongue, the twelfth, Petrus Compostelanus in his *De Consolatione Rationis* furnishes a surprising parallel to the productions of later times.† As hinted in the title, the work is indebted to Boethius, who through the whole extent of Spanish literature, in Latin and in the vernacular, exercised an important influence, suggesting especially the allegorical female as guide. It bears some relation also to the *Synonyma* of St. Isidore, another work after the type of the *De Consolatione Philosophiae*, in which Ratio comforts men in desperation.* Petrus, besieged by the seductive figures of the World and the Flesh, is succoured by Reason, who shows to him the purer beauty of seven damsels typifying the seven Virtues. Forthwith appear four Vices, and enter into a debate with the Virtues, Reason acting as arbiter. The unabated enthusiasm for the figures of the Virtues and the combat against the Vices prepares the way for Imperial's *Decir de las Siete Virtudes*. In the course of the poem are introduced, in true Dantesque fashion, explanations of the Christian mysteries, abstruse discussions of free will, of the nature of sanctity, of original sin, of the Immaculate Conception, and of the Hypostatic Union, and descriptions of hell, the terrestrial paradise, and the blessedness of the saints.

Although Spanish literature in the vernacular occasionally reveals a knowledge of Latin allegory in other countries, it is plainly not necessary to seek the impetus for the *genre*, and especially for visions, in any other than the prototypes of the peninsula itself. In Spain, more than elsewhere, vigorous monastic life tended to perpetuate a knowledge of Christian literature in Latin ; and the earliest allegories in Castilian are indissolubly linked with the past.

CHAPTER IX

THE THIRTEENTH CENTURY

GONZALO DE BERCEO

IN the use of allegory by Gonzalo de Berceo, the chief versifier of the century, three different stages of development may be discerned. The *Milagros de Nuestra Señora* exemplifies the first: the mystical garden, the constituents of which are elucidated as the attributes of the Blessed Virgin, is attached only very loosely and clumsily to the body of the work, which relates twenty-five of her miracles, and it is not an integral part of the composition. The vision of the three crowns in the *Vida de Santo Domingo de Silos*, illustrating the second phase, is an artistic entity wherein the allegorical narrative is sustained to the end and its exegesis inextricably woven into the fabric. The more skilful treatment of allegory would tend to discredit the view of Amador de los Ríos,* who, following Sánchez,† believes this the earliest of Berceo's poems; but the point should not be pressed too far, since for such progress he is indebted to his Latin source, Grimaldus.‡ In any case, he continued to pursue the better course in the *Santa Oria*, explicitly declared by the poet himself to be a work of

his old age,* throughout which the visionary becomes the principal interest and is disturbed by no
prosaic elucidation. It is not necessary to inquire
whether to Berceo himself the visions in this instance
and in the *Santo Domingo* were allegories or absolute
realities. Inasmuch as his successors were to employ such visions as mere fictions, the increase of
the visionary in the later period of his production
is identical, from our standpoint, with an increase
of the allegorical, and constitutes a further step
in the evolution of the type. The dependence in
the *Santa Oria* upon the lost Latin biography
of the nun† does not diminish the significance of
his achievement, nor does it affect my theory
of his chronological development. The important
question is, not whether he derived the visionary
from his own brain or from another writer's, but
whether he deliberately chose, in his maturity, to
introduce more of it and to treat it more artistically.
Even if the Latin originals had been left untrans-
lated, their existence in the Iberian peninsula would
have been noteworthy as indicative at least of a
monastic and cultured interest in the visionary.
When they appear in the vernacular of Berceo, they
acquire additional significance as actual monuments
in the evolution of Spanish literature, the effect of
which was to infuse a taste for this literary form
and its peculiarities into more popular and untu-

tored minds. The acquaintance with previous Latin literature, revealed by these translations, demonstrates anew the unbroken connection between the allegory of the two ages.

The chief importance of the *Miracles of Our Lady** is that it exhibits the first clumsy method of allegorical presentation. The mystical garden is an early instance, in the vernacular, of those vernal bowers, constructed upon the model of monastic paradises, which in French and in later Spanish literature so often form the setting to agreeable allegories. There are the customary verdure, the shade, the flowers, the soft odours, the streams of cold and warm water, the music of the birds. The evidence is almost cogent enough to suggest a direct imitation of Berceo by Imperial in the verses upon the Seven Virtues : both, in a single line, use *olor* and one of its cognates, and both have the unique conception of the disappearance of all perspiration upon entering the garden.

The *Vida de Santa Oria,*† in which the visionary factors are no longer episodic, may be used to controvert those critics who believe that Spanish allegory really begins in the fifteenth century, generated by Italian influence. The chief ecstasy, in which the nun beholds her seat in heaven, is the centre of the poem, the converging point of all other incidents, occupying over one-third of the total number of lines. In addition to this, two other visions of the saint are related, one of the Blessed Virgin announcing her death, the other of the Mount of Olives, apparently conceived as the earthly paradise; likewise two visions are assigned to the mother, Amuña, the first of her deceased husband, Don García, foretelling the death of Oria, and the second of the daughter herself in glory. The visions absorb about five-eighths of the poem ; * there is a brief introductory sketch of the nun's antecedents and early life, and what small part of the remainder is not visionary is composed chiefly of transitional passages. The kernel of the piece is evidently the long vision of the seat prepared for the Saint in heaven : the short biography leads up to it, and upon it depend the other visions, — the announcement by the Virgin of the approaching exaltation to the throne, the sight of the Mount of Olives just before Oria's death, the second announcement by Don García, and the view vouchsafed Amuña of her daughter after she has been translated to the glory of the throne. In a composition, the centre and four auxiliary incidents of which are visions, the visionary element, equivalent, for our purpose, to the allegorical, instead of sporadic, is characteristic.

Some details are prototypes of elements existing in the allegory of the fifteenth century, which otherwise might be, and indeed, in many instances, actually have been, ascribed to the influence of the *Divine Comedy*. The accurate dating of such visions as those related in Imperial's *Decir* on the birth of John II or in Ruy Páez de Ribera's upon the regency has been alleged as evidence of Dantesque imitation, but out of the five visions of the *Santa Oria*, the principal one and three others are thus introduced. Oria is vouchsafed a sight of her celestial seat upon the third night after Christmas, the feast of St. Eugenia ; the Blessed Virgin appears upon the third night before the feast of St. Saturninus, " which falleth in November close to St. Andrew's " ; Amuña beholds her deceased spouse in the second week of March on the feast of St. Gregory the Great, and her beatified daughter in the middle of May on Whitsunday. The scrupulous observance of the date is a commonplace of European allegory,* and may be prompted by a desire for realism, the lack of which the mediaeval poet must have recognized when he contemplated the whimsicalities of the usual vision.

Another cog of mediaeval machinery is the guide. At first, Oria has three, SS. Agatha, Eulalia of Merida, and Cecilia, the last of whom also appears in a subordinate vision to prepare the nun for the visitation of the Virgin. The three celestial damsels in the second canto of the *Inferno* and

Beatrice in the *Paradiso* are the analogues that immediately suggest themselves; and there is a maiden
conductor, Providencia, in Juan de Mena's *Laberinto*. As in Dante, queries are made by the writer
and answered by the guides. The analogy becomes
even more exact * when Oria, though timid before,
is emboldened, as she rises in holiness, to inquire
for her old nurse. The group are admitted through
three windows to heaven by three *sanctos varones*,
who, as keepers of paradise, are not too remote from
Cato in the *Purgatorio*. A surer and more surprising
similarity to the Italian poem is the ascent of Oria
into the supernal regions by concentrating her
gaze upon a dove, the symbol of the Holy Spirit,
here probably typifying Oria's divine inspiration,
just as Dante is drawn up by steadfastly looking
into the eyes of Beatrice.†

The earthly paradise is painted in the colours of
a French garden, but heaven itself is parallel in many
respects to Dante's. Some system is evident in
the division of the blessed into six categories: canons
(52–56), bishops (57–62), virgins (63–79), martyrs
(80–82), hermits (83–85), and apostles (86–87).
There pass *muchas honradas processiones;* above the
whole scene Christ is heard but not seen; and
like Dante,‡ Berceo demurs before the lofty theme:

> Dexemos lo al todo, a la siella tornemos,
> La materia es alta, temo que pecaremos.

The celestial host, as at the happy outcome of Dante's examination,* rejoices at the return of the three virgin saints with Oria, and the company of virgins itself receives her with the honour that the poets give to Dante in Limbo. Again, Oria meets many contemporaries, some in each category, except naturally in those of the martyrs and the apostles. The author vents his indignation against an unworthy bishop by failing to find him among the beatified prelates and by denouncing him with Dantesque virulence. Among the hermits she discovers, with others whom she recognizes, her own father, and in her second vision, among the glorified mortals, a certain Don Sancho. With still closer parallelism to the *Divine Comedy*, she hears amidst the virgins the voice of her old nurse Urraca, in a happier environment, however, than that in which Dante encounters his master, Brunetto Latini. As in the case of Henry VII in the *Paradiso*,† a splendid throne awaits Oria, watched over by the mysterious damsel Voxmea. Since so many elements of later allegory here find a first manifestation before a word of the *Divine Comedy* was written, greater caution than has been the custom should be observed in relegating them forthwith to the category of Dantesque imitations.

The description of hell in the *Libro de Alex-*

andre, whether Baist's attribution to Berceo is correct or not,* likewise presents curious analogies both to the *Divine Comedy* and to later Castilian allegory; but it is perhaps more significant to note that here in the first of the many Spanish journeys to the infernal regions there is an approximation to passages in Virgil. The imitation, to be sure, is derived from the Latin original, the *Alexandreis* of Gautier de Châtillon, and, considering the vast popularity of Virgil in the Middle Ages, was to be expected in any attempt at the epic, however falsely classical in tone; but with the translation into the vernacular the seeds were implanted in Spain.

Nature finds the mouth of hell beset with the Vices, like the dread allegorical figures of the *Æneid*,† and the author cannot resist the mediaeval temptation to dilate upon these favourite personifications until he makes their analysis the chief part of the episode. The monsters whom Æneas encounters at the entrance ‡ are paralleled by the *muchas malas serpientes* which, as in the grotesque mediaeval frescoes, wait with hideously gaping jaws amidst the infernal thorns and thistles to devour the victims. Though the scheme of hell is only dimly outlined, an outer region seems to exist for punishing certain sins, some of which are casually mentioned in connection with the description of the Vices, as if the writer had some system in his own mind that he forgets to reveal. For example, the perjurers stand naked, their tongues devoured by worms; the gluttons suffer the condemnation of Tantalus; the slothful are boiled in pitch and lead. This region corresponds to the outer circle in Hades,* and analagous to the classical and Virgilian conception of an inner abyss or Tartarus,† in the midst of hell is a fiery furnace, where burn the devil and abandoned souls, like the presumptuous Titans of old, and where indeed the Virgilian Tityus appears in strange mediaeval company. Finally, the whole incident of the descent of Nature to inspire sedition against Alexander may be modelled upon that of the *Æneid* in which Juno arouses the Fury Alecto against the Trojans.‡

Some fortuitous resemblances to the *Divine Comedy* again establish the tradition of details in later allegory for an explanation of which an appeal is usually but erroneously made to Dante. Savi-Lopez § discerns a greater elaboration and a more careful division of punishments than appear in the original *Alexandreis*. Outer hell, as may be gleaned from vague suggestions, seems to be separated into different circles of the several vices, and in the furnace of hell are varying degrees of torment according to desert. The entrance to hell,

like that of the *Inferno*,* admits of no escape ; the
damned, like the souls upon the banks of Acheron,†
curse their destiny ; and unbaptized infants, as in
Limbo,‡ do not suffer but are enveloped in gruesome darkness. The most significant analogy to
the fifteenth century is the painstaking and disproportionate digression upon the nature of the
Vices. The analysis is as minute as in the *Decir
de las Siete Virtudes*, and after the same fashion as
the Virtues, almost every Vice is accompanied by
personified subordinates. Thus Avarice and her
sister Covetousness are followed by the hand-
maiden Ambition, and Lust is pictured in the
midst of her foul crew. The didactic tendency is
so ingrained that the writer cannot refrain, even in
a vision which purports to be realistic and is an
integral part of the general plot, from an explanation of the purely accessory figures of the Vices that
in its length and perspicacity obscures the main
theme and destroys the harmony of the whole.

The figures of the four Seasons upon Achilles's
shield constitute another allegorical element,§
and the signs of the zodiac and the seven planets,
represented in the same place, though not strictly
allegorical, are to be put to such uses in subsequent
literature. The pictures of heaven and hell upon
the top of Alexander's tent, the description of
which seems to be original with the author, and

the passages in Berceo's composition, entitled, *Of the Signs that shall appear before the Judgment*, depicting the punishments of the damned and the delights of the blessed, show the mediaeval mind so besieged by these concepts that their adaptation to allegorical purposes was inevitable. In the latter instance, the torments in general are first outlined, — fire and darkness, hunger and cold, bad food, smoke for the eyes, a stench for the nose, vinegar for the lips, gall for the palate, gripes for the bowels, and Dantesque serpents which gnaw through to the heart. Special penalties are next measured out to different sins: evil speakers are suspended by their tongues, the mouths of the covetous stuffed with gold, dishonest officials loaded with iron, unworthy clerics beset by angry beasts; proud tyrants, as in the *Purgatorio*, are bent low and go about begging, the envious are spurned by the kicks of all. Into heaven the blessed enter in procession after Christ, singing hymns, free from anxiety, and enjoying five graces: immortality, an effulgence greater than of seven suns, unobstructed vision, lightness of body to facilitate flight, and security from harm. Some of these details are again noteworthy as direct prototypes of fifteenth-century peculiarities.

OTHER ALLEGORIES OF THE THIRTEENTH CENTURY

Two anonymous compositions, though hitherto inexplicably slighted in discussions of Spanish allegory, are of prime importance in their relation to French models and to the productions of the fifteenth century: the *Disputa del Alma y el Cuerpo*, and what is generally known now from the name of the scribe as the *Romance de Lope de Moros*. The first of these, written across a Latin document of 1201 and belonging to at least as early a date as the opening of that century, falls into the large mediaeval class known as the *Debate of the Body and the Soul* or the *Vision of Philibertus*, and is the earliest of a series in Spain upon this subject.* Its dependence upon an Anglo-Norman original is a link in the chain of evidence which proves that what extraneous influences exist in Spanish allegory are of northern rather than Italian derivation; and it affords, two centuries before the assumed introduction of Dantesque motives, a plain example of a dream used as the framework to didactic matter. The author, dating his vision with customary exactness at the end of a Saturday and the dawn of a Sunday, explicitly declares that it occurred in his sleep. Somewhat differently from the ordinary type, in which the body starts by upbraiding the soul, the soul here commences the abuse; but since all except the opening tirade is lost, we must resort for the rest to the Anglo-Norman source.

Much discussion has been spent upon the other two fragments, comprised under the name *Romance de Lope de Moros* and published for the first time by Morel-Fatio* as separate compositions under the titles of *Poème d'Amour* and *Débat du Vin et de l'Eau*. The *Poème d'Amour*, usually called now from the opening lines the *Razón de Amor*, is an idyll describing a scholar's more or less imaginary encounter with his lady, and thus belongs to a class which, as I have sought to demonstrate, may be regarded as allegorical; the *Debate of Water and Wine* is seen by its name to be a member of a large and well known category of mediaeval verse. It is a question whether they are to be considered as separate poems or parts of the same poem.† The protagonists of disunion are Petraglione and Carolina Michaëlis de Vasconcellos, who ascribe the awkward juncture to some lumbering copyist; the latter differs from the former only in suppressing certain lines that she regards as added to the original compositions for a makeshift at a transition. Monaci, Gorra, Baist, and lastly Menéndez Pidal maintain that the two fragments were meant by the author to constitute

a single poem. Gorra surmises that he has translated and united two foreign pieces without heed
to the artistic discord. Baist, on what ground I do
not know, would trace the juncture to the French
original. Monaci and Menéndez Pidal suggest
that the author had the specific intent of exhibiting the dexterity of his trade by joining two incongruous scenes. Though the links between the
love poem and the debate, adduced by Menéndez
Pidal as impossible for a mere copyist, are by no
means conclusive evidence, they tend to inspire
a belief in the unity of the whole composition.
The difficulties, however, are of little importance
to us : whether the two parts are to be conceived
as originally distinct, or one as a digression within
the other, for our present purpose we need only note
the two diverse themes. It is, in any case, an error,
as Petraglione was the first to point out, to print
the whole first part separately and to call it with
Morel-Fatio *Poème d'Amour* or with Menéndez y
Pelayo *Aventura Amorosa;* * for this also is subdivided into two separate parts, the one forming an
introduction and setting to the Debate, the other
consisting of the detached amorous episode and
having no apparent logical connection with the
theme of the Debate.

After a preface in which he discusses the excellence of his poem and his own cosmopolitan

education in courtliness, the writer imagines himself, in the month of April, a popular time for such
experiences, as lying down after his meal under
an olive tree and as seeing in the branches of an
apple orchard a silver vessel full of red wine,
placed there by the mistress of the garden and
possessing the magical property of curing whoso-
ever drinks of it daily. He discerns also, in some
vague spot above the wine, a vessel of cold
water, which rises from the apple orchard and
which he hesitates to drink for fear of enchant-
ment. Here commences the long digression of
the meeting with his mistress, which for the moment I pass over. When she has departed, he
continues without transition the allegorical setting to the Debate by describing the appearance
of a dove, which, frightened from bathing in the
spring of the olive orchard by the sight of the
author, seeks the vessel of water in the apple orchard.* Having refreshed itself, the bird in its
rapid flight overturns the water into the wine below,
thus precipitating the encounter and consequent
quarrel of the two liquids. The introduction and
the Debate itself are further riveted together by a
double reference in the latter to the commixture
as the motive for the argument.

The mingling of the two liquids is a common
setting for the mediaeval subject of a debate

between Wine and Water. Thus in the French *Débat du Vin et de l'Eaue*,* Pierre Jamec, also after a meal, provokes the dispute by mixing the two in his glass. In our anonymous composition† the device of the dove and the basins of wine and water hidden away amidst the foliage of an orchard is more ingenious and poetical, and possesses a certain charm of mystery. Although, strictly, Wine and Water are personifications rather than allegorical figures, the treatment does not differ from that of the ordinary allegorical debate. The introductory fiction, though somewhat more extended, serves the purpose, as in the debates of Ruy Páez de Ribera, of a framework for a didactic argument. It is an instructive comment on the attempt of those who would trace Ribera's inclination for allegory to Dantesque influence that there exists in Spain two centuries before his day, not a general, but an exact prototype to his poems, and that the imaginative setting in the identical sort of composition plays a more important rôle prior to the entrance of Dante into Spain.

The erotic episode itself is more or less on the plane of allegory. Lying in a meadow bedight with varied flowers, and watered by a spring the coolness of which spreads a hundred feet around, the writer, as he is about to sing of *fin amor*, beholds a fair lady approaching and likewise singing of love. After the mediaeval fashion, he describes her loveliness in most scrupulous detail. Her song is of the scholar who is unfaithful to her. She does not perceive the writer until, grasping her by the hand, he draws her to his side beneath the olive tree and questions her of her lover. Learning that she does not know him except by reputation, and by the gloves, hat, coral, and ring that he has sent her, he recognizes her forthwith by his own gifts, and she him by the belt that she has embroidered with her own hands. Like Basiliola in D'Annunzio's *La Nave*, she slips the mantle from her shoulders, they have their pleasure, and she leaves him.

The background of the episode is one of the conventional gardens that are to form so frequent a feature of literary landscape in the fifteenth century. The first lines, assigning the events to the springtime and laying the scene in an orchard, belong both to the erotic episode and to the Debate, but in the former they are later much augmented by a lengthy description of the fountain and a detailed list of the flowers. The whole passage is closely parallel to the beginning of the *Decir de las Siete Virtudes*. Just as the earlier poet is surprised by the lady of his heart, so, in the midst of a garden surrounded by a sweetly murmuring stream, carpeted by flowers, and redolent with soft odours, Imperial perceives Leah singing and gathering blossoms. The similarity to the dream of the twenty-seventh canto of the *Purgatorio* and to the fulfilment of the dream in the twenty-eighth might seem exact enough to suggest a relationship, were that possible, and once more proves how hazardous it is to dogmatize about specific imitations, unless they be extended or verbal.

The lapse of two centuries brings with it no appreciable difference in the verses that tell of Imperial's amorous wound and captivity. The same emphasis is given to the flowers and their perfume, and the many and varied constituents of the lady's beauty are enumerated with the same meticulous care. The surprisingly unmasculine familiarity with feminine costume finds an analogue in the description of the French lady whom Imperial in another poem discovers hunting along the bank of the Guadalquivir.

The presence of all this material in the thirteenth century renders it absurd to speak in very decided terms about any new allegorical school at the beginning of the fifteenth century. Since the Marquis of Santillana, the chief exponent of allegory during the later period, does not employ this form in at least half of his productions, if we are to speak at all of a Spanish allegorical school, Berceo should not improperly have a place in it. If he is responsible for the *Alexandre*, his title is all the stronger; if not, allegory of these early days occupies a still broader field, for another poet not only imports allegorical elements from his sources but adds touches of his own.

FRENCH INFLUENCES

In this discussion of primitive Spanish allegory, it has been necessary often to allude to French sources; these may now be recapitulated and grouped with others, in order to demonstrate for the whole early period the very general reliance upon the north. It has not yet been determined whether the legends themselves of Berceo's *Milagros de Nuestra Señora* are to be derived from the collection of Gautier de Coincy or from two Latin collections, one published by Bernhard Pez and the other in a Paris manuscript;* the setting of the garden can in any case be paralleled by countless examples across the Pyrenees. The *Santa Oria* and the *Santo Domingo* are amplified translations, one from a lost Latin biography by the nun's confessor, the other from Grimaldus, and some of the ornaments may have been filched from France. In the former I have already alluded to the pedantic dating of the visions as a suggestion of French methods; and the poet, according to the prevalent custom, degrades the earthly paradise into the ordinary French bower with a mystical tree in the centre. The sources of the *Alexandre* we have already seen to be French. Likewise, the pleasing though conventional picture of May and summer,* for which no source has been discovered, is thoroughly Gallic.

The *Disputa del Alma y el Cuerpo* is a translation, not of the Latin original, but of an Anglo-Norman version. The two parts of the composition published by Morel-Fatio are related to productions across the Pyrenees. He himself comments upon the analogy between this and certain French debates of Wine and Water, adding other Latin and Spanish parallels.† The two chief French analogues are the earlier *Desputoison du Vin et de l'Iaue* ‡ and the later *Débat du Vin et de l'Eaue*. The mere circumstances of the debate in the former are not analogous, for Water puts in his voice only after he is weary of hearing the several wines of France bicker about their respective merits. But certain similarities in the setting of the latter have already been indicated, and further similarities in the presentation of the cases of both Wine and Water may be found in the footnotes of Morel-Fatio. Finally, the digression upon the meeting with the lady is connected with the *pastourelles*.§

CHAPTER X

THE type that has appeared in the earlier period with the *Disputa del Alma y el Cuerpo* is reimbodied in a prose version called by its first editor, Octavio de Toledo, *Visión de Filiberto.** Assigned by him to a date after 1330, it is based directly on the Latin *Dialogus inter Corpus et Animam*, known also by the name *Rixa Animi et Corporis.†* The tradition of a visionary framework for the debate still persists, and the interest in the infernal regions, which is manifested in the early Christian ecstasies and in the *Alexandre* and which was to express itself in the many examples of the Erotic Hell, here crops out again. The picture of the demons descending upon the doomed soul is amplified with greater terror and grotesqueness than in the Latin text, and the occasional allusions to the pains of hell, like the detailed descriptions of the *Alexandre,* are more frightful than the original. There is no more hope in hell than Dante admits in his *Inferno,* and the penal system is very naïve in its regulation of punishment according to the wealth of the condemned. The *Visión* *de Filiberto*, constituting a link between the *Disputa del Alma y el Cuerpo* of the thirteenth century and the *Revelación de un Ermitaño* of the late fourteenth, proves again the continuity of Spanish allegory.

JUAN RUIZ

The *Libro de Buen Amor* by Juan Ruiz, Archpriest of Hita,* is saturated with allegorical elements, greater in number and more distinct in nature than those of the *Alexandre* or the undoubted works of Berceo. As the most momentous poetical composition of the time, the work surely can be assumed to voice some of its main tendencies and to possess a strong formative influence in the evolution of Spanish letters.

Considered as a whole, the *Libro de Buen Amor* could almost be said to be constructed on a single allegorical background. Although the erotic escapades of the Archpriest constitute the substance of the poem, they are accompanied through a large part by a species of allegory that at the same time illustrates and unifies them; or to put it another way, the vicissitudes of the author's passion, which form the main theme, are allegorically set forth, and then liberally punctuated with actual episodes. The scheme, in broad outline, is the following. When in the beginning he is constantly

unsuccessful in his amorous attempts, he symbolizes his deliberation and mental upheaval by a
debate between Love and himself, in which the
former is roundly scored as the source of all wickedness and misfortune and as bringing in his train
the mortal Sins. Love responds by a long instruc-
tion upon the proper mode of conduct for winning
feminine acquiescence. Ruiz proceeds further to
symbolize his deliberation by the admonitions
that he puts into the mouth of " Sennora donna
Venus muger de don Amor," to whom he conceives that he has now betaken himself.* All this
purely allegorical passage consumes about one-
fourth of the entire work. After several peccadil-
loes, he illustrates the restraint of Lent by the
temporary victory of Cuaresma over Don Carnal,
and the relaxation from discipline at Easter by the
triumphal return of Flesh † and Love and a vision of the latter's tent, in which sit the twelve
months engaged in their various occupations.
Many lapses from virtue, which follow, are thus
allegorically prophesied ; but when the procuress,
Trotaconvientos, has been laid away with an epi-
taph, a final allegorical passage, a detailed statement of the spiritual armour to be used against
the seven deadly Sins, suggests that the higher
nature in the end is victorious. Neither this nor
any other of the Archpriest's moralizations, how-

ever, is to be taken very seriously but rather as a concession to the temper of the age, and it is obvious that what he truly relishes is the retrospect upon his scabrous intrigues. The varied incidents are thus cast into relief against the allegorical setting and are bound together by it into a real unity, the supposed lack of which has been so often deprecated. Not only is the general plan allegorical, but in actual figures the allegorical passages amount to slightly less than half the poem.* Since Santillana himself cannot show a much better proportion, the *Book of True Love* indicates a lively interest in allegory persisting through the fourteenth century.

The production of Juan Ruiz looks backward to the *Alexandre* and forward to John II's court, and may be considered a link in the chain of allegorical development that extends unbroken from the thirteenth to the fifteenth century. The description of Love's tent is derived from the *Alexandre*,† and the triumphant procession of Love is said to reflect Alexander's entry into Babylon.‡ There is a parallelism also in the presentation of the capital sins through an allegorical framework. As the Vices in the *Alexandre* appear in the form of Furies at the entrance to Hell, and as the Virtues in Imperial's composition take the form of ladies amidst the beauties of a French garden, so in the *Libro de Buen Amor* the Vices assume the rôle of Love's retainers. No essential distinction exists between the use of allegory in the three cases to embody didactic matter. The famous mythological and Biblical examples under each Vice * point forward to the analogous lists of the fifteenth century and forestall the influence upon later Spanish literature of similar passages in the sculptured or chanted illustrations of Dante's *Purgatorio*, in the processions of Petrarch's *Triumphs*, or in such works as Boccaccio's *De Claris Mulieribus*.

Several episodes anticipate certain poems of the fifteenth century. The procession of Love and Flesh, if isolated, might very well be mistaken for a production of John II's court. Don Carnal, exalted upon a seat of skins and leathers, slaughtering axe and knife in hand, holding in leash his hunting dogs, is received with a barbecue of cattle and great merrymaking. Don Amor, in the midst of a vast mediaeval orchestra of the most bewildering instruments, the names and queer variety of which supply an interesting precedent to Richard Strauss, is met (with a subtle irony) by the different monastic Orders, singing, in a not uncommon mediaeval form of bad taste, excerpts from Latin hymns, some from the most sacred moments of the Mass. It is a veritable Triumph of the Petrarchan type, and obviates the necessity of deriving such poems as Santillana's *Triunphete de Amor* unreservedly from Italian models. The theme contained in a single stanza about the wound from his lady's arrow and its great pain received extended development, probably with additional influence from French originals, in the most thoroughly Gallic of all Imperial's compositions, and, with a change to the arrow of Venus, in the most thoroughly Gallic of Santillana's compositions, *El Sueño*. The armour against the seven deadly Sins, discussed at great length and paralleled by the armour against the devil in the *Castigos y Documentos del Rey Don Sancho*,* furnishes a Spanish prototype for the very graceful conceit of Imperial, whereby he arms himself against his literary enemies with the beauties of his lady.

Not only is the proportion of allegory greater than in Berceo, but partly through French influence, partly through a natural development, its type is well defined and close to that of John II's court. The incidents are now invariably regarded as absolutely fictitious. The dispute between the Archpriest and Love, the lectures of Love and of Venus, the battle of Flesh and Lent, are mere inventions concocted for the purely literary purpose of crystallizing and enhancing what might otherwise be the somewhat tedious musings of the poet's conscience. When once transported, however, to this confessedly fictitious world, he describes allegorical personages and happenings with a vigour that produces the illusion of reality. Don Carnal and Cuaresma have an existence of their own, so that sometimes they even perform acts that have no direct allegorical connotation. The former dispatches two letters, one warning all sinners against Don Carnal and announcing the imminent conflict, another challenging Don Carnal himself. The imprisonment and penance of the latter are related with as much perspicacity * as if they constituted one of the author's immoral escapades. Don Carnal duplicates the action of Cuaresma by a counter-challenge and a notification to society in general. After the Triumph of Love and Flesh and the housing of the former with the Archpriest, the figures of the Months in Love's tent are sketched with the same realism as the actual characters in the tale. In the description of Alexander's tent in the *Alexandre*, from which this passage seems to be derived, the Months are only depicted upon one of the four sides as decoration. In Juan Ruiz, once granted the allegory, they take on individuality and become concrete personalities seated in the tent of Love, the winter Months, beginning with January, appearing as three *caba-*

lleros at a gaming-board, the spring Months, beginning with April, as three *fijosdalgo* at a table, the summer Months, beginning with July, as three *ricos hombres* engaged in a dance, and the autumn Months as three labourers. The vision of the three crowns and the ecstasies of the saintly virgin in Berceo, and the descent into hell in the *Alexandre*, have life and movement, and are interesting in themselves, but the didactic purpose is everywhere uppermost. The *Libro de Buen Amor* approximates yet more closely the mature type of the fifteenth century, surpassing even the works of Imperial and his contemporaries, in the increased vividness of the mystic world and the unadulterated joy experienced in the account of its delights. When this attitude is attained, allegory becomes absolutely a thing by itself, significant and pleasurable in itself.

The fourteenth century emphasizes the innocent plagiarism from France. The principal allegorical episode of the *Libro de Buen Amor*, the strife of Lent and Flesh, a member of the large and popular class of *débats*, is imitated, not from French methods in general, nor from a Latin version in France, but directly from a well known French poem in the vernacular,* the *Bataille de Carême et de Charnage*. The alliance of Love and Flesh is probably to be traced to the *fabliau, Des Cha-*

noinesses et des Bernardines.* The presentation of the Months is drawn from the passage in the *Alexandre*, and this in turn from the French *Roman d'Alexandre*. For the covert satire of making the several religious Orders welcome the procession of Love, there is a general precedent in the frequent attacks of French literature upon the clergy, especially on those in the regular life, and possibly a direct source in Rutebeuf's arraignment of the different Orders, one after the other, in such works as *Les Ordres de Paris* and *La Chanson des Ordres*. The long list of musical instruments in the Triumph is also of French origin, either taken, through the French and Spanish epics of Alexander, from the Pygmalion episode in the *Roman de la Rose*,† or modelled upon such categories, which were common enough in France during the Middle Ages.‡

CHAPTER XI

THE FIFTEENTH CENTURY

FRANCISCO IMPERIAL

THE FIRST PERIOD

THE study of the great century of allegory, the fifteenth, naturally begins with the Sevillan school, which flourished from about 1400 to 1450, and in that school with its leader, Imperial. As the first in Spain to exhibit traces of Dantesque imitation, he imposes upon us forthwith the task of determining the precise nature and significance of the foreign influence at its entrance into the peninsula.

With respect to his employment of allegory, Imperial's career may be divided into three stages. In the first, he reveals a strict subservience to French ideals and an utter absence of Dantesque interest; the second is marked by a tendency to a more original use of French form and to its adornment by a few reminiscences from the *Divine Comedy*, in the third, he continues the basic allegory of French provenience, but decks it out meretriciously and extensively with Dantesque borrowings. Since some of his compositions form transitions from one period to the other, it is not advisable to pigeonhole each of them in one of these categories. Nor may the categories be regarded as severely chronological. Imperial may whimsically have composed verses wholly in the French style when his originality had already hazarded certain flights; and an interval of some indifference to Dantesque decoration may very well have succeeded a period of greater devotion. My chronology, however, is not affected by the description of his age in the first stanza of the *Decir de las Siete Virtudes*, which I assign to his last phase : *De la mi hedat non aun en el ssomo;* for, as Amador de los Ríos suggests,* this may be only a recollection of Dante's *Nel mezzo del cammin di nostra vita;* or even if the phrase is taken literally as referring to middle life, it is by no means extraordinary that a writer should attain the plenitude of his style before the age of forty or fifty years. In general, therefore, I would cling to the three stages of development, the more scrupulous preceding the freer Gallic imitation, and the fewer preceding the more extensive borrowings from Dante.

Of the first category the *Decir* on Love's wound is the most perfect example.† At dawn, in an arbour of flowers, amidst the songs of nightingales, the writer hears a voice summoning him to surrender himself its prisoner. Turning his eyes, he beholds

a lady bright as the sun, with countenance out-
shining the flowers. After he has dilated upon her
varied beauties and compared her to the flowers
to the latter's disadvantage, he describes her bow
and arrow, explaining the allegorical significance of
the several parts. Supplicated in vain for mercy, the
lady lets fly with all her might an arrow poisoned
by the herb of love and lays him low in the
meadow. Still pitiless, she unlooses her lovely
girdle, winds it about his neck, and drags him
captive after her through the garden. Having be-
sought once more in vain for release, he asks her
name, revealing enigmatically some letters of his
own. Forthwith at her cruelty the nightingales
beat their wings and call for vengeance, the roses
wither, the laurels drop their foliage, and the water
loses its sweetness.

Two aspects of this poem require particular
stress, the continuity of the tradition that binds it
to previous allegory and the already mentioned
Gallic flavour. Its close resemblance to the *Aventura Amorosa* of the thirteenth century I have already noted. The bower includes all the proper-
ties of a French garden. The detailed analysis of
the loved one's charms and the emphasis upon the
flowers are also French. The elucidation of the
several parts of the bow and arrow as concomi-
tants of the condition of love is the amorous and

rather paltry allegory that finds its most perma-
nent expression in the *Roman de la Rose*. The cord,
for instance, is explained as " various thoughts,"
and the iron as " torment with sweet odours." The
central event of the wound from the arrow brings
the whole composition into a large class that emanates probably more or less directly from the long
episode in the *Roman de la Rose* in which Amour
wounds Amant with the five arrows of Biauté,
Simplece, Courtoisie, Franchise, and Biau-Sem-
blant.* Ovid, however, may have helped to suggest the idea of the amorous wound in Spanish as
in other mediaeval allegory.† The very fact that
the *Decir* is completely in the French manner endows it with an aesthetic unity characteristic of
similar compositions across the Pyrenees and not
possessed by those other works of Imperial upon
which Dantesque reminiscences are often incon-
gruously grafted.

A considerable number of shorter poems are
still wholly in the French mode. They are not so
thoroughly allegorical as the *Decir* just discussed.
Some are symbolic meetings of the same kind as the
Romance de Lope de Moros, one or two are simply
addresses to ladies on special occasions; but with
a single exception they all contain allegorical matter. Although in two or three may perhaps be
discerned the beginning of a tendency to adopt

Dantesque ornaments, no one of these few possibilities will prove to be a certain reminiscence, and they are in any case so slight as not to affect at all the general character of the compositions.

I begin with three that do not betray even the remotest trace of Dantesque leanings. If I quote the prose heading of the first,* which comprises only four strophes, its substance will be evident: " This Decir was made by the said Micer Francisco Imperial for love and praise of the said Isabel González, mistress of the Count Don Juan Alfonso, inasmuch as she had sent to ask him to visit her at the convent of St. Clement, and he dared not go for the reason that she was a very splendid and gracious lady." The following details are especially indicative of French influence. The allusions to the Court of Love we need not recapitulate. The second strophe mentions definitely a prison of love, confinement in which the author seeks to avoid. In the last strophe he speaks of Isabel's allurements as allegorical armour, an idea which we shall see him employing for the central theme of another poem. The conceit underlying the whole composition, the danger that lurks in the mistress's charms, is closely allied with the allegory of amorous captivity that received an ampler expression in the former *Decir*.

Although the other two compositions † are

anonymous in the *Cancionero de Baena,* I have little hesitancy in ascribing them to Imperial. First, they occur in the regular series of his poems, which stretches from no. 226 through no. 250, broken only by replies from other versifiers or by compositions on related subjects. With the exception of such interruptions, it is Baena's general scheme to present all the works of each author as a separate and continuous collection; and the two poems in question do not constitute interruptions of either kind. Secondly, they follow immediately upon four anonymous strophes, assigned by the editor, Pidal, to Imperial,* whether on the same grounds as mine or on others, I do not know. Thirdly, the first poem takes place at Seville, the abode of Imperial. Fourthly, since no other contributor to the *Cancionero de Baena* exhibits allegory of this particular French variety, the attribution to Imperial becomes virtual certainty. Although hitherto neglected by scholars, the compositions are of prime importance in determining the provenience of Imperial's characteristics. Even could it be proved that they were not his, they would belong to some related poet and would still justify my contentions about allegory of that period.

The first, curiously like the long *Decir* upon the amorous wound, I have already discussed as a member of the class of *pastourelles.* The Guadal-

quivir as the place of the encounter with the lady
suggests an analogy to the series of poems addressed to Estrella Diana; and the longer *Decir*,
related by its substance to the poem in question,
might then belong to the same group.

The second of the anonymous compositions
recounts a meeting with four allegorical ladies,
each appropriately gowned, Chastity in *alvo cen-
dal*, Humility in *un paño gris*, Patience in *xamete
prieto*, and Loyalty in *color de un fyno çafyr oriental*. Having engaged in the conventional debate as to precedence, they choose Philosophy as
judge. Leaping forth from a rose bush in which
he has been hidden, the writer proffers himself as
their legal representative before the judge, and,
after performing his mission, comes to the conclusion * that whomever of the four his eyes light
upon he judges her of greater worth. The dispute takes place in a French landscape, and, fettered by the memory of conventional descriptions,
he cannot refrain from attaching to his bush the
fragrant rose, though the point has no bearing
upon the substance of the poem.

We now come to a series of four compositions
upon the Sevillan lady whom he dubs Estrella
Diana. Despite the fact that the first of these †
contains three possible recollections of Dante,‡ it
is completely French in general character and in

detail, and the other two in the series, also wholly
in the French manner, exhibit no trace of the *Divine Comedy*. Even if, then, the certainty of the
Dantesque allusions might be admitted, this first
member of the " sequence " could not be classified in the second division of Imperial's works,
where the Dantesque has acquired some importance, however superficial. The name of the lady
is itself derived from the northern romance of
Paris et Vienne, which Imperial shows other evidence of having read. Diane, the name of Vienne's
mother, is thus glossed at the very beginning of
the oldest French manuscript of the work : *C'est
le nom d'une tres belle estelle, qui se moustre chascun
matin au point du jour, et certes, celuy nom lui afferoit
bien quar elle estoit si garnye de toutes beautes et de
cortoysie, que c'estoit a merveilles, et sa beaute res-
plandisoit cy fort que quasi estoit semblant a celle
estelle que je dys.* Imperial translates from the first
part of an earlier text when he introduces his lady :

> A la muy fermosa Estrella Diana,
> Qual sale por mayo al alva del dia.†

In the first strophe Imperial represents himself
as meeting her upon a bridge over the Guadalquivir, as she goes to the church of Santa Ana.
Having been honoured with her gracious smile,
he bursts forth into ecstatic eulogy, in the second

strophe comparing her countenance to that of the angel Gabriel at the Annunciation, in the third commanding the famous poets of antiquity to keep silence about their heroines, and concluding by begging the indulgence of Iphigenia and Helen for thus exalting his love.

The main substance and form of the work are in no wise Dantesque, unless it is to be supposed that Imperial caught the idea of a meeting with his lady from the *Vita Nuova*. The motive, however, is not confined to Dante, but is a commonplace of French and Provençal pastorals. The tone of the four stanzas, with the constant comparison of the lady to a rose, savours rather of the poem of Guillaume de Lorris.

By a consideration of the next two poems belonging to the sequence, the reliance upon French sources becomes the more evident.

To replies of Fernán Pérez de Guzmán * and Diego Martínez de Medina, censuring him for the extravagance of his eulogies, Imperial responds with a poem † in which, after reviewing the substance of the attacks upon him, he swears, in the presence of Venus, that he will champion his assertions before the God of Love. Through a series of conceits, he entreats her to construct armour for him from her many traits of beauty and virtue: from her hair a coat of mail; with her arms a girth;

from her eyes a lance; from her gentle demeanour a shield, in the midst of which shall be set her mouth and teeth as a device; from her countenance a helmet; from her nose an arrow feathered by her eyelashes, with her brow for his bow; and from her neatness his special insignia. The references to the Court of Love in Fernán Pérez de Guzmán and in Imperial again exhibit very plainly the connection with France, which is also indicated by other details. In the first strophe, he addresses his mistress as *estrella del norte*, a phrase which in all probability, especially when taken in relation to the other members of the series, denotes her French origin; and the testimony is complete when, with a reference to Arthurian romance, in speaking of the token he desires from his lady, he contrasts it with those of Guinevere and Iseult.

In the third poem of the sequence,* the Gallic flavour is unmistakably given, despite a possible recollection of Dante in a single line, by the confessedly French nationality of the lady, who dresses after a foreign fashion, in one whole strophe actually lapsing into her mother tongue, and by the meticulous description of her garments, a trait that had already entered Spanish tradition as early as the *Romance de Lope de Moros*. The setting on the banks of the Guadalquivir suggests a relationship to the poems that are explicitly addressed to

Estrella Diana, and another bit of proof occurs in
the explanation of her desire to show him honour :

> Vous êtes le bien venu
> Et le bien trouvé, bien servi ;
> Tant honneur m'avez fait vous
> Que je m'esjouy d'esprit.

The honour that the poet had done her would
naturally refer to his former productions, — why
not the two in the series we have already discussed ? It would seem natural, then, to conclude
that the two ladies are identical, and the probability becomes almost a certainty, when in the
second of the sequence, which is explicitly directed
to Estrella Diana, she is styled *estrella del norte*.
The chain of circumstantial evidence conduces to
a belief that the first and the second poems are
written to the same lady as this third ; and, since
she is here stated to be French and the whole
piece is completely northern in character, the
French aspect of the other two is corroborated.

There is yet a fourth composition that may
be assigned with even greater confidence to the
series. After Diego Martínez has concocted a
second limping *respuesta*, in which he seeks to
attack Imperial with armour from Venus, and a
juryman of Seville, Alfonso Vidal, has decided in
favour of Imperial, and, after the strange interpo-
lation of a mismated wife's complaint,* Imperial

returns to his original theme, undaunted, extolling his lady in more extreme language than ever.* In the heading itself three persons are suggested as possible recipients of the honour, one of whom is Estrella Diana. The details of the piece bear out my ascription. Lauding the God of Love and Apollo, here conceived under the figure of planets, because they have united in their most auspicious moment to shed benign influences upon his mistress, he boasts that the stars pale before her light and that Diana and Helen must yield in their attractions, and concludes by apostrophizing Poetry and Rhetoric, who have enthroned themselves in her. The relation to the first of the series must be manifest to the most casual observer, and the renewed allusions to the Court of Love continue the fiction that has been preserved throughout.

Since all the formative influences of the first period prove to be French or the natural heritage from an indigenous tradition already perceptible in the *Romance de Lope de Moros*, it cannot be maintained, at least for this class of Imperial's works, that the impetus to allegorize is imparted by the incipient popularity of the *Divine Comedy*. No impetus was needed for a type the vogue of which was already assured by the innate appreciation of the Spanish people for all varieties of mysticism, by its previous use in Spain for two hundred years, and by the prestige that it had acquired from the greatest poets of that period. Even if an impetus had been required, it would surely have been given by the literature to which Spanish was closely allied.

THE SECOND PERIOD

In the second phase of Imperial's activity the presence of Dantesque elements has become a certainty, but they cannot be said to characterize the compositions. The general scheme and most of the substance are evolved by Imperial himself upon French models, upon former Spanish tradition, and upon his own initiative; the Dantesque is confined to inorganic decorations. The chief representative of this phase, the *Decir* on the birth of John II,* is marked by a much more complicated use of allegory than the short love-poems. In these it is a petty though attractive exposition of amorous relations with more or less of a basis in fact throughout, or at least with a pretence of the writer that the basis is fact, and with the background of an actual geographical spot, or at least a world not remote from our own. In the above-mentioned *Decir* there is no idealization of a concrete fact, such as the meeting with the lady, but the event of the King's birth is taken as a starting-point and about it is woven an elaborate veil of fictitious circumstance, largely unconnected with reality and occurring in a purely imaginary world. We have passed, in other words, from the *pastourelle* to the type of the longer allegorical French *dit*.

It is, then, not at all the kind of allegory that appears in the *Divine Comedy*. There the conception is a journey through three supernatural states, the nature of which was more concrete and material to the mediaeval mind than to ours, containing numerous encounters with historical personages, many of them contemporaries, and the whole is composed with a serious and lofty purpose ; here the episode takes place in an atmosphere that is playful and fantastic, and the intent is flattery or didacticism. Again, the diction of the Italian epic is terse and compressed to the extreme ; Imperial, in accord with the general Spanish tendency of his day, is prolix and expansive. On *a priori* grounds it was not likely that he could adopt from the *Divine Comedy* much of its style or anything of its titanic scheme and thought.

The *Decir* I have already summarized as an important stage in the evolution of the Panegyric, and I have pointed out its dependence, in fundamental idea, upon the *Anticlaudianus*.

The influence of the planets, one of the central

concepts of the poem, is to be traced to French or general mediaeval sources rather than to the *Paradiso*. The idea of the heavens of the seven planets as the abode of the blessed is too diverse from that of the planets themselves as allegorical females moulding an infant's destiny to permit the assumption of any interrelation. In several instances, moreover, Imperial's analysis of the celestial activities is at variance with Dante's. The heaven of Saturn in the *Divine Comedy* belongs to the contemplative. As was inevitable when both writers were drawing from the common stock of *Planetenlehre*, a suggestion of this conception occurs in Imperial's analysis, but it is rather the ordinary mediaeval idea of the planet's gift of mature reflection before action than Dante's lofty transformation of this influence into a religious symbol of the contemplative life, and in the next lines the endowment from Saturn is, indeed, materialized into a long life and architectural enterprise. Likewise the planet of Jupiter, after bestowing upon the young King the characteristics of a just ruler, descends to the paltry addition of fine apparel and accoutrement. The gifts of the Sun and Moon are totally at variance with the Dantesque system. The heaven of the Sun in the Italian is the abode of doctors of philosophy and theology; the Sun in the *Decir* blesses the child with beauty of person, an unruffled private life, and a prosperous reign. The heaven of the Moon in Dante is the abode of the redeemed who have repented of their broken vows of chastity; the Moon in Imperial promises to the child the traditionally lunar qualities of good health, favourable weather, and success in the chase. Although the episode of Mercury commences in the Spanish with a simile that after the Dantesque fashion explains the effulgence of the planet as a manifestation of its joy, and although there is a reference to Justinian, who in the *Divine Comedy* is the chief figure of the second heaven, the qualities imparted are not those of the active life, but the conventional legal knowledge, subtlety, and courtliness, while the active life is mentioned only incidentally at the end.

Imperial's ideas are significantly parallel to the petty attitude towards the planets in French verse. In an anonymous *Dit des Planètes* of the thirteenth century,* their influences are correlated with the different professions and days of the week, as the Moon with Monday and the clergyman, Mars with Tuesday and the warrior, Mercury with Wednesday and the merchant; and in a long passage from Froissart's *Joli Buisson de Jonece*,† the planets are correlated with the seven ages of man. Imperial in every case walks with his eyes downward, intent upon the dead level of mediaeval commonplace; Dante has his feet upon the mediaeval plane, but his gaze is constantly upward.

Nor is the Spaniard's conception of Fortune more ethereal. She is the stereotyped personification who exercises a whimsical control over the possessions and fates of men, and, as was to be expected in a work that drew so largely upon the *Anticlaudianus*, especially in this very subject of Fortune's activity, she is described in much the same terms as in the poem of Alanus de Insulis. Dante,* following somewhat in the steps of Boethius,† but actuated most by a lofty and consistent Providential theory of the universe, elevates Fortune into God's minister of earthly splendours, whose operation, though secret and surpassing mortal comprehension, is yet the result of reflection and judgment. Imperial's conception is so obviously humdrum that it would be unnecessary to deny any interrelation, were it not for the assertions of Sanvisenti and even of so eminent a scholar as Farinelli. In the account of Fortune's caprices, the single line, *De linage en linage, de gentes en gentes* may or may not be a reminiscence of Dantesque phraseology. The question has no bearing upon the character of the whole description, for the line occurs in a passage like half a hundred others that impugn the permutations of Fortune, and at any rate is of no significance in determining the trend of its context.

Sanvisenti insinuates vaguely that what Imperial has derived from the *Divine Comedy* is the belief in Fortune as a superior power. But surely this is a commonplace of mediaeval verse. In the *Anticlaudianus*, the very office of Fortune is to complete the gifts of Nobility, which without her coöperation are of no avail. In the *Roman de la Rose*, although her divinity is expressly denied, and in opposition to Imperial's idea, she is not irresistible for the strong of mind and heart, she nevertheless receives honour as the mistress of worldly possessions. It is not, however, in accordance with the ordinary mediaeval attitude to limit her sovereignty. At the beginning of Thibaut's *Roman de la Poire*, to which the *Decir* of Imperial is bound by several ties, Fortune proclaims her powers in no ambiguous terms. Baudouin de Condé in the *Prison d'Amours* represents her as ruler of the world, with a wheel of four spokes, each of which symbolizes a different degree of prosperity, whirling men from the heights to the abyss of love. In Nicole de Margival's *Panthère d'Amours*, Happiness and Unhappiness keep the house of Fortune, but they are subject to her command. Finally, in the *Escharbote* of Watriquet de Couvin, the world is represented as a city under her capricious domination, and the words defining her despotism are unmistakable.

Sanvisenti suggests also that, as in the *Divine Comedy*, she is God's agent, thinking of I know not what, except, perhaps, the semblance of an analogy in Imperial's representation of Fortune as the friend of the diligent. But she immediately restricts her kindness by the line:

Pero contra mí non val fuerça é sesso.

Boethius had already held a brief for Fortune; and the idea of some excellence in her is as early in French as the *Roman de la Poire*, where she is depicted as the protectress of the righteous and the benefactress of faithful lovers. As far as any Dantesque influence goes, the whole discussion is futile; that Fortune is to a certain degree the friend of the diligent is not implicit in the Providential system of the passage from the *Inferno*, nor indeed is it a Christian tenet that the good prosper materially.

The ordinary mediaeval and French character of Fortune in Imperial is further illustrated by her connection with Fame and with Love.* Boethius joins very closely, and Chaucer in the *House of Fame* confuses, Fortune and Fame; Imperial causes Fortune to bestow as her last gift immortal renown. The bonds between Fortune and Love were tightly drawn in almost all the French allegorical poems. Nicole de Margival utilizes Fortune as the *dea ex machina* for the lover. Baudouin de Condé endows her with a wheel that sweeps lovers from the summit of joy to the depths of despair. In the *Roman de la Poire* she is concerned with the welfare of lovers, and at the opening of the poem, Love himself states his alliance with the goddess. Imperial causes her to bestow upon the young prince the fairest of wives.

In other shorter compositions devoted wholly to the topic of Fortune, Imperial expressly and categorically denies an agreement with Dante's ideal. A *requesta* to Fray Alfonso de la Monja * for an elucidation of her nature, although it contains possibly one or two flickering reminiscences of the Italian's wording, yet constitutes in substance just the kind of stereotyped complaint that Dante decries :

> Quest' è colei ch' è tanto posta in croce
> Pur da color che le dovrian dar lode.

After the Friar has responded, defending her and asserting, like Dante, her divinity, Imperial frames a very clever rejoinder,† using humility as a foil and yet meeting his adversary at every thrust, until with a double mention of the allegation of divinity, he sets it down as opposed to his own conclusions. A reply to a *pregunta* of Fernán Pérez de Guzmán upon the same subject of Fortune is a closer approximation to the passage of the *Inferno*.* The secrecy of Fortune, which is prominent in this and in the *requesta* to Fray Alfonso, is not peculiar to Dante, as is shown by Boccaccio's colloquy with her in the *De Casibus*.†

The *Decir* upon the birth of John II exhibits a great preponderance of French details, many of which had already been planted in Spain during the preceding centuries. There is the old vernal bower, suggested by countless previous descriptions, though not, I think, definitely, as has been claimed,‡ by the *Roman de la Rose*. The manner in which Imperial's mind was obsessed by Gallic literature is revealed by his references to the Arthurian matter, to the romances of *Paris et Vienne* § and *Flor et Blancheflor*, and to Narcissus, who is so important a figure in French verse that in the *Roman de la Rose* the author, coming upon the fountain, his sepulchre, digresses to relate his sad story. Much in the same way, also, as Dangier in the *Roman de la Rose* ejects the Lover, the gardener at the end casts out the writer.

It is superfluous to examine again the double mention of Dante's name and the few more or less certain verbal reminiscences of the *Divine Comedy*, which I have partially indicated in a former essay upon Dante and Imperial and which have often been discussed by critics of Spanish literature;

they do not affect the essential nature of the composition. Several parallelisms exist also in imaginative details. The general manifestation of joy by each planet when it is her turn to bless is analogous to that shown by the redeemed souls in satisfying Dante's desires, and the Sun's benignity is actually compared to the smile of Beatrice in heaven. The probability of a relationship is strengthened by the symbolization of actual charity through greater effulgence. An instance, important enough to be considered separately, is afforded by the twelve handmaidens who, representing the signs of the zodiac, are enveloped in sparkling flame and encircle one another beneath the steady gaze of the eight planets, singing antiphonally the *Te Deum*. Imperial expresses his conception very vaguely and inadequately; but if we postulate the influence of the *doppia danza* of the twenty-four holy doctors in the heaven of the Sun,* we may understand that two bands of six move one within the other, and that he neglects to explain the exact situation because he himself has the Dantesque description vividly in mind and forgets that his reader has not always the same advantage. In the next strophe, the Virtues greet the newborn King with Latin hymns in the same fashion as the mystical processions greet Beatrice in the terrestrial paradise. But a precedent exists already within Spanish itself in the triumphal procession which meets Love in the *Libro de Buen Amor* and which uses the very *Benedictus qui venit* from the Mass that occurs both in Imperial and Dante.

These hypothetical cases, however, are insignificant, as compared with Dante's stylistic influence upon Imperial, which has been strangely slighted by those who would make of him a slavish disciple of the Italian. The Spanish versifier now begins to enliven his compositions with conscious extended similes, unknown hitherto in the vernacular. As the Renaissance had not yet introduced into the peninsula the great vogue of classical authors, and Imperial reveals no familiarity with Petrarch or Boccaccio, they are probably to be ascribed to a perusal of the *Divine Comedy*. But even if we add the stylistic to the verbal and conceptual imitations, the examples of an interrelation remain very few. Despite these Italian slashes of the brush, the finished picture presents the appearance of a French production.

THE THIRD PERIOD

The *Decir de las Siete Virtudes* * is Imperial's most mature and ambitious work. Beginning with a quotation from the *Divine Comedy*, glossed as a suitable prelude in the most proper pedantic fashion, he conceives himself as dreaming at dawn beside a rose-grown spring. After an elaborate invocation to Apollo, he finds himself in the stereotyped French bower, here described at length. He is met by Dante himself who, as guide, is modelled upon Cato of the *Purgatorio*, and holds the *Divine Comedy* itself in his hand. The voices of the three theological Virtues are heard uttering appropriate Latin texts, the four cardinal Virtues chant *cantares morales*, and Leah sings as she gathers flowers. Dante indicates and analyzes for him seven starry feminine figures much like those in the *Decir* on John II, the Virtues, of course, whose mother is Discretion and whose handmaidens are represented in their rays. While he explains one of Imperial's doubts, he alludes to seven serpents, which, though they accompanied the author until he entered the garden, were rendered invisible by a veil that is generated through excessive contemplation of them. They are the seven deadly Sins, whom the guide endows with the most outlandish names and elucidates.* He then bursts forth into a fiery denunciation of Seville as the abode of all these Vices, and solves Imperial's doubt as to their invisibility. In the midst of canticles of praise to the Blessed Virgin, issuing from all the roses, considered as the seats of the different orders of angels, Imperial is struck by a soft breeze and awakes to find the *Divine Comedy* open in his hands, —

> ' En el capítulo que la Virgen salva.

The analogues in the earlier history of the peninsula I have already discussed ; in France they are even closer. Of first importance is the *Tesoretto* of Brunetto Latini, which, though written about 1262 or 1263 in Italian, is largely a condensation of his longer work in French, *Li Livres dou Trésor*, and is wholly in the French mould. After wandering through a desolate forest, he comes upon a court of Virtue, which is situated, like Imperial's, in

> Un grande pian giocondo
> Lo più gaio del mondo.*

Her four daughters, the cardinal Virtues, dwell in separate palaces, each, as in the Spanish poem, with her own train of Graces. Only four of these latter, Cortesia, Larghezza, Leanza, and Prodezza, are analyzed in the fashion of Imperial. At the end of the poem, having described his own penitence, Brunetto tells a friend how to examine himself for confession according to the seven Vices, constructing a kind of devotional manual of possible violations in each sin. Since Brunetto Latini was read and translated in Spain and actually happened to be in Castile before he wrote his Italian poem, it is not unlikely that Imperial had the *Tesoretto* in mind for the *Decir de las Siete Virtudes*.

In Robert de l'Oulme's *Dit des VII Serpens* of 1266, the deadly Sins are represented in a debate with the devil, and compared to seven serpents and the seven roots of the tree of evil.* The allegorical framework of Rutebeuf's *Voie de Paradis*,† modelled possibly upon the *Tesoretto*, is only an excuse for a wearisome exposition of the Vices and Virtues. When he comes to the town of Penitence, Pity, his guide, describes to him the abodes of the former, and then those of the latter. For Luxury and Humility, certain subordinate abstractions, as in the two longer poems of Imperial, are named as servants. The importance of the *Somme des Vices et Vertus*, which was published about 1279 by Frère Lorens, I have already stressed. During this same century was composed another presentation of the subject, the unpublished *Songe du Castel*, where the struggle of man against evil is symbolized through the beleaguering of a castle by seven giants.‡

In the fourteenth century, Froissart's *Temple d'Onnour* § belongs to the same class. The marriage of Desir, the son of Onnour, and Plaisance, the daughter of Courtoisie, takes place in a temple upon seven steps of which stand fourteen Virtues, whose nature is expounded by Onnour. Gower's *Mirour de l'Omme*, which was written before the summer of 1381,‖ presents another excessively prolix allegorical treatment of the Virtues and Vices, especially from the standpoint of their genesis. The Devil, by an incestuous union with his daughter Sin, engenders Death; and by the intermarriage of the two last, are born the seven deadly Sins. To defeat the ends of Providence, the Devil unites the Vices in turn with the World, whence are born to each Vice five daughters, symbolizing five subordinate sins. In symmetrical opposition, the seven Virtues are married in turn to Reason, each bringing forth five ancillary Virtues. The length of all this section of the *Mirour*, 18,372 lines, affords an index to the mediaeval interest in the subject. So late in the fifteenth century that it could have had no influence upon Imperial's *Decir* and yet important as indicating that the evolution of the French forms in France itself produced a composition exactly parallel to the Spanish example, Antoine de la Salle's *Journée d'Onneur et de Prouesse* presents an allegorical garden in which these two Virtues and their numerous attendants are explained to him.*

Finally, in the consideration of prototypes, we may turn, as so often for Spanish allegory, to later Italian adaptations of Dante rather than to Dante himself. In the fourth book of the *Quadriregio*,† Federigo Frezzi is conducted by Humility through the realms of the four cardinal Virtues, who, ensconced in regal state, expound to him their own characteristics and those of their attendant handmaidens. Though the personifications of the subordinate Virtues are not always the same and there is nowhere any verbal similarity, yet Imperial may very well have known an Italian composition that was completed between 1400 and 1403 ; at least he did not derive from it any inspiration other than what he found in Brunetto Latini, whom Frezzi himself evidently imitated.

The Gallic skeleton of his poem Imperial adorns with certain ideas borrowed from Dante. The invocation is an ingenious fusion of the similar passages in the first and thirty-third cantos of the *Paradiso ;* but an invocation is a commonplace of the classical writers, of Claudian, Alanus de Insulis, and mediaeval Latinists in general, and is not unusual in French allegorical versifiers, especially Froissart.* Imperial himself had already used an invocation to Apollo in the verses upon John II, and in the present instance he may be considered as applying the Dantesque form to what otherwise would not differ from the ordinary mediaeval type.

Whether the first idea of representing the Virtues by starry figures came to him from the *Divine Comedy*, it is impossible to determine. Dante, as he enters purgatory, beholds the four stars of the Cross of the South, figuring the four cardinal Vir-

tues. At the beginning of his vision Imperial sees
in the East four stellar circles which intertwine
to form three crosses, figuring the seven Virtues,
and when he is once within the garden he actually
encounters the heavenly females whom the constellation symbolizes. The idea of the juncture of
four circles doubtless came to him from the first
canto of the *Paradiso*, where the sun is said to rise
most propitiously from the spot which "joins
four circles with three crosses," betokening, for
some commentators, the seven Virtues.* In Dante,
the four circles are the horizon, the zodiac, the
equator, and the colure of the equinoxes; in Imperial, they are evidently a constellation of some
sort, for he describes them as shining, and afterwards identifies them with the seven allegorical
stars. Thus, while the geometrical arrangement
is derived from the *Paradiso*, the idea of the stars
and of their relation to the vision may be derived
from the *Purgatorio*. Since, however, in his earlier
Decir upon the birth of John II he has already
evolved the conception of astral women, denoting,
not the Virtues, but celestial influences, and since
throughout his works he exhibits a predilection
for effects of light, it is not improbable that he
himself invented the designation of the Virtues by
stars. Imperial's conceptions would, then, have coincided with those of Dante; and this, I suspect,

inasmuch as they were both steeped in mediaeval conventions, was not infrequently the case, so that it was easy for him to deck his French or his original ideas with Dantesque hangings. In the present instance he would have derived from the Italian poet the device of prefiguring his allegorical personages by the constellation.

The divergence in wellnigh every detail, especially in the colours with which the Virtues are dressed, makes it very doubtful whether Imperial recalled distinctly their description in the mystical procession of the *Purgatorio*.

When once within the garden, he finds Dante as guide, suggested to some extent by the guardian angel of the *Purgatorio*, by the sages of Limbo, and by the Dantesque Cato and Virgil. But an old man as a guide with white hair and beard are by no means extraordinary in the mediaeval journey. In the *Vision of the Monk of Eynsham*, the guide is the aged St. Nicholas; in the *Vision of Alberic*, the protagonist is conducted by St. Peter; or if we pass to French allegory, Baudouin de Condé in his *Voie de Paradis* encounters an old man with a long white beard, who directs him. Farinelli's statement, then, that the vogue of the old man as guide is initiated in Spain by Imperial's imitation of Dante's Cato is to be accepted with a grain of salt.

Of the preparatory phenomena, the voices in the air may possibly be suggested by the unembodied allusions to charity and envy in the second circle of the *Purgatorio*. Leah gathering flowers at daybreak is doubtless derived from Dante's mystic dream before he enters the terrestrial paradise, but her presence, though it offers the opportunity for a bad pun and a *rime équivoque*, has a very dubious connection with the scheme of the poem, and seems only a perfunctory and incongruous importation. The obviously exotic character of this detail brings into relief the general attitude of Imperial in his other borrowings, which are only somewhat less superficial. The invective against Seville, a fusion of the opening of *Inferno* xxvi and the arraignment of Italy, and especially Florence, in *Purgatorio* vi, is purely a digression.

The guide Dante anticipates and satisfies two of Imperial's doubts after the manner of Beatrice, first, the question of the Virtues' equality despite their variance in beauty, and second his perplexity because the serpents of vice were invisible to him. Although it is a commonplace for guides to read the thoughts of those entrusted to their protection,* we may suppose that here, as in some other instances, since the *Divine Comedy* individualizes and sublimates ordinary mediaeval devices, Imperial is somewhat affected by Dante's example, but not so far as to alter the general tone of the composition.

The exact provenience of the closing details is as problematical. It seems to have been Imperial's method to choose those elements that struck his fancy from the immediate vicinity of the passage he was reading, and to adapt them as best he could to the piece in hand. According to this principle, since he fits the description of the guardian angel in *Purgatorio* ix to the guide Dante, the sound of organs that accompanies the salutation of the Virgin at the close of the *Decir* is probably drawn from the sweet music at the end of the same canto. Similar logic would conduce to a belief that the salutation of the Virgin with which the work concludes is derived from the *valle fiorita* of the seventh and eighth cantos of the *Purgatorio* instead of the thirty-third canto of the *Paradiso*, for it is here that Dante introduces the serpent, typical of temptation, which, together with those in the *Dit* of Robert de l'Oulme, was perhaps in Imperial's mind. Some of the elements that appear also in French gardens, such as the flowers, odours, and especially the precious metals and stones, are possibly to be traced to the *valle fiorita* rather than to the terrestrial paradise. The spirits of the negligent princes sit upon the grass and upon the flowers, singing the *Salve Regina* much in the same way

as Imperial in his *Decir* conceives the orders of
angels upon the roses of the bush. The idea is
doubtless influenced to some degree by the Celestial Rose of the *Paradiso;* but Imperial's angels
are not seated upon the petals of one vast rose like
the Blessed in the *Divine Comedy*, but upon separate roses of a bush, and the hymn to the Virgin
in the thirty-third canto of the *Paradiso* is intoned
not by a group of souls but by St. Bernard alone.
It was, then, at the page containing the *Salve Regina* of the valley of princes that he found the
book open when he awoke. The fact that he
borrows almost wholly from the adjacent cantos
is cumulative evidence. The opening sentence he
takes from the third canto of the *Purgatorio*, the
device of the constellations from the first, and then
passing to the series of cantos from the sixth to
the ninth, upon which his eye chiefly rested when
he was composing the *Decir*, from the sixth he
takes the invective against Seville, from the *valle
fiorita* of the seventh he adds a few touches to
his general scheme, from the eighth he remembers the serpent, and from the ninth he retains
certain details for the description of the guide
and the music.

Upon this growth, which remains in all essentials a French allegory, Imperial attempts to en-
graft, not always successfully, rhetorical flowers

that he has culled from reading the *Divine Comedy*. These verbal imitations are considerable in number, but in almost every instance betray poetic inferiority by reducing the brilliantly figurative language of his model to prosaic and lengthy explicitness. They are but foreign trappings, often chosen promiscuously without regard for artistic harmony, but occasionally transferred rather skilfully from their Italian setting.* The most important effect of the *Divine Comedy* upon Imperial, as in the *Decir* for John II, is again to be sought in the introduction of similes, which here increase in number and extent, and, like Dante's, are often taken from atmospheric phenomena or the picturesque minutiae of daily experience.

In determinative features, however, the *Decir de las Siete Virtudes* does not differ from the ordinary mediaeval output. It is merely a didactic presentation of an Aristotelian catalogue of Virtues and Vices, cast in the favourite mould of allegory and enshrined in the framework of an imaginary journey to a fanciful garden. The framework amounts to little more than an introductory device, so that in kind the poem does not differ from Berceo's primitive composition on the Miracles of Our Lady. Haunted with memories of the *Divine Comedy*, Imperial would fain increase the attraction and erudition of his piece by imitative and inor-

ganic ornaments, such as a Dantesque modelling
of the invocation, Dantesque touches upon the
guide or the Virtues, or stylistic flourishes in dis-
torted reflection of the Italian poem. Even though
in this product of his third period the Dantesque
assumes its largest proportions, the substance is no
more vitally affected by the *Divine Comedy* than is
Chaucer's *House of Fame*.

CONCLUSIONS

Imperial's whole temperament was utterly in-
capable of appreciating Dante. The playfulness
and pettiness of his amorous lyrics are far removed from the gravity and sublimity of Dante's
love. His patriotism does not rise above the
profession of a courtier. The invective against
Seville sounds artificial upon his lips. His shal-
lowness prevented him from ever immersing and
saturating himself in the master's nature sufficiently to become an intelligent disciple. With a
poetical talent which, to say the least, was not superior to that of the ordinary French versifier,
with little or no originality of matter, with no
marked ability for the adaptation and manipulation of what he borrowed, neither endowed by
nature with an unusual wit nor blessed with
learning adequate to the comprehension of Dante,
Imperial was not the man to achieve more than a

superficial imitation of the great Italian.* His significance lies rather in his emphasis at the beginning of the great allegorical century, the fifteenth, upon the already long existing tradition of copying from France. But the emphasis upon French models should not be interpreted as in any sense the creation of a new allegorical school. A cursory study of earlier literature in the peninsula is all that is required to refute Puymaigre's and Baist's allegations about the extension of allegory, with Imperial, from isolated episodes to whole compositions. Even if this change could be conceded, it would be futile, inasmuch as the characteristic note and the great mass of Imperial's work are not Dantesque, to make Dante responsible; and it would be an anomaly if a man of so light a nature and of such meagre attainments as Imperial should, apart from a transmission of Dante's influence, effect a revolution by dint of establishing his own or French methods.

CHAPTER XII

THE FIFTEENTH CENTURY

THE CONTEMPORARIES OF IMPERIAL

RUY PÁEZ DE RIBERA

CRITICISM has presented Ruy Páez de Ribera in the mutually dependent characters of a follower of Imperial and a Dantesque innovator. For neither of these characters, however, is any confirmation afforded either by his works or by our inadequate knowledge of his biography.*

Three poems suggest a possible relation to Imperial. Two of these are somewhat like the *Decir* upon the birth of the King and have to do with the childhood of John II. The substance of the first, upon the regency,† I have already given in discussing the genesis of the Panegyric. The garden setting of two lines and the accurate dating of the vision (here, in any case, perfectly natural, since the poem embodies a definite historical event) are such trite mediaevalisms that they have no force as proof.

From a broader point of view, the very fact that Ruy Páez wrote political allegory might be considered a sign of Imperial's influence. French precedents, however, are not infrequent. Though not a vision, Philippe de Vitry's *Chapel des Trois Fleurs de Lis* (1335) represents Science, Foy, and Chevalerie under the form of three lilies in order to show Philippe de Valois and his knights the spirit in which the Crusade should be undertaken.* Another political allegory is Philippe de Maizières' *Songe du Vergier* (1376-8), in which an allegorical dispute between clerics and knights takes place in a garden before Charles V, over the old crux of the relations of church and state.† A nearer approximation to the Spanish piece in machinery and in eulogistic intent is Watriquet's *Dit des Quatre Sièges*, where, in a vision on Ascension Day, 1319, the writer sees four seats, the guardians of which tell him that they are reserved for Arthur, Alexander, the Duke Naimes, and Girard du Fraite, who are reincarnate in the living Charles of Valois, the Count of Hainaut, the Constable of France, and the Count of Flanders.‡ The exaltation of the King and his regents upon three thrones is not so close to Imperial's endowment of the newborn King with different blessings as to imply an interrelation, and each poet may have had in mind French models. Ribera's poem, to be sure, was written shortly after Imperial's; but this circumstance is offset by the fact that Ruy Páez presents in its shortest and simplest form the framework that Imperial elaborates.

May not Imperial have borrowed the basic elements from Ribera?

The second composition in question * offers in its last part an analogy to Imperial's *Decir*. *En un deleytoso vergel espaciado*, the author is present at a debate between Soberbia and Mesura. Each mentions her allegorical attendants and states before Justicia her respective claims to preëminence. Justicia decides in favour of Mesura and decrees that the young King shall put to death Soberbia and her brood and that Mesura and her maidens shall follow in his train. The composition as a whole belongs to the large and dreary class of *débats*. The accompaniment of the two chief figures by their subordinates, a commonplace of French and Spanish literature, does not necessarily reflect the *Decir de las Siete Virtudes*. The assignment of the Virtues to the young King does not parallel closely the planetary influence in Imperial's other long *Decir*, it might naturally suggest itself, and, occurring only in the last two stanzas, appears as an agreeable device for rounding off the poem.

The third work, though it contains more definite marks of a relation to Imperial, has hitherto been strangely disregarded.† A heavenly appearance, denoted by an effusion of light, stands before his bed and asks him whether he sleeps or is awake. Aroused, he makes the excuse that he was stricken with terror by the evils of the world; whereupon the celestial messenger reassures him by enumerating the necessary qualities for a prosperous nation and its king. Finally, the spirit disappears, blessing him with the sign of the cross and a Latin benediction. As in the two former compositions, we have here a didactic and political purpose enshrined in a very slight allegorical frame.

One or two phrases in the poem may be taken from Dante or from Imperial's reflection of Dante ; but inasmuch as Imperial has translated not a few passages from the *Divine Comedy*, and Ribera otherwise none, it is reasonable to accept the latter alternative. The adoption of a few words, however, does not constitute literary discipleship, and Imperial may have indeed been the pupil, borrowing the idea for his *Decir* upon the birth of John II. Ribera is the stronger personality and has juster claims to poetic eminence. A sincerity and enthusiasm of definite purpose are more clearly discernible. Amador admits that he has greater descriptive talent. Puymaigre calls him more original. His form is undoubtedly more artistic in that he does not sacrifice congruity to a passion for weaving into the introductions to his poems as many Dantesque threads

as possible. Devoting only one or two quatrains
to the unessential details of the vision, he proceeds
directly to the substance of the composition, so
that the final product obeys the rules of proportion. His sinister temperament fixed a wide gulf
between him and Imperial. The contention that
his contemporary set him to composing in the
allegorical form is absolutely contrary to the evidence.

In another place* I have sufficiently disproved
the possibility of Dantesque influence for the
poem in which it has been chiefly asserted to exist,
namely, the Debate, within a gloomy valley, of
Grief, Old Age, Exile, and Poverty, upon the pre-
eminence of the last as a curse.†

This and Ribera's two other tirades upon Poverty certainly are connected with the passage in the
Roman de la Rose in which Ami warns the author
against her. Professor Luquiens, who considers
the relation only as possible, has indicated some
of the similarities.‡ I would add from the Debate
the very important analogy of the idea that Death
is pleasanter than Poverty.§ The thoughts of the
first poem of the series recur in the second, where
Ruy Páez compares Poverty to dangers he has experienced.‖ The third of the series ¶ reveals such
exact parallelisms to the *Roman*, even in unique
ideas, that the relation seems to me indubitable

and strengthens a like derivation for the others. The general statements about the preferability of all other torments correspond in the Spanish and French. The fundamental and by no means ordinary conception of Fortune as the source of Poverty is common to both, and the contrast with Wealth in the second half of the *Decir* again recalls the *Roman*, in which Richesse is represented as a guide and Pauvreté as an obstacle along the road of Trop-Donner.*

The relation to a *canzone* of Fazio degli Uberti against Poverty,† suggested by Puymaigre, is open to grave suspicion. The idea that Poverty plunges her victim into hell is not unusual enough to preclude originality in both writers; it appears also in the *Roman de la Rose*, where the diction is similar to that of the Spanish; and it is approached differently in the Italian by a passage discussing the ruin that she wreaks upon morality. The important details of the derivation of Poverty from Fortune and of the loss of friends and relatives are not found in Fazio degli Uberti at all.

Since Ribera's attitude towards life coincided in so many ways with Dante's, the absence of verbal or conceptual parallels is all the more remarkable. The depression at the condition of his country, and the settled gloom, manifested in the three denunciations of Poverty and in the *Decir* upon the overweening pride of mortals, arose, perhaps, as in the case of Dante, from sad personal experience, and formed a bond of sympathy between the two poets. Ruy Páez is a kind of Spanish Theognis. His depression is not pessimism. It is distinguished from pessimism by patriotism and the desire for amelioration which ring forth from his exhortations to the young King and to the Queen Regent and which draw him nearer to the Florentine zealot. His seriousness, which is not marred by a single amorous lyric, — a strange phenomenon, indeed, in those days when even friars must imagine for themselves a literary mistress,* and almost unique in the *Cancionero de Baena* — was better suited to receive the Dantesque heritage than was the playfulness of Imperial. If he had known the *Divine Comedy* at all, would he not surely have been eager to imitate those passages that expressed in so final a form his own ideas? The absence, then, of Dantesque elements would tend to prove that acquaintance with the sovereign poet was not so widespread in Seville at the beginning of the fifteenth century as is generally assumed.

VILLASANDINO

Alfonso Álvarez de Villasandino has usually been regarded as the chief representative of the artificial and stereotyped verse of the old Galician

manner, and therefore the head of a circle opposed
to the allegorical and Dantesque innovations of
the coterie that included Imperial and Ribera. It
has been demonstrated, however, that neither of
these poets altered the current of Spanish tradition;
and the allotment to Villasandino of the first place
and the longest space in the *Cancionero de Baena*
indicates that its compiler did not deem him the
last of an antiquated and decaying school. Un-
questionably much of his output is on the dead
level of tedious Galician conventionalism; but, in
the process of borrowing the artificialities of French
and Provencal courtly verse, the Galician rhymesters had also managed to import something that
was pretty and fresh, the *pastourelle;* and in the
use of this type, at least, Villasandino is not to be
classified in a movement opposed to Imperial, who
here once more harks back to the earlier literary
history of the peninsula.

Seven compositions of Villasandino deserve
comment as approximating more or less the *pastourelle,* which I have described as partially allegorical. The first,* dedicated to Juana de Sosa, the
mistress of Henry II, represents the author as
counselled by the nightingale not to grieve but to
hope in the lady's kindness, and as answering that
he finds a certain pleasure in his very sorrow.
In the second,† with the conventional setting of a

mountain approached through a forest, the writer, hearing two nightingales and a magpie urging to boldness in love, comforts himself with the thought of his loyalty but laments his procrastination. The four poems inscribed directly to ladies are closer to Imperial. In the regular garden along the Guadalquivir, as in Imperial's fancies about Estrella Diana, he sees three lovely flowers, symbolizing three ladies whom he resolves to serve for the sake of Doña Juana.* Again, in the orange grove of the Alcázar at Cordova, he beholds her conversing with other damsels upon the tender passion; and though these murmur against him, he hastens to the side of his beloved, concluding with a vituperation of his eyes for having brought him into such dire straits.† In still another, he describes his meeting with her in a Cordovan bower, calling her, like Imperial, a rose.‡ In the fourth, he discovers in a dark forest the Queen of Navarre and two of her maidens dancing a French figure, and though they realize that he is smitten with love for one of them, he refuses to reveal her name.§ Somewhat different is the seventh composition, in which he hears Love complaining of Spain and threatening to abandon the country, and is told by a maiden that the reason is to be sought in a lady who was praised but whom now he will revile.‖

Several other poems of Villasandino do not

vary appreciably from contemporary and later allegory. He adopts the favourite form of Ribera, the *débat*, representing the body as the accuser of the heart, for having reduced him to the torment of passion.[*] Santillana's debate of the heart and mind in the *Sueño* supplies a convenient parallel. Villasandino writes in the vein of Imperial's *Decir* upon the royal birth in symbolizing the young ruler under the form of a Lion.[†] Twice he approaches the visionary works of Imperial. In the first instance,[‡] dreaming at the conventional time just before dawn, he beholds the toils that are woven for the destruction of the realm, and in the second stanza introduces the familiar fiction of the ship of state.

The second instance, being a fanciful presentation of Henry III's death,[§] is to be grouped in the same political class with Imperial's *Decir* upon the birth of John II and Ribera's upon the regency. It acquires additional importance as a Spanish precursor of Santillana's *Visión* and as the first example of the allegorical type in which feminine figures (here Queen Catherine, Justice, and the Church of Toledo) are consoled in some fashion by the author. A precedent for the type is first offered by the lovely Provençal poem in which Guiraut de Bornelh imagines an encounter with three maidens, probably not allegorical, who

lament with him over the distressed condition of
the land bereft of song, delight, and chivalry. An
exact and notable analogy, early enough to have
influenced Villasandino, occurs in a passage of
Froissart's *Prison Amoureuse*, where the author
beholds in a dream three ladies, Justice, Pité,
and Raison, exiled and stricken with grief, especially the first, who arouses him to a battle against
her arch-enemy, Orgoel.*

It is difficult to accept Farinelli's derivation of
the Spanish composition from Dante's famous
canzone which depicts Drittura, Larghezza, and
Temperanza bewailing their exile from Florence to
Love within his heart. The personal equation of
Dante's passion is introduced to vivify the Italian
poem; but the didactic *banalité* of the Spanish is
quite at variance with the ethereal fiction of the
dolce stil nuovo and the mysteriously beautiful descriptions. There are the French and Provençal
analogues, and the poems of Villasandino himself
bristle with such allegory in cases where no question of Dantesque influence is involved. A short
poem already discussed depicts Love stricken with
grief after the same fashion as in this longer elegy.†
One of his all too numerous complaints about his
sad plight represents him as living night and day
with Poverty and as having Age for a mistress.‡
In an apology to the Archbishop of Toledo, Don

Pedro de Luna, for not having been so frequent in attendance upon him, he again personifies Age, Poverty, and Sorrow as his companions.* One of the series of addresses to Don Gutierre and Doña Constanza about a present of fruit even contains an exact miniature of the verses upon Henry III's death, and this in a case where the absence of the visionary form, the different circumstances, and the casual nature of the passage admit no possibility of a relation to Dante's lyrics.† The expansion of the stanza in which three allegorical ladies in distress complain against the exaltation of wickedness to power would easily result in such a *Decir* as that under discussion, without the interposition of foreign influence, and yet with a still greater resemblance to Dante's *canzone.* Whereas in the poem on the death of Henry III one personification is the Church and a second figure is only the Queen herself, in this shorter passage and in the Italian there are three Virtues, Mesura, Franqueza, and Bondad in the former, Drittura, Larghezza, and Temperanza in the latter. A similar piece of allegory occurs in one of the Bachiller of Salamanca's questions to Villasandino, where, more nearly as in Dante's lyric, Franqueza is represented as banished from Spain.‡

The improbability of Dantesque imitation increases when no trace either of the *Canzoniere* or of the *Divine Comedy* can be disclosed in the rest of Villasandino's production. Four times he mentions Dante, but only as a traditionally great name, a synonym for a poet, affording a convenient rhyme in "ante." He shows no proof of having read this remote luminary, actually ascribing to him once an aphorism that cannot be unearthed in his works. The interchange of verses between him, Ferrant Manuel de Lando, and Alfonso de Baena has been seized as evidence that he combatted the allegorical school for which certain innovations are postulated as derived from Dante. But what he really champions in the dispute is the restriction of poetic activity to the erudite and the aristocratic, moved by rancour against those who were supplanting him in his own methods, and he evidently does not regard Dante as the inspiration of his rivals, for he praises him highly in those very compositions in which he takes up the sword against the so-called opposing faction.

FERRANT MANUEL DE LANDO

Santillana in his *Proemio* and Villasandino in a quatrain from the literary contest * denominate Ferrant Manuel as a disciple of Imperial, but nowhere in his preserved works is there a trace of the Sevillan poet's manner. Twice he upbraids Fortune in the conventional mediaeval style,† and once he speaks of her as subject to God,* but without any approximation to the diction of the *Divine Comedy*. Maintaining in a reply to Baena that the mere glance of Love suffices without conversation,† he appeals to Dante's authority, possibly with a vague allusion to his gaze at Beatrice in the *Vita Nuova* or the *Divine Comedy*, probably, however, in a desire to lend weight to his statement, and, like Villasandino, with no scruple about the absence of the actual words in the Italian text. The ease with which any great name at this time could be disingenuously coerced into service is betrayed by Baena's citation of the same authority for exactly the opposite opinion. Villasandino, on the other hand, had already reprimanded Lando ‡ for having abused Dante ; and in none of his compositions does Lando adopt from Imperial the custom of giving a Dantesque colouring to the language. What ground, then, remains on which the assertions of discipleship to Imperial may rest? It is not unlikely that in one or more of the numerous quarrels in verse that were typical of the day, Ferrant Manuel had supported his contentions on subjects that are unknown to us.

FRAY DIEGO DE VALENCIA

Although Fray Diego frames an elaborate reply to Imperial's *Decir* on John II, his rare imaginative productions are usually not strict allegories but what I have defined as extended metaphors. He once more accentuates the tradition of purloining from French, deriving the garden to which he likens his mistress from the *Roman de la Rose*.* In a single instance he resorts to ordinary allegory, enumerating the changes and chances of life at the palace under the figure of a capricious wheel, like the conventional attribute of Fortune, and at the end personifying the deadly Sins and their subdivisions.†

GONZALO MARTÍNEZ DE MEDINA

The bare didacticism of Gonzalo Martínez would not detain us, were it not that by an imitation of Boccaccio he first signalizes definitely for Spain a greater interest in the Italian successors of Dante than in the master himself. In a *Decir* upon the deaths of Diego López and Juan de Velasco,‡ commenting upon the dealings of Fortune, he alludes to the similar matter of the *De Casibus*; and in a second *Decir* to Juan Hurtado de Mendoza, warning him against the uncertainty of this mortal life,§ he actually imitates the *De Casibus* with a series of famous downfalls, comprising those of Lucifer, Adam, Nimrod, Hercules, Hecuba, Hannibal, Scipio, Pompey, Caesar, Alexander, the tribes expelled by the Goths, Murad I,* Popes John XII and Benedict XIII, almost all of whom are treated by Boccaccio. The unusual example of Pope John XII emphasizes the derivation from Boccaccio. The conception of Fortune has its source also in the *De Casibus*, where she figures prominently, first in a debate with Poverty † and second in a colloquy with the author, who solicits her aid.‡ In the Spanish she is not, as in the *Inferno*, a beneficent agent, but a whimsical force, and it is Divine Grace that, overruling her actions, operates with the purpose of final good, chastising the virtuous for their salvation, exalting the humble, and putting down the mighty from their seat. Perhaps the idea of the composition was partly suggested to Gonzalo by such clauses in Boccaccio as *gygantes opprimo imperatoresque deicio; quos meae manus ad sydera evexere et demum mersere sub inferis;* or *quocunque modo sentiant potentes e culmine lapsos, indeque se deici posse quandoque.* The two lines about the permutations and ministrations of Fortune are drawn more probably from the *rerum revolutrix egregia* and the *rerum mortalium ministra* of Boccaccio, who is mentioned by name in the Spanish, than from the similar phrases of Dante, who, despite the contrary assertions of certain critics, seems to have exerted no influence upon the other works of Gonzalo Martínez.

ALONSO ENRÍQUEZ

The verses ascribed to the great noble, Alonso Enríquez, are all of more or less doubtful authenticity.* The *Vergel de Pensamiento* † is a debate between himself and his Reason upon the question of loyalty to his obdurate lady, in which the latter is ultimately victorious in persuading him to renounce his allegiance. The name is derived from the setting in the garden of amorous thought, the trees of which are persistence, the flowers hope, and the fruit great joy. At the end, discovering that Pallas, Venus, and Cupid have listened to the discussion, he succeeds in obtaining pardon from the first two deities, but by the third is required to undergo a penance. To him also is attributed a Testament couched in amorous terms, establishing the precedent for a type of allegory that was to enjoy considerable popularity in Spain.‡ With the Archbishop of Lisbon as executor, he bestows upon Love his soul and body, and asks that the parts of his tomb be constructed of his several sweethearts and that burial be granted him in the house of another lady, whom, in recompense, he endows with his whole estate.

THE DANCE OF DEATH AND THE REVELATION OF A
HERMIT

Before proceeding to a study of the great exemplars of Spanish letters in this century, the
Marquis of Santillana and Juan de Mena, I pause
to consider briefly two compositions contemporary
to the productions of the Sevillan School, which,
though isolated and anonymous, are none the less
important as affording evidence of the real literary
trend of the day, the *Danza de la Muerte* and the
Revelación de un Ermitaño. The former* is germane to our purpose for two reasons. First, as a
free translation or manipulation of an old French
original, it emphasizes the still persistent connection of Spanish allegory with France. Second,
though it does not relate an actual descent into
the nether regions, it signalizes in Spain, without
Dantesque influence, that spirit of ghostly terror
and that dread of future retribution which characterize the usual visionary journey. Besides the general
gruesome atmosphere pervading the whole work,
there are specific allusions to punishment in the
other world. The allegory is identical with that of
the journey to hell, except that an earlier moment,
the article of death, instead of the penal state after
death, is chosen for representation, and vengeance
is prophesied rather than meted out to the different
classes of evil-doers.

The Revelation of a Hermit * constitutes the third link in the chain of debates of body and soul, the two other sections of which appear in the earlier literature.† The hermit discovers in the usual sinister valley a putrefying corpse engaged in the ordinary dispute with the spirit. Like the earliest of the series, it is dated with the exactness that writers of the Middle Ages assign to their visions. Two or three passages are of interest as revealing in Spanish tradition apart from Dante mediaeval elements that also find expression in the *Divine Comedy*. The author in vain seeks exit from the valley; *coplas* twelve and thirteen are devoted to a debate between a demon and an angel for the wretched soul; ‡ and the last part consists of a most violent denunciation directed by the soul against the falseness of the world, the flesh, and the devil.

CHAPTER XIII

THE GREAT MASTERS OF THE FIFTEENTH CENTURY

THE MARQUIS OF SANTILLANA

THE *PROEMIO*

FORTUNATELY we may institute an examination of Santillana with no surmises but with his own explicit literary manifesto, the celebrated *Proemio* for the collection of his works that he presented to Dom Pedro of Portugal.* What is to be gleaned about his attitude towards allegory may conveniently be grouped under the three headings of his observations upon his compatriots, upon Frenchmen, and upon Italians.

It is a satisfaction to possess a writer's direct statement as testimony of a relation to the past. One is likely to infer that because the literary men of this century revealed broad lacunae both in their knowledge and appreciation of their predecessors, they cared for them not at all and owed them no debt; but of the first three Spanish works that the Marquis mentions — *el Libro de Alixandre, Los votos del Pavon, é aun el libro del Archipreste de Hita* — the first and the third contain extensive allegorical elements, that are specifically paralleled in his own compositions.

From France, he mentions the authors of the *Roman de la Rose*, Pierre Michault, Oton de Granson, and Alain Chartier, all of whom he imitated. Of the works of Alain Chartier that he names, two, the *Livre des Quatre Dames* and the *Hospital d'Amours*, are particularly important in the formation of Santillana's methods. After the catalogue of French authors, he proceeds with a comparison of the French and Italians, assigning the preference to the latter, but with the significant restriction that the former are superior in "art." He cannot be attaching to the word "art" its usual sense, in which surely he would have recognized that the Italians excel; he seems to give it the more general meaning of "form." It is to be extended beyond mere style, for he immediately distinguishes one of its departments, stating that in questions of art the Italians pay heed only to the perfection of their prosody and to the musical accompaniment. May it not include allegorical framework, which in his definition of poetry Santillana has described, again in direct connection with metre, as a "very beautiful covering" for didactic substance? The French would then surpass the Italians in that very detail in which we have seen Imperial and his fellows construct-

204 MEDIAEVAL SPANISH ALLEGORY

ing their works upon northern models. The Dantesque form was too abstruse, and Santillana, with the rest of his compatriots, as he would here acknowledge and as he exemplifies in his compositions, found French allegory, or the allegory of Petrarch and Boccaccio based upon French models, easier to comprehend and more pleasing to write.

There was, nevertheless, one adornment of substance in which they could imitate the Italians, namely, "fair and strange stories." These are to be understood as historical and classical references, which, with the flood of the incoming Renaissance, begin to overrun Spanish poetry, and which form a part of the new kind of literature that endows old allegorical concepts with mythological nomenclature. Such an interpretation is corroborated by a passage at the beginning of Cámara's *Siervo Libre de Amor*. Dedicating the work to Gonzalo de Medina, the author promises to follow the methods of a long list of the ancients, Dante among them, "drawing fictions . . . from gods . . . and goddesses . . . for the poetical purpose of being useful and pleasant to thee with the stories which will afford that profit which plain statement does not allow, by the allegorical sense that carries with it the rude letter, although it seems wholly lacking." These words, by the express statement of the author, refer to the classic investiture of the allegory, such as the symbolization of the three amorous conditions by trees consecrated to Venus, Hercules, and Minerva, the resort to Seneca for advice, the representation of hell as Virgilian, and the thronging historical and mythological allusions. The phrase, "allegorical sense," is not here employed in its broader meaning but is equivalent to the allegorical interpretation of the classical references, described as "fictions" and (corresponding to the word that Santillana uses) "fables."

By nature and literary inheritance, the Marquis would be more concerned with the allegorical than with the other works of the Italians. Of Dante he names only the three parts of the *Divine Comedy*; of Petrarch's Italian compositions, only the *Triumphs*; and when he comes to Boccaccio, he exhibits once more the chief attraction that the Italians had for the poets at the court of John II by singling out the *Ameto*, which is an allegory in classical dress.* Several passages point to a greater interest in Petrarch and Boccaccio than in Dante. Speaking of great princes' patronage of letters, he mentions Petrarch's visit to Robert of Naples and Boccaccio's praise of John of Cyprus, but has naught to say of the courts with which Dante had any connection. Petrarch he calls " poet laureate " and Boccaccio " excellent poet and distinguished orator," terms of honour that he does not accord to their more illustrious predecessor.

THE EROTIC TRILOGY. *EL SUEÑO*

Three poems by Santillana, the *Dream*, the *Little Triumph*, and the *Hell of Lovers*, form, as I shall subsequently seek to prove, a trilogy. We may begin, as in the case of Imperial, with the one that displays no traces of the Dantesque but is in character thoroughly French. Like Imperial's early *Decir*, the *Sueño*, or *Dream*, the substance of which I have already epitomized, belongs to the large class of mediaeval compositions that end with a wound from Love's dart.

The familiar allegorical battle embodied in this piece emanated from Spain itself in the *Psychomachia* of Prudentius. The likeness of the *Sueño* to the conclusion of the *Roman de la Rose* has already been pointed out by others.* At the first Amant is wounded by Amour and swoons; † and in the last part there is a combat, though in this case Venus and Cupid fight on the side of the lover against the castle of Jalousie. Huon de Mery's *Tornoiement d'Antéchrist* ‡ contains an exactly parallel conflict of Chastity and Love with similar details. In both, the lover journeys several days before he comes to the scene of the chief event, a blast of martial music summons to the strife, and the victim, wounded by the arrow of Venus, sinks fainting upon the turf. Froissart's *Prison Amoureuse* represents the hero Rose and allegorical personifications championing Justice, Pité, and Raison against Orgoel and his followers. In the *Echecs Amoureux*, Diana warns the lover against Venus.* The *Fimerodia* of Jacopo da Montepulciano, written before 1395,† depicts also a struggle of Venus and Diana over Luigi Davanzati, but the parallelism is not close. In Petrarch's *Trionfi*, Love is put to rout by Laura, the incarnation of Chastity. The debate of the Heart and the Mind in the *Sueño* upon the reality of dreams points, in the previous literary history of the peninsula, to the debates of the Body and Soul and the Body and Heart.

Spanish itself affords a close and curious analogue to the *Sueño*, where it would least be expected, in a versifier, the rest of whose meagre extant works are of the dullest Galician type, Santillana's older contemporary, Macías, more famed in legend than in literature. Four short stanzas ‡ present in a nutshell all of the Marquis's matter: Beauty, leading Moderation, Courtesy, Prudence, and Vigour, wounds and captures the writer as a prisoner of Love, assigning him as guards Sorrow and Care. Santillana, however, may not have known this uncharacteristic bit from

Macías, for in the *Proemio* he does not include it in the four poems of his that he declares to be current. If he had modelled one of his own compositions upon the piece, it is hardly possible that he would have forgotten it. For us the question is not pertinent, inasmuch as the mere existence of a tendency to this special kind of allegory in a poet in no sense influenced by Dante proves that Santillana cannot be isolated from past Spanish tradition, or considered as an innovator suddenly looming up on the horizon of literature. What details of the *Sueño* are not French or original are to be sought in Boccaccio rather than in Dante.

I suspect that not long before he had read the *Fiammetta* and the *Corbaccio*. To the former he definitely alludes in the *Comedieta*.* Fiammetta's sorrow, after the fashion of Senecan drama, is foreshadowed by a dream analogous in almost every factor to the Marquis's premonitory vision. Lying in her bed, after gathering flowers in the traditional meadow, she seems to see herself sink upon the thickest grass to rest; whereupon a serpent immediately bites her, as in the Spanish poem, beneath her left breast. In both compositions the snake's wound is accompanied by a great upheaval of nature; and on awaking from the nightmare each instinctively feels for the wound. The parallelism of language, joined to the general similarities in thought, implies a direct relation between the two passages. A final analogy is found in the ominous visions that Fiammetta experiences just before the unhappy news.

Although the opening of the *Corbaccio* has no serpent, certain details are even closer. Boccaccio, like the Marquis, sets out over a pleasant path, but finds the way suddenly changing character. In the Italian, the grass and flowers become rocks and thistles; in the Spanish, the trees of the orchard are transmuted into gnarled and savage trunks. Like Santillana in the raging storm, Boccaccio is enveloped by a dark cloud, from which he finally emerges to find himself in the Labyrinth of Love. Dante has no monopoly upon old men as guides, so that Tiresias need not be taken with Menéndez y Pelayo from the Cato of the *Purgatorio*; the parallelism of the earlier passages and the peculiar choice in both authors of the age when the hair is just turning white suggest a derivation rather from the unhappy husband, Boccaccio's conductor.

THE EROTIC TRILOGY. *EL TRIUNPHETE DE AMOR*

In the *Triunphete de Amor*,* the Italian influence is more considerable but, as the title betrays, emanates from Petrarch. Early in summer, at midday, the author encounters in a forest two sumptuously dressed pages with their steeds, and learns from them of the approach of Cupid and Venus in triumph. Both deities file past with their respective trains of lovers, and at the goddess's command he is pierced by the arrow of one of the ladies.

Two fairly distinct streams of derivation can be discerned, one, French, extending as far as the appearance of the amorous deities and including the final episode of the wound, the other, Italian, covering the triumph itself. Though each stream overlaps the other, Santillana may be said in the specified places to have felt the effect of one more strongly than of the other. The introductory framework is northern; I cite three analogies, one Latin, the second Provençal, the third French. In a portion of his *De Amore*, Andreas Capellanus describes a procession led by Love in the guise of a richly caparisoned knight and moving toward a meadow in which are set gorgeous thrones for the deity and his spouse.* Peire Guilhem, astray, like the Marquis, in a luxuriant landscape, is met by a resplendent knight corresponding to Santillana's pages, who does not, as in the *Triunphete*, point out to him the Court of Love, but, as in Andreas Capellanus, is himself the god, and together with Mercy, Loyalty, and

Modesty, follows him to a kind of improvised Court of Love, where he answers his erotic queries.* Eustache Deschamps, in his *Lay Amoureux*,† wandering through a fair meadow after the same fashion, encounters Love in the form of an hermaphrodite, accompanied by a great throng of famous lovers. Of the wound we have already seen examples, both in French and Spanish.

The *Triunphete* may be considered a Court of Love with additions from Petrarch. As soon as the procession passes before him, the Marquis is carried away by Italian reminiscences. That Petrarch is definitely in his mind is shown by the title itself, by his own comparison of the experience to the Italian work, and by the parallelism and classicism of the lists of lovers. Many of the women, and with the exception of Mark Antony and Galeot, all the men, appear in Petrarch's Triumph of Cupid. It is unnecessary to derive so famous a figure as Galeot from the *Divine Comedy*, especially when Tristan and Lancelot, who figure also in Petrarch, have just been mentioned; and the name of Dante himself is simply repeated from the Italian *Trionfo*.‡ The greater classicism may be demonstrated by a glance at the lists in the *Lay Amoureux* or in such a French Court as Froissart's *Paradys d'Amour*.§

THE EROTIC TRILOGY. *EL INFIERNO DE LOS ENAMORADOS*

From this strong tradition of French and later Italian borrowing, as the discussion of the Erotic Hell has already demonstrated, the *Infierno* does not depart. The marked increase in rhetorical adornment, producing eight distinct and elaborate similes in contrast to the one of the *Sueño*, is to be traced as much to Petrarch, Boccaccio, and the classics as to Dante.

The general structural connection of the *Infierno* with Petrarch's *Triumph of Love* is corroborated by the fact that these three poems of Santillana seem to form a kind of trilogy, figuring different stages in the vicissitudes of passion. We need not suppose that one is a direct continuation of the other, but only that Santillana composed each with the definite idea of a relation to the others. As in Petrarch, there is depicted first in the *Triunphete* the victorious procession and then in the *Infierno* the suffering of lovers. The undoubted dependence of the former upon Petrarch increases the probability that in the latter the Marquis was reproducing the Prison of Love in the *Triumphs*. Like Juan Rodríguez de la Cámara's *Siervo Libre de Amor*, the trilogy would represent the author's servitude to Love and then his rejection of that servitude by the example of amorous woes. In the *Sueño*, the Marquis is defeated, captured, and wounded by Cupid and Venus ; in the *Triunphete*, he beholds the triumph of his conquerors, and is wounded again, this time by his lady; in the *Infierno*, he is healed of his passion by the sight of so much distress. In the first, the French influence is paramount; in the second, a Petrarchan strain is also discerned; and in the third, a few Dantesque elements are engrafted upon the French and Petrarchan stock.

Many considerations strengthen this theory. Both in the *Sueño* and *Infierno*, it is evident that Santillana has been reading Boccaccio, and especially the *Corbaccio*. The interest in Petrarch unites the two latter members of the series. The same playful tone of the French Court of Love characterizes all three. Diana, as well as the deities of the tender passion, makes her presence felt throughout. In the first she is most prominent as the protectress of the author in the strife. The second opens with the following lines :

> Siguiendo el plaçiente estilo
> Á la grand deessa Diana.

Since there is no other reference to this goddess in the poem, the lines utterly lose their point unless we connect them with some other poem in which she is important. If the *Sueño* immediately preceded, the lines would become pregnant with meaning: despite his capture by Love in the previous composition, Santillana would wish still to assert his allegiance to the patroness of chastity, and since he has to be wounded again at the end of the *Triunphete*, he evidently considered himself at the beginning as persisting in her service. In the third composition, Diana, who in the first of the triad has encountered a serious hindrance to her purpose, is enabled finally to effect the Marquis's salvation through her favourite Hippolytus. She is here again regarded as the opponent of Venus, for she is mentioned as the protector of Cephalus, one of the chaste who are allowed to walk immune in the gruesome valley. If this interrelation, which is at least plausible, may be conceded as a fact, the influence of the French poets and of Petrarch and Boccaccio throughout the trilogy receives additional confirmation by cumulative and reflected evidence.*

THE *QUERELLA DE AMOR*

The substance of these verses † is the complaint of Macías wounded by Love, to which the Marquis listens in a nocturnal vision. It is compiled of extracts from Macías, Juan Rodríguez de la Cámara, Pero González de Mendoza, Villasandino, and an unknown author. The subject of an amorous wound

had often been treated before in Spain, notably by
Imperial in his first period; and the indubitable
reliance upon earlier literature in the peninsula
demonstrates that such a work as the *Infierno*,
the theme of which, the agony of love, is the
same, does not develop wholly under exotic influences.

THE *VISIÓN*

Political in its body, erotic in its conclusion, the
Visión * affords a convenient transition to the second division of Santillana's works. My desire is
to prove the instability of the general theory that
would connect this poem, the best example of the
class in which personifications appear in distress
and are consoled, with Dante's *canzone, Tre donne
intorno al cor mi son venute.*

The points of similarity are the encounter with
three figurative ladies and their grief. But, as in
Villasandino's poem of the same type, the acci-
dents of the number three and the sorrow rather
than the joy of the personifications are insufficient
proof of a relation to the Italian lyric. If Villasandino had imitated Dante, he would probably
have indulged in some verbal reminiscences; and
their absence is all the more striking when it here
occurs a second time. No question of Italian influence could arise in the analogous Spanish pas-

sages, to which reference has been made in the discussion of the verses upon Henry III's death; and with still less reason may the *Visión* be derived from Dante, when so close a parallel as Villasandino's poem exists in Spanish literature itself. Santillana surely knew this composition. In the *Proemio* he speaks of its author with the highest esteem, and reveals thorough familiarity with his works by referring to him as the literary opponent of Manuel de Lando. There is also a verbal relation between the two poems. In the Italian it is only said that the Virtues are questioned, and even then, not by the writer, but by Love, and the question itself is not given; in both Spanish poems the question is expressed at length with stylistic parallelism, and the diction at other points is so similar as to establish a connection. Santillana himself, in the *Defunción de Don Enrique de Villena*, presents the Muses mourning the royal poet, and in the *Comedieta de Ponza*, four princesses grieving for their relatives who have been captured in the battle.

The absence of Italian imitation from either poem becomes more conspicuous when to the Spanish are added French analogues. Some of these have been mentioned in the treatment of Villasandino's composition. The passage in Froissart's *Prison Amoureuse* has an even more striking resemblance to the *Visión*: in both emphasis

is laid upon the tears, and the Virtues, when interrogated, respond in the same fashion. Other
French compositions also are closer to Santillana than Villasandino. Puymaigre * has already
pointed out the similarity in Pierre Michault's
Doctrinal de Cour (composed in 1466 after the
Marquis's death), where the author in a wood,
like the *valle espantoso* of the Spanish, encounters
exiled Virtue, who guides him first to the chief
Vices and thence to the four cardinal Virtues
asleep in the School of Truth. In the *Livre des
Quatre Dames*,† Alain Chartier, finding four ladies
engaged in a rivalry as to who is the greatest suf-
ferer from the respective misfortunes of their lovers at the battle of Agincourt, is unable to decide
among them, and turns over the question to his
mistress ; and in his *Esperance ou Consolation des
Trois Vertus*, it is the personifications, Faith, Hope,
and Charity that resuscitate him from despair over
the distraught condition of his country.‡

With these analogues in mind, it is impossible
to believe in the Dantesque derivation. There are,
moreover, important points of divergence. The
Spanish Castidat is a division of the Italian Temperanza, but the Italian Drittura and Larghezza
bear no similarity to the Spanish Firmeza and
Lealtad. In Dante the Virtues are three different
generations, and Drittura, the oldest, is sister to

Love's mother; in Santillana this intricate family-tree does not exist, the Virtues being simply sisters. The two compositions conclude quite differently : in the Italian, Love unites himself in sorrow to the three ladies, making really four unhappy personifications, and Dante in such comradeship comforts himself for his own exile ; in the Spanish, the three figures, as in Chartier's *Livre des Quatre Dames*, are merely bidden to take refuge with his Lady, who is the home of all Virtues.

Santillana is utterly unable to attain the delicacy that surrounds the conceptions of the *dolce stil nuovo*, manifested here especially in the assignment of the vision to Dante's heart and in the choice of Love and not the writer as the interlocutor. Again the complex and exquisite mystery that hovers over the whole *canzone*, sometimes intangible, sometimes finding expression in such details as the account of the birth of Larghezza and Temperanza, is replaced by a mediaeval perspicacity. The Spanish dream is located, not in so vaguely enchanting a place as the heart, but in the definite setting of a dread valley beside a fountain. The Italian Virtues are sketched with a weird indistinctness, and the reader does not learn what becomes of them ; the Spanish are accurately drawn, and the reader leaves them safe in the lady's bosom. Dante's lofty picturesqueness of expression is far removed from Santillana's reach. The former describes his figures nobly by reference to their mental state; Santillana stresses their physical plight and, with a pedantic tendency engendered by the Renaissance, compares their grief to classical examples, the laments of the Roman matrons after Cannae, of the Greek women for Capaneus, and of the Trojan dames after the destruction of their city. While the Marquis scrupulously names their garments, Dante is painting with ineffable loveliness the very soul of sorrow, employing, instead of direct statement, accidental and impressive symbols of the emotion :

> Dolesi l'una con parole molto,
> E'n sulla man si posa
> Come succisa rosa :
> Il nudo braccio, di dolor colonna,
> Sente lo raggio che cade del volto :
> L'altra man tiene ascosa
> La faccia lagrimosa ;
> Discinta e scalza, e sol di sè par donna.

THE PANEGYRICS. THE *CORONACIÓN DE MOSSÉN JORDÍ*

Closely connected with this erotic verse, because uniting the love and Coronation themes, is the first* of the two poems that the Marquis composed in eulogy of two great literary figures of his day. Only the provenience of certain items need be discussed here.

The influence of Dante is even slighter than in the *Infierno*. Santillana decides to compose an allegory of the Court of Love in honour of a fellow poet, and happening to recall a striking reference to a dream in the ninth canto of the *Purgatorio*, he exhibits his wide reading and pads out his substance by an allusion to the Italian passage. In reviewing the canto he is impressed by the intricacy of the opening temporal circumlocution, where the dawn is described as the concubine of Tithonus,* and since his custom was to begin his visions with these pedantries, in imitation of Boccaccio, with whom they became a mannerism, he utilizes that one which is ready at hand, the *tiempo poetico*, as he calls it. He then goes on to copy the immediately succeeding metaphor of the winged night, and with this the influence of Dante ends. One might as well call the piece an imitation of Virgil, for Venus is compared to that apparition of her which was vouchsafed to Æneas at Carthage, and the happiness of the company to the felicity of the inhabitants of the Elysian fields.†

THE PANEGYRICS. THE *DEFUNCIÓN DE DON ENRIQUE DE VILLENA* ‡

Here again an earlier chapter leaves for discussion only the derivation of certain details. The *Divine Comedy* is responsible for isolated and insignificant parts of the framework. The attempted ascent of the mountain in the first *Inferno* is quite diverse in its circumstances. Dante's climb has the profound allegorical meaning of spiritual effort, and it is noteworthy that he advances only a short space; but Santillana conceives the mountain to be simply the place of the vision, destitute of any such *moralem sensum* as celestial blessings or a virtuous life, and he succeeds in reaching the top. The Marquis probably had in mind, as the abode of the Muses, Parnassus, which is actually named in Juan de Mena's *Coronación*. He was doubtless affected also by the location of so many allegorical journeys upon heights. In Claudian's *De Nuptiis Honorii et Mariae* and in the *Architrenius*, the house of Venus is upon a mountain. In the *Anticlaudianus*, the palace of Nature is upon a mountain and that of Fortune upon a cliff. In the *Roman de la Rose*, Fortune lives *en haut, ou chief de la montaingne*.* A still more important analogy is afforded by Chaucer, who fixes his House of Fame, parallel in some respects to Santillana's place of honour, upon a mountain of ice. Nor is the description of the site itself necessarily from the *Divine Comedy*; † the diction is as close to that applied to the similar waste in the *Corbaccio*. The three animals that dispute the way in the *Inferno* are named, but in the *Corbaccio* and the *Defunción* only the generic terms are used. Farther along the way the Marquis encounters classical monsters, modelled, surely, upon the prodigies that prowl about the entrance to Virgil's Hades, since in the next *copla* he makes an express comparison to Æneas and the Harpies. The obscurity of the atmosphere might as well be derived from the thick cloud that befogs Boccaccio's sight as from the *Inferno.**

The gloom of the journey was bound to suggest similar passages in the *Inferno*. The Marquis compares his fatigue from climbing to that of the Italian poet at Acheron, either reading it between the lines, since Dante says nothing of weariness, or misinterpreting the swoon, which is really caused by terror, or confusing this third canto with the first, where fatigue is strongly suggested and even explicitly stated. He remembers one or two fine descriptive phrases, and perhaps here and there shapes the form of his sentence upon the master's precedent. The wealth of imagery and classical lore, which assigns the *Defunción*, like the *Infierno* to a more Italianate period than the *Sueño* and *Coronación*, is extracted from Petrarch, Boccaccio, and the ancients, as well as from Dante.

THE *COMEDIETA DE PONZA*

The *Planto de la Reina Doña Margarida* and the *Comedieta* are likewise fanciful expressions of

sorrow. Of the former I have nothing further to
say. The latter, like so much Spanish allegory,
has an historical interest.* At the dead of night the
author beholds Queen Eleanor, the Queens of
Navarre and Aragon, and the Infanta Catherine
plunged in the deepest grief. They beseech Boccaccio, who in his *De Casibus* had catalogued such
terrible misfortunes, to write their story, and
Eleanor recounts to him at length the names and
virtues of her different children, her portentous
dream of drowning at sea, and following close
upon it the letter reporting the disastrous naval
battle, in which her sons Alfonso of Aragon, John
of Navarre, and the Infantes Don Enrique and
Don Pedro were taken prisoners by the Italians.
The aged queen falls dead at the news; but at
dawn Fortune appears in triumph with her train
of subjects, and by vaunting her own fickleness
comforts the other royal ladies with the hope that
a better fate awaits them. The vision ends with the
appearance of the four captives returned to freedom.

There is no doubt in this case that the fundamental source is a French poem, the *Livre des
Quatre Dames*, which, since it was composed by
Alain Chartier, makes more probable the derivation of the *Infierno* from the *Hospital d'Amours*,
believed by the Marquis at any rate to be by the
same author; its possible relation to the *Visión*

has already been noted. A parallel dating from a few years after Santillana's death is furnished by Chastellain's *Temple de Bocace*,* written like the *Comedieta* for the consolation of a queen, Margaret of Anjou, whose husband Henry VI of England, is captive, deposed, and insane. Transported to a temple, he perceives first a procession of famous unfortunates, then the royal lady herself, who conjures Boccaccio from his grave, as the reporter of so many mischances in the *De Casibus*, to listen to her complaint. In a long harangue he comforts her with the thought that she suffers guiltless and that she may hope for a happier lot, and he consigns to her the seven Virtues that she may cherish them.

The Spanish poem is not so fittingly named as the French, for the influence of Boccaccio is of considerably more moment than that of Dante, which is suggested in the title. The basic conception, the insecurity of human life, is derived from the *De Casibus*, and the important rôle of Fortune is partly traceable to her position in Boccaccio's work. Reminiscences of the Fortune in the *Amorosa Visione* also linger in Santillana's mind: for example, she overthrows the cities of Thebes and Troy, as in the Italian, and her victims are partially identical with those in Boccaccio's poem whom Fortune and Fame have influenced.

Such attendants upon allegorical personifications are, of course, as the Marquis specifically declares, also derived from Petrarch, who, though Fortune is not one of his characters, suggested the general idea of a triumphal procession.

The conception of the goddess is very doubtfully Dantesque. The only approximation to the thought of *Inferno* VII is Fortune's own statement that she has been assigned her capricious task by God's commandment. But this I take to be merely an attempt to lend authority to her whims, very remote from Dante's idea of a beneficent minister. The rest of Fortune's long analysis of her actions is concerned with the conventional topic of her continual permutations; and a very strong savour of French rather than of Dantesque mediaevalism is attached to the elaborate description of her dress. Two parts are especially noteworthy, a girdle upon which are wrought the twelve signs of the zodiac, and a circlet for the hair in which are seven medallions representing the seven planetary deities. Her rôle as comforter may be partly explained by the like office of Philosophy in Boethius.

Some details also are from Boccaccio. The company that the Queen Eleanor gathers together for tale-telling, to help her to forget her anxiety, is probably suggested by the merrymakers whom

Florio in the *Filocolo* finds at Naples, or the group of ten in the *Decameron*.* Although the Marquis mentions the authorities, Macrobius, Guido delle Colonne, and Valerius Maximus, the Queen's monitory dream may be imitated from the *Fiammetta*, which has already been seen to be efficacious in the *Sueño*, for the lady-in-waiting who presents to the Queen the fatal letter about the battle is compared to the heroine informed of Panfilo's perfidy.† A general influence of Boccaccio is to be discerned in the exaggerated number of classical allusions, a good example of which Fiammetta herself supplies in the whole chapter of ancient mischances mentioned in comparison to her own plight.

Upon this structure are hung a very few Dantesque ornaments. The title itself is doubtless somewhat coloured by that of the great Italian epic, but, as appears from the short introductory *Proemio*, in which he dedicates this and some other poems to Doña Violante de Prades, the connection is most superficial and unessential. In the conventional manner he divides poetry into three classes, tragedy, satire, and comedy ; then, defining comedy as the type that begins in sorrow and ends in joy, he classes together Terence and Dante as its exponents and suggests that his composition is of the same sort. According to Santillana's own implication, there is no need, from the similar title, of supposing a nearer relation between Dante and himself than between Dante and Terence. The *Proemio* itself does not rely upon the questionably authentic letter to Can Grande, but upon the analogous discussions in the commentaries of Benvenuto da Imola and Pietro Alighieri, or at least upon a closely similar commentary. Some half dozen lines, especially in the invocations, perhaps reflect Dantesque phraseology, none of them such as to modify the framework or general effect of the composition; it is rather an extravagant antiquarianism that gives the tonality to the French and later Italian grounding.

CANONIZACIÓN DE LOS BIENAVENTURADOS SANTOS MA-ESTRE VICENTE FERRER, PREDICADOR, Y MAESTRE PEDRO DE VILLACRECES, FRAILE MENOR

Farinelli has related this composition* to the *Paradiso* upon vague and indecisive grounds, such as an invocation concerning the difficulty of the subject, the presence of light and song in heaven, or the beatific vision; but there exists more trustworthy evidence of which he might have taken advantage and yet not have characterized it as even an indistinct echo of the third *cantica*. Its genesis may be traced within the peninsula itself. The basic idea of a canonization is surely not derived from the Italian poet but from the common custom of the Church; the *raison d'être* is the popularity of these saints, especially Vincent Ferrer, whose name resounds through the literature of the fifteenth century. As the apotheosis of the Coronation form, the structure is affected also by the constituents of that Spanish type. The visionary framework of the celestial journey is a mediaeval commonplace. Paulus Emeritanus and St. Valerius furnish examples within the limits of Spain, and the emphasis upon the surpassing brightness of heaven in the vision of Maximus, described by the latter, creates a precedent for Santillana's, —

> La su claridat vençía
> Á todos otros clarores.

In the vernacular an exact prototype is afforded by Berceo, whose St. Oria is borne through the categories of the blessed to behold the place of her own beatification.

The starting point, and, indeed, the ending point, for the assertion of Dantesque influence is a simile not observed by Farinelli. Describing the refulgence of the twelve apostles in the midst of the celestial brilliancy, the Marquis seems to take his figure of sparks discerned in a flame from the *Paradiso.** Upon this, certain other relations are contingent. It is possible that *Tú, solo Sancto, Osanna filii María,* as a hymn of praise was suggested by the *Osanna*, which the souls in the third heaven intone (in the context* immediately adjoining the above-mentioned simile) or by the longer *Osanna* at the beginning of the preceding canto. The equal glory that St. Thomas Aquinas in the heaven of the Sun ascribes to SS. Francis and Dominic may have led the Marquis, having once ideated a celestial Coronation, to group a Franciscan with the Dominican saint and to conceive of a double championship as again saving the church. The metaphor of the ship is used of the religious champions in both the Italian and Spanish, but it is so usual a way of setting forth the church as to be of slight probative value. Although the four beasts of the Gospels that Santillana beholds are also part of the mystic procession in the *Purgatorio*, they are probably taken directly from the fourth chapter of the *Apocalypse*. Dante represents them in the terrestrial paradise, and the Marquis, with St. John, in heaven; and whereas Dante does not name the four beasts, the Marquis follows the Revelator in identifying them. Even if these few contingent reminiscences, however, could be proved certain, they still would not alter the architectonic scheme.

The simplicity of style militates against the Italian influence. The classical element is very slight,† and the similes have not the effect, all too common in Santillana's work, of borrowed finery, inappropriate to the general dress. They are singularly in accord with the religious subject. The orders of angels are compared to the three crowns of the papal tiara; and the silence of the celestial host, when God speaks, to that of earthly choirs when the priest chants alone. Of all Santillana's compositions hitherto considered, this, by reason of its unaffected and homogeneous character, should be referred, if anywhere, to a persistent indigenous tradition, emanating from the Latin allegorists of the peninsula and developing in Berceo.

EL DIÁLOGO DE BÍAS CONTRA FORTUNA

Santillana's only other long allegorical poem, *The Dialogue of Bias against Fortune,* is of a totally different nature.* The title indicates that it belongs to the class of *débats.* The author, as he himself states in the special *Proemio* to the Conde de Alva, takes advantage of the legend that represents the philosopher of Priene, while his fellow citizens are fleeing in panic from the sack of the city, calmly encountering Fortune at the town gate and satisfying her curiosity at his placidity with the famous words: *Omnia mea bona mecum porto.* The Marquis imagines a dialogue in which Bias discredits one by one all of Fortune's pretensions. Farinelli †

would see in the consolation against the blows of
the goddess the influence of Dante, but surely
very little connection exists between the idea that
there is some protection against her caprices and
the idea that they are part of God's providence.
He could with a greater semblance of probability
have pointed to the description of hell, which
Fortune reserves as her last weapon to terrify
Bias; but what might seem at first glance reminiscences of the *Inferno* prove to be elements of
a Virgilian Hades, which in general was more in
the minds of Spanish poets during the fifteenth
century than the first *cantica* of the Italian poem,
and large sections of which, together with the description of the Elysian fields, the Marquis translates or adapts line by line.

CONCLUSIONS

I have stressed the sources of Santillana's works in
order to refute the general tendency to derive them
only from Dantesque precedents; but they are by
no means mere mosaics compounded of foreign
materials. He is a direct inheritor of former alle-
gorizers in the peninsula and adds an important
contribution of his own to the glory of the line.
I have sought to indicate the many legacies that
he received from his predecessors; it is only necessary to recall, for example, his indebtedness in

the *Canonización* to Gonzalo de Berceo, in the *Visión* to Villasandino, and in the *Sueño* and *Coronación* to Imperial, in order to realize the continuity of Spanish allegorical wealth. He enriches this heritage, to be sure, with acquisitions from French and Italian treasures : he owes much less to the *Divine Comedy* than to Petrarch and Boccaccio, who adapt Dante's material to the French spirit. It is significant that he does not concern himself with the allegorical mechanism of the *Divine Comedy* in his annotations around the margin of the so-called translation of Enrique de Villena. His general tone, nevertheless, is thoroughly and essentially Spanish. He writes with that grave didacticism, manifesting itself, now in stern arraignment of vice, now in religious and sententious ardor, and now in learned compilations, and with that fervent patriotism, finding expression in bitter condemnation of overweening nobles, in loyalty to his sovereign, and in grief for national disaster, which have always been the peculiar characteristics of Castilian literature.

He himself augments the general patrimony more than any individual predecessor. By setting the impress of his authority upon the Erotic Hell, he ensures it a vast popularity in the peninsula ; and by constructing, partly from his own invention, the *Defunción* and *Coronación*, he establishes the norm for poetic Panegyrics. But his influence upon Castilian literature is still broader and deeper. The compositions of Imperial and the other versifiers of the *Cancionero de Baena* had been more or less uneven, disjointed, disproportionate in their parts, and generally rude; Santillana, guided by the spell of the Italian spirit and his own innate sense of harmony, is the first in Castile to endow allegory with artistic form. It required this truly literary expression before it could obtain a reputable standing among men of letters. To the fact that the Marquis, high in the state and reverenced for his magnanimity, threw his weight into the scale of allegory, is largely due its great vogue in Castile during the fifteenth century.

CHAPTER XIV

THE GREAT MASTERS OF THE FIFTEENTH CENTURY

JUAN DE MENA

THE *LABERINTO DE FORTUNA*

JUAN DE MENA,* by his travels in Italy, studies at Rome, and close approximation in time to the Spanish Renaissance, might be expected to have become so thoroughly Italianate as to break with the long established indigenous tradition of allegory ; but the *Laberinto* † is parallel to the ordinary mediaeval journey to the House of Fortune or Fame, or to the Court of Love, and his Italianism is restricted to augmented classical reminiscence. The chief importance of the poem lies in its extension of the allegorical form to a lengthy composition.

After a dedication to the King and an invocation of Calliope and Apollo, in the midst of a denunciation of Fortune, the writer finds himself snatched up by the chariot of Bellona to a great desert, before a shining marble wall surrounding the Palace of Fortune. Out of a dark cloud there appears to him the lovely guide for his journey, Providencia. She transports him through the great crush at the portal and sets him down inside, whence he can indulge in one of those geographical outlooks so dear to the mediaeval mind, here constituting a digression of inordinate length. Within the palace are three wheels, two motionless, symbolizing the past and future, one in movement, symbolizing the present, and beneath are the unfortunate who have fallen to the ground. On the wheels of the past and present are fixed seven circles, to represent the different planets, and upon each planet its appropriate group of the blessed according to the conceptions of planetary efficacy. With Providencia as lecturer, he inspects the inhabitants of each circle, and in some cases discovers under the wheel those condemned for the corresponding vices. The Moon is the abode of the chaste, Mercury of good counsellors and traders, Venus of pure lovers, the Sun of those who have attained wisdom in any capacity, Mars of valiant warriors, Jupiter of great rulers, and Saturn of righteous nobles, not sharply distinguished from the preceding circle. The end of each division contains a careful definition of the virtue in question and an exhortation to the King to repress the opposite vice, except in the case of Mercury, where Avarice is defined. The poem concludes with a Panegyric, in the mouth of Providencia, upon the historic glories of Spain.

Seeking to embrace her knees in reverence, Juan
de Mena finds, like Virgil and Dante, only thin
air between his arms. To the original three hundred strophes* were afterwards added twenty-
four, usually printed separately and perhaps by
a later hand, bewailing the oppression of the
King by his nobles and having no real connection
with the substance of *Las Trescientas*.

The details of this experience are suggested by
a great number of Latin and French prototypes,
chiefly the *Anticlaudianus*, the *Roman de la Rose*,
Baudouin de Condé's *Prison d'Amours*, Watriquet
de Couvin's *Escharbote*, and Tommaso di Saluzzo's
Chevalier Errant. A more direct source was doubtless the hall of Fortune in Boccaccio's *Amorosa
Visione*, but the closest analogy is Frezzi's *Quadriregio*, which Juan de Mena may have read while
in Italy. In the second book the author is vouchsafed a glimpse of Fortune ensconced in the midst
of seven wheels, upon the upper section of which,
as usual, the happy rejoice, and upon the lower
section of which the unfortunate suffer. Most
noteworthy is the presence on each wheel of famous mortals, ancient and modern.

The architecture and material of the poem seldom rise above mediaeval commonplace. Mena's
system of the three wheels and their circlets shrink
into trivialities before Dante's towering conception.

He does not attain even to Imperial's vague re-
membrance of the Italian's Fortune, paralleling
the *Anticlaudianus* too closely not to imply a me-
diate or immediate relation. Dante considers the
goddess beneficent, Juan de Mena brands her as
essentially evil but controlled by Providence. Sanvisenti's derivation of the classification upon the
wheels from the Italian heavens may be categorically denied. There are certain similarities, but
only in cases where Dante agrees with current
ideas; the dissimilarities are much more striking.
Sanvisenti fails to understand one of the fundamental distinctions between Dante and Juan de
Mena, and, indeed, between the Italian and Spanish mind and the literature that each produced.
The former usually chooses and develops with
singleness of purpose one of that multitude of
traits which the latter, in conjunction with Imperial and most mediaeval poets, careless of artistic unity and concerned only with the momentary
effect of luxuriance, represents as produced by the
influence of each planet. Consistently with his
purpose Dante admits to his celestial spheres only
those who have exhibited this trait within the
pale and according to the principles of Christianity;
the Spaniard with little thought for congruity admits Christian and Pagan alike who have exhibited
any remotest ramification of the trait. The mere

subdivision of the supernatural abodes is the normal method of visionary literature. The figure of the guide Providencia presents one of the cases where it is hard to determine whether the poet owes more to his own originality, to Dante, or to Boccaccio. The constant dependence upon Boccaccio throughout the *Laberinto* would tip the scale in favour of the Lady in the *Amorosa Visione*.

We seem to catch the surest and brightest glimmer of the *Divine Comedy* in the historical personages who are discovered upon the mysterious wheels and whose tragic stories, like those of Francesca or Ugolino, are related by the guide. It is of course in no sense a Dantesque anomaly for mortals lately defunct or represented as defunct at the time of the vision to appear in journeys to the other world; but the vividness and power with which Juan de Mena relates these episodes certainly reflect a profitable study of the Italian epic and instil life into the fantastic unreality of the allegorical type that he borrowed from France and from Boccaccio and Petrarch. In some instances, however, the narratives are based rather upon classical prototypes. The tale of the Count of Niebla is in part an imitation, with additional Virgilian borrowings, of Caesar's attempted sail in the fifth book of Lucan's *Pharsalia*, and the resuscitation of a corpse by a witch to prophecy about Alvaro de Luna is copied, often with exact translation, from the visit of Sextus Pompeius to Erichtho in the sixth book of the same work. The general debt to antiquity is as great as that to the Middle Ages, provoking, for instance, the pedantic intrusion from *Æneid* VI of certain monstrous shapes at the entrance to Fortune's palace. One or two passages are possible, but not indubitable, recollections of Dante's phraseology; several lines, which might at first sight appear to have their source in the *Divine Comedy*, are in reality again taken from Virgil's journey to the realms beyond. In an unreflecting imitation of the ancients, figurative language reaches in Juan de Mena a fulsomeness and artificiality unprecedented in Spain, but certain similes, perhaps under the spell of Dante, are drawn from the homely familiarities of ordinary existence, especially from the life of children.

THE *CORONACIÓN* OR *CALAMICLEOS*

Of this developed example of the Panegyric* I need indicate here only the strong classical colouring. The hell that he has added to the heaven of coronation is derived from ancient lore, particularly from the sixth book of the *Æneid*. There are not more than one or two hypothetical reminiscences of the *Inferno*, as, for instance, the souls who, crying out to the author in his crossing of

Acheron, might be suggested by Filippo Argenti
in the pool of Styx. In his own tedious and des-
perately precious commentary, based in its definition of tragedy, comedy, and satire, like Santillana's *Proemio* to the *Comedieta*, upon Benvenuto
da Imola, he indulges in long mythological and
historical digressions about the ancient worthies
that people the domain of the dead, and interprets
the whole in the spirit of the mytho-allegorical
school, making Jason into personified Incon-
stancy or Ixion into personified Avarice. The
absurd Latin vocabulary and periodic involutions
bring the *Calamicleos* even nearer than the *Laberinto* to the stylistic extravagances of Boccaccio. The
secondary title itself is evidently imitated from such
anomalous formations as Boccaccio's *Filocolo :* as
Juan de Mena avers in the first preamble, it is compounded of the Latin *calamitas* and the Greek κλέος,
and thus signifies the combination of infernal pains
and celestial delights that the poem involves.

MINOR WORKS

The *Debate of Reason Against Will** was held
in such high repute with contemporaries that, left
unfinished at the author's death, it was honoured
by three separate continuations at the hands of the
chief literary lights of the day, Gómez Manrique,
Pero Guillén, and Jerónimo de Artés. Mena be-

holds in a vision fair Reason and foul Desire, whose seven faces symbolize the deadly Sins. Reason meets and vanquishes the arguments that each face advances in support of a claim to man's esteem. Juan de Mena's portion comes to an end in Reason's tirade against Wrath. It is to be classed within the same tradition as the category of sins in the *Alexandre*, the debates of Body and Soul, or particularly, the debates of just such personifications as Reason and Desire in the works of Ruy Páez de Ribera. It contains some analogies to Fazio degli Uberti's series of sonnets upon the mortal Sins but not close enough to postulate a relationship. Foulché-Delbosc has published, from a manuscript of the fifteenth century in a private library, a *Conversation that Juan de Mena Holds with Death*,* in which, after the fashion of the *Dance of Death*, the gruesome personification recounts to the poet her ruthless impartiality, and he answers with a pedantic list of the great who have been her victims. He adduces Ovid and Dante as authorities that she has slain Hercules, but he must have read the statement in no work of Dante that the world has ever known. He slips here into the common peccadillo of fifteenth-century Spanish *littérateurs*, who like to strengthen their assertions by an appeal to Dante, or any other famous name, without regard to facts.†

CHAPTER XV

OTHER ALLEGORIES OF THE FIFTEENTH AND EARLY SIXTEENTH CENTURIES

THE PANEGYRISTS

STRANGELY enough, Santillana's nephew, Gómez Manrique, reveals an interest in the intricate allegorical machinery and stylistic license popular at the period only when, in his Panegyric upon his uncle, he is strongly under his influence. To the dependence upon the *Defunción* and the *Infierno* I have already alluded, and there are parallelisms also to the *Comedieta*, which is somewhat analogous in subject. The shields of the cardinal Virtues may be a reminiscence of the princesses' escutcheons, and Manrique actually reproduces Queen Eleanor's confession of her helplessness to depict her daughter's merits when he refers to his own inability to comply with Poetry's demand.

His other sepulchral poem* is an unvarnished narrative of Garcilaso de la Vega's death,† the mourning for him, and his burial, — a kind of *Comedieta de Ponza* stripped of its allegorical frame and rhetoric. In no visionary vale, but at an actual place in Moorish Spain, the author hears the

Christians lamenting and learns of Garcilaso's death by an arrow. He assists at the obsequies, and describes the agony of the women at the messenger's report, and their resignation to the divine will.

In several less pretentious compositions he reduces allegory to its lowest terms. Two of these consist of verses written for dramatic masques and are the simplest possible embodiment of the idea underlying Imperial's *Decir* on John II. The first, upon the birth of a nephew,* includes only seven *coplas*, one assigned to the benediction of each of the Virtues, who are disguised as godparents or fairies; the second, in honour of the fourteenth birthday of Alfonso, Isabella's brother,† includes an induction and eight *coplas* spoken by the beneficent Muses, the last of whom the Princess herself acted. Another composition, the *Batalla de Amores*,‡ sets forth allegorically the struggle between an old and new passion in Manrique's heart. In the very first stanza, without the introductory journey of Santillana's *Sueño* and without the description of the imaginary time and place, the author at once catches the sound of hostile trumpets advancing to attack him, and pits Loyalty, Truth, and Fear against *Breçaida*, who marches upon him amidst her women; but he is wounded and despite his supplications haled off to prison.

Since these are poems of the same class as Imperial's *Decir* and the *Sueño*, the complete absence of the usual extensive machinery is tangible evidence of the discrepancy between Manrique's attitude towards allegory and that of his immediate predecessors.

The *Triumph of the Marquis*, by Diego de Burgos, betrays more influence of the *Divine Comedy* than any work since the compositions of Imperial, confined for the most part, as usual, to style. It is a strange and significant coincidence that Diego de Burgos also chooses Dante as the visionary guide, who compliments him for his frequent reading of the Italian poem and acknowledges to him a debt of fame. The enthronement of the Marquis, with the theological Virtues on his right and the cardinal Virtues on his left, and the subsequent triumph in the midst of sacred song, may be somewhat affected by the symbolic procession of the twenty-ninth canto of the *Purgatorio*. The encounter with Juan de Mena is constructed upon Dantesque models. Diego sues for permission to address him, as Dante to address Francesca, and when he explains how it is that he journeys through the spiritual world being still in the flesh, he recalls Dante's reply to Marco Lombardo.* The frequent invocations at important points in the poem, as at the beginning before the description of hell, and before

the long catalogue of famous men, may also be a
reflection of the *Divine Comedy*.

We do not discover, however, a Dantesque colouring in the passages where we should most expect it. The diction about the lorn wood reveals
nothing of the *Inferno* except the phrase that was
echoed down perhaps from Santillana,—

> Venimos en parte do no sé tal hombre
> Qu'en sólo pensarlo no quede espantado.

It is rather to be compared, like so many passages
in contemporary Spanish literature, to the forest
above the entrance to Hades in the *Æneid*, where
are to be found similar abnormal beasts and monsters. Diego does not penetrate into hell, but as
in the vision of Maximus by St. Valerius, he is
shown its yawning gulf and is instructed about its
terrors. Though the guide Dante declares it to be
the place he visited with Virgil, and though, as
in the *Inferno*, the abyss becomes continually nar-
rower, it is exclusively classical. The condemned
consist of those concerned in the war of the Seven
against Thebes, of Atreus and Thyestes, of Chiron
and Phlegyas, of the Lapithae, of " him by whom
language was confused at Babel," of the Assyrians,
of the prodigies slain by Hercules, of many Greeks
at Troy, of the Titans, of Tereus, Pasiphae, Scylla
and Myrrha, Nero, Tullia and the Danaids. The
amphitheatre may be slightly affected by the ce-

lestial rose,* but its long list of classical occupants suggests the Elysian fields of the *Æneid*.

It is the style that reflects the *Divine Comedy*, not in direct translation, but in an occasional shaping of the phrase caused by a constant perusal of the poem. The guide Dante intimates his identity in cryptic terms like those of Virgil in the *Inferno*. Like Dante spurred to the fiery tirade *Ahi, serva Italia* by the embrace of Virgil and Sordello, Diego no sooner beholds Godfrey of Bouillon in the amphitheatre than he bursts into a denunciation of modern lassitude in regard to the Holy Land. One or two of these echoes, however, had already been sounded by Santillana in the *Comedieta*. The similes are also sometimes Dantesque in tone, several drawn from curious psychological conditions, and three, in close juxtaposition at the end, from the experience of children.

The Panegyric upon Alonso Carrillo, by Diego Guillén de Avila, is more than ordinarily enclosed in a Virgilian wrapping. Although in the introduction the author asserts that he has chosen Dante for a guide because of his cantos upon the nether regions, the Hades is taken *in toto* from the *Æneid*. Tartarus becomes the *casa infernal*, guarded by Tisiphone; haunted by hideous monsters, Centaurs, Chimeras, Harpies, the Hydra, Briareus, the Gorgons, and Cerberus; inhabited by Ixion,

Tityus, Salmoneus, Phlegyas reiterating the Virgilian admonition, the Titans and the Aloidae; and ruled by the inexorable judge, Rhadamanthus. The midway place between purgatory and paradise Diego Guillén definitely names the Elysian fields. He is met by Carrillo, as Æneas by Anchises, and the branch which the Bishop bears is compared to that carried by the Latin hero. The forest in which the first glorification of the deceased takes place is paralleled by the *seclusum nemus et virgulta sonantia silvae.* He mentions only Greek and Latin worthies, excusing himself from allusion to moderns and especially Spaniards on the plea of lack of time.

In many ways the poem is united to the general allegorical tradition of the peninsula. The nature of the vision is analyzed with a definiteness totally opposed to the mystery spread about the *Divine Comedy,* and the journey is dated with the usual exactness. As in the works of Juan Rodríguez de la Cámara, certain details are elucidated at once: the valley is the symbol of *Tristuras,* and each of the Virtues in the celestial mansion has a name inscribed upon her.

Inheriting the form of the Panegyric, Diego Guillén, attracted, like some of his predecessors, by the masterful treatment of similar material in Dante, filched a few ornaments for his own com-

position from the *Divine Comedy*. The denunciation of Fortune, which may have been suggested by
the introduction to the *Laberinto*, presents a nearer
approximation to the conception of *Inferno* VII
than has been afforded hitherto in Spanish literature. Though the similarity is not verbal, it is
acknowledged that as the minister of Providence
she acts according to law, however inscrutable.
The guide Dante shapes his actions partially after
the Virgil of the *Inferno*. Heretics are punished
by fire, but the analogy is not exact, for they are
not sunk in burning tombs, but consumed, and,
phoenix-like, reborn from the ashes. Hypocrites
are punished by leaden burdens, but leaden garments are not mentioned, and the lead itself is
heated. The figure of Divine Grace is influenced
by Beatrice, taking charge of the writer after the
less exalted guide has conducted him through the
two lower realms. The only stanza that deals with
the passage through the heavenly spheres is probably inspired by the *Paradiso*, but the whole ma-
terialistic conception of the heavenly abode is utterly foreign to Dante's lofty and spiritual system.
If the work could be considered as an isolated
phenomenon, it would be natural, inasmuch as
Dantesque elements are found both in hell and
heaven, to derive at least the conception of a journey to the three spiritual realms from the *Divine*

Comedy; but coming as late in the century as 1483*
and paralleling so closely other Panegyrics, the composition of Diego Guillén de Ávila should not be
traced directly to the Italian epic but to the other
pieces of the same Spanish type, which were largely
constructed from general mediaeval sources. There
is little or nothing of the strong stylistic colouring exemplified in Diego de Burgos.

The imitation of Dante is abandoned altogether
a few years later in the eulogy of Queen Isabella,†
differing widely from the ordinary Panegyric, and
influenced principally by the *Laberinto* of Juan de
Mena. Journeying through a wood, he comes
upon the house of the three Fates, the first of
whom relates the former history of Spain, the second Isabella's birth, marriage, and early life, the
third some past events as if they were prophecy.
The piece is heavy-laden with the Renaissance
erudition of which we have discovered many traces
in the earlier Panegyric, and which he exaggerated,
the more saturated he became in the humanistic
atmosphere of Rome. The idea of Imperial's *Decir*
upon the birth of John II is employed again in
Clotho's catalogue of the benedictions shed upon
the young Queen by different allegorical and mythological figures. The analogy to Juan de Mena
appears in the patriotic account of Spanish history
and in the encomium upon the sovereign.

Another peculiar ramification of the Panegyric is Diego del Castillo's *Vision on the Death of the King Don Alfonso*,* modelled closely upon Santillana's *Comedieta de Ponza*. The author imagines that in the midst of a frightful tempest he hears the Fate Atropos threatening mortals and Alfonso V of Aragon in particular, and he passes forthwith to a report of the wails of the royal suite and the Queen at the approaching death. Atropos responds asserting her inexorable will and extenuating her funereal actions. The composition concludes with a description of the King's dissolution and with his encomium by the author. The eulogistic purpose of the *Defunción* is accommodated to the form of the *Comedieta*. The several members of the royal family are praised in Santillana's poem, but sorrow for the naval disaster is the chief motive. Diego del Castillo imitates the structure of the *Comedieta* in the outcries for the King's decease and in the manipulation of a feminine figure to upbraid and console the mourners, but he utilizes this structure for a personal eulogy such as that of the *Defunción*, which is a series of lamentations for Enrique de Villena. On the other hand, the general substance resembles that of Gómez Manrique's verses on the death of Garcilaso de la Vega ; but, whereas these relate nothing that is not historically possible, the *Visión* of Diego del Castillo is more fanciful because it reproduces the Fortune of the *Comedieta* in Atropos as arbitrator of the issues of life and death.

Like Gómez Manrique, however, Diego del Castillo retains very little of the Marquis's machinery and nothing of his Dantesque pilferings. The introductory hocus-pocus he wellnigh abandons and proceeds directly to the substance of the vision. The decoration is almost wholly classical. The grief of the King's retinue is likened to that of Phaethon's sisters; the royal widow is compared to Hecuba; inexorable Atropos to the cruel Pyrrhus; and the Queen wishes to sacrifice her own life like Alcestis.

Juan del Encina harks back to the Middle Ages, not only in the Panegyric, but also in his velleity for amorous allegories. Of these the most extensive is the *Triumph of Love.* On a May evening the author is awakened from sleep by Cupid and started on the way to his palace. Passing the house of Liberty and avoiding the dwelling of Reason, they arrive at the foot of a walled mountain, and are admitted by the porter Sensuality. As they climb, they come to the habitation of Good Fortune, near which is a sinister forest, serving the purpose of an Erotic Hell. Aided by Good Fortune, he attains the castle at the summit, where are gathered the ordinary quota of famous ancient lovers, and where are celebrated festivities in honour of Venus and her son, ending in a pompous banquet, at which Fortitude, Liberality, Beauty, and Prudence dispute the seat of honour next to the god. Cupid intervenes, even in one of his dramatic compositions, to speak the prologue, vaunting his powers and virtues, and to wound one of the shepherds; * a Testament, Confession, and Joust of Love may be read in his *Cancionero.*

DON ENRIQUE DE VILLENA

If anyone in the fifteenth century might be expected to prove a thorough *Dantista,* that man should be Don Enrique de Villena, the translator, at Santillana's solicitation, of the *Divine Comedy.* It is, then, most significant of Dante's really slight influence upon Castilian literature that, though Villena several times employs the allegorical form, he never reproduces Dantesque details.

Two of his works are cast in already existing moulds. If he really composed the verses for the morality play at the coronation of Ferdinand of Aragon,† he showed himself in his early period an exponent of the widespread custom of personifying the Virtues. The *Tratado de la Lepra* is preceded by a letter from his friend Alfonso de Cuenca, using the allegorical veil to ask him for an explanation of the Biblical phenomenon of leprosy in garments and walls. Alfonso dreams that he attempts in an orchard to pluck a lovely fruit, bending the branch with one hand and reaching with the other. He is interrupted by the entrance of an old woman coughing, who bids him write to Don Enrique for an explanation of the troublesome texts in *Leviticus*. Villena answers, elucidating the sleep as of the intellect and the orchard as wisdom; the fruit is the knowledge of truth and good manners, the part of the branch that he holds down is his sensual appetite, the other part still in the air is careful study, and the old woman typifies the Mosaic law. After this involved introduction, Villena finally proceeds to the real question at hand. From the days of Gonzalo de Berceo the Spaniard had sought to relieve the dullness of his didactic matter with exactly such fantasies.

Villena's chief allegorical work, the *Doce Trabajos de Hércules* belongs to the type of mythological exegesis, discussed by Santillana and Juan Rodríguez de la Cámara. The twelve labours represent the respective duties of certain classes of mortals: the Centaurs are the wicked whom princes should punish; the Nemean lion symbolizes the proud whom prelates should seek to crush; the Caledonian boar the body which the hermit should strive to overcome by humility, figured in Atalanta; the apple of the Hesperides betokens knowledge, the acquisition of which is the duty of monks. In the glosses to his translation of the *Æneid* he betrays himself again the victim of the mytho-allegorical school, discerning in the epic such hidden meanings as the ages of man, the Virtues and Vices, or the brevity of human life. The sentence about the sixth book, presents his whole attitude in a nutshell: "Virgil disseminated such secrets under the poetic integument that only the loftiest spirits, who attain to angelic thoughts, can comprehend it." The Florentine academician, Landini, is not more ingenious in discovering in the *Æneid* a Neo-Platonic allegory.

JUAN RODRÍGUEZ DE LA CÁMARA

The attempt at the Erotic Hell is not Cámara's only indulgence in allegory. He wrote two poems of the French type that depends for interest upon the adaptation of ecclesiastical forms to erotic conceptions, the *Siete Gozos de Amor* mimicking the seven joys of the Virgin, and the *Diez Mandamientos de Amor*, mimicking the Decalogue. The allegorical framework of the two compositions, *Triunfo de las Donas* and *Cadira del Honor*, formerly believed to be distinct works, but now convincingly demonstrated to be parts of one,* may be partly

suggested by Boccaccio's *Ameto*. At a loss whether
he should dedicate the latter, which is a treatise on
the vexed question of true nobility, to a man or a
woman, the author imagines that he is repeating
aloud in a retired spot Boccaccio's tirades against
the other sex, with the intent of afterward enumerating their virtues, when a nymph, who has been
transformed into a fountain of tears, interrupts him,
and declares fifty reasons for the preëminence of her
kind. The *Triunfo de las Donas* is thus a sort of
long digression woven into the main fabric of the
Cadira del Honor. Juan Rodríguez, who ranges himself on the more conservative and feudal side of
the dispute about aristocracy, alludes to Dante's
opinion three times, but only as he knows it in the
citations of Bartolo.*

He describes the throne of Honour with the
same unrealistic allegorical method as in the *Siervo
Libre de Amor*. "On the mountain of good desires
is the forest of effort, at the end of which is the
orchard of merit, whence spring those two fruitful
plants, virtue and nobility, different in name, similar in fruit; from which with perfect hand is wrought
the very high throne of Honour, which so few in
our age occupy that, rightly considered, they perhaps do not exceed the number of the Theban
gates; although under false pretences innumerable
persons are seen to sit upon it, who more truly

occupy the seat of False Honour, made of those two wild plants, fiction and fortune, which take root in the valley of vices and are their work."

In one passage of the *Cadira del Honor*, he alludes to an intended Panegyric, a *Coronación* of Macías, from the composition of which, however, he was deterred by the reflection that only kings may bestow the crown of laurel and by indignation at his contemporaries who arrogated to themselves, even though allegorically, the prerogative of judging and rewarding literary prowess. One would like to see what would have been the result of applying his mannerism of labeling to the *genre* of Coronations. The author would have wandered through the gloomy vale of literary Obscurity across the bridge of Ambition to the meadow of Reputation, in the midst of which he would have discerned the Temple of Fame. Thither he would have been conducted by the Muses, to behold the crowning of Macías by the four maidens, Prudence, Justice, Fortitude, and Temperance, and his enthronement in the Seat of Honour, built from the strong timbers of High Birth and Morality.

ALFONSO DE LA TORRE

The *Visión Delectable*,* an encyclopaedic work in prose upon philosophy, theology, and the seven

Liberal Arts, composed probably in the fourth de-
cade of the fifteenth century, is the most eminent
example in Spain of the old tradition of sugaring
didacticism with a liberal coating of allegory. Alfonso de la Torre first beholds in a vision and describes with ponderous mythological pedantry the
corruption and confusion of the world. He then
pictures the child, Understanding, accompanied
by Instinct, at the foot of a lofty mountain, in
quest of knowledge about the true end of man.
Understanding resorts on successive days to the
abodes of the sisters of the Trivium, Grammar,
Logic, and Rhetoric, and listens to lengthy expositions of their different branches. Abandoning the
first road and guided to a side path by Rhetoric,
he finally attains another marvellous road at the
top of the mountain, which on the fourth, fifth,
sixth, and seventh days brings him to the no less
instructive sisters of the Quadrivium, Arithmetic,
Geometry, Music, and Astrology. The appearance, attributes, and dwellings of the Arts are all
described with a meticulous regard for allegorical
detail, except in the case of Astrology, who reserves her information until he has entered within
the enclosure of Truth.

The account of Rhetoric is typical: "Going
now along this road with great joy, they arrived
at a town built with wondrous artifice, the houses

of which were more sumptuous in the accessory adornment of paintings than in the intrinsic principal foundations. When he had entered a great and very beautiful hall, Understanding saw a maiden, who, although she was not of such profundity or subtlety as the second (Logic), was at first glance infinitely more striking, as well in the expression of the face, features, and proportions of her person, as in the extent and price of her garments. Her hair appeared gold, divided and disposed in a most suitable arrangement. There was a colour in all her face, which one could not determine from afar to be pink or some exotic shade; but observed at close range, the greater part of the colour was fallacious and simulated. The words of this maiden were so sweet and so delightful that she surpassed the human manner of speech. At times she had a look of such exceeding merriment that the house seemed to laugh, and at other times she had so perturbed a look that all trembled before her. Now she would extol you to the skies, and again she would humble you to the abyss. Now she made you believe a thing and grant it to be good, and next she made you abhor it as evil. In her right hand she held a Moorish flute (*añafil*), in her left a closed book, and on the upper edge of her garments there were some Greek and Latin letters that read: *Ornatus persuasio.*"

Much of the apparatus is allegorical. Instinct starts enveloped in a cloud which the light has completely dispersed by the time that they have reached the dwelling of Arithmetic. Upon the walls of the several houses are depicted many subjects germane to each discussion, together with the famous exponents of each Liberal Art conceived as her progenitors or as the builders of the edifice. Exceptionally but properly, Understanding finds almost no painting in the habitation of Geometry, but is introduced into the closed chamber of her daughter Perspective, where he sees (how we are not told) the explanation of certain optical problems. Little or no space is allotted to the description of Astrology and her abode.

At the summit are the queen of the sacred mount, Truth, and her three sisters, Wisdom, Nature, and Reason, surrounded by the famous sages of antiquity. The constituents of the earthly paradise in which they live, such as the dazzling light, the heat, the rich fruits, and the tree of life, possess a patent significance. The first of the two gates is opened by Music; through the second Understanding is admitted only after some delay. As a result of the four ladies' deliberation in answer to his messenger, Astrology, he has first to be lectured by Reason, and then to despoil himself of his old and sordid vesture of vain opinions. He is now subjected to the even lengthier teaching of these four new personifications, whose aspects and habitations are described with the same scrupulous care. From time to time he is granted a glance at Truth's mirror, which, closely paralleling the frescoed walls of the Liberal Arts, reflects both the matters that have been explained and other new topics. At the beginning of the second book, which is devoted to ethics, Wisdom and Truth are enthroned in courtly fashion with the rest grouped round about. Soon the four cardinal Virtues at the four corners of Reason's mansion deliver their sermons, and eight other minor Virtues are explained, Magnanimity, Mildness, Magnificence, Liberality, Moderation, Friendship, Prudent Administration of Justice, and Heroism. Finally, the mirror becomes so refulgent with the exposition of the Trinity that Understanding and even Reason are blinded, and the end of man is proved to be the Beatific Vision.

The allegory of the *Visión Delectable* is a consequence of the mania for personification rife in the Middle Ages, here carried to the extreme. The standard for the seven Liberal Arts had been set as early as the fourth century by Martianus Capella in the *De Nuptiis Philologiae et Mercurii*. J. P. W. Crawford has shown in an excellent article that Alfonso de la Torre is partly indebted for his account of them to the *Anticlaudianus* of Alanus de Insulis.* The Virtues and other figures, the very idea of a journey through these fanciful realms, are mediaeval commonplaces. He is doubtless recalling also the preaching of Philosophy in the *De Consolatione*, for Reason, like the heroine of Boethius, sometimes appears to reach to heaven, sometimes shrinks to human compass. It was inevitable that the old school of critics, led by Amador de los Ríos, should suggest here an analogy to the *Divine Comedy*, and the analogy does in some instances become rather striking, as in the dazzling effect of a contemplation of the Trinity. But there is no trace of verbal imitation, and the similarities in idea are to be ascribed only to the fact that both are the products of the Middle Ages.

ALFONSO FERNÁNDEZ DE PALENCIA AND POLITICAL ALLEGORY

This chronicler of Henry IV's reign, in his *Tratado de la Perfección del Triunfo Militar* of 1459,† employs the allegorical form for rather original material, a study of Spanish military qualities and defects. Conscious of Spanish courage and therefore at a loss to explain Spanish failures in arms, Ejercicio (personified military drill) starts forth on a quest of Triunfo, who has so long abandoned the Iberian peninsula. Resorting first to the aged Experiencia, he is directed to seek out her daughter, Discreción, in Italy. On his journey he encounters several persons who suggest to him reasons for the martial imperfection of his native land, and he has some instructive adventures. When he has finally arrived at the house of Discreción in Tuscany, he is vouchsafed by her a long lecture, which resolves itself largely into an elucidation of ancient military successes. He proceeds to Rome with letters of introduction from his hostess, and profitably witnesses the ideal warfare waged by the captain Gloridoneo with the assistance of Orden, Obediencia, and the Italian Ejercicio. Triunfo, whom he has at last found, celebrates Gloridoneo's victory. An extended *débat* now ensues between Orden, Obediencia, and the Italian Ejercicio for the place of honour nearest to Triunfo, but the question is satisfactorily solved when, in the concluding Petrarchan Triumph of Triumph, Orden rides before the chariot, Ejercicio at the right, and Obediencia at the left. The implication of the whole involved work is that the Spaniards require other virtues besides courage to attain military perfection. The passion for allegory in the fifteenth century could not better be demonstrated than by its forced application to substance that befits rather the sober pen of Machiavelli.

Alfonso de Palencia's other long treatise, composed before 1455, the *Batalla Campal entre los Lobos y los Perros*,* describes in great detail a war between the wolves and dogs. It is impossible to determine how far it is an allegory of contemporary events, how far it is an allegory of the struggle of life in general, or how far it is merely a preliminary exercise in narrative, without a concealed meaning, in order to prove his ability for the coveted post of royal chronicler. Pedro de Escávias, in any case, does actually set forth in verse the civil strife under John II by the picture of a battle between many beasts and monsters. Through the agency of Fortune, he witnesses the combat at the foot of the usual mountain, and he concludes his vision with the appearance of the defunct worthies of Spain, led by Henry III, to bewail the unhappy confusion of the realm.† In a way somewhat similar to that of Alfonso de Palencia, Alonso Hernández of Seville in the *Historia Parthenopea* (1516) seeks to enliven historical material, a eulogistic account of the Great Captain, Gonzalo de Córdoba, by a liberal injection of such mythological sap as an appearance of Pallas Athene to Ferdinand and Isabella, the activity of Aeolus in raising a tempest, or a journey of Mercury through the kingdom of Naples.‡

The desperate condition of the kingdom under

Henry IV is again the topic for allegorical treatment in the satirical *Coplas de Mingo Revulgo*, ascribed variously to Juan de Mena, Rodrigo Cota, and Hernando del Pulgar.* The interest in the eclogue aroused by the Renaissance throws the work into the form of a dialogue between two rustics, the seer Gil Arribato, typifying the higher classes of society, and the herdsman Mingo Revulgo, typifying the lower. The latter, interrogated by the former as to the cause of his dishevelled appearance, bursts into an extended Phillipic against the indolent and vicious chief shepherd, i.e., Henry IV, but Gil Arribato retorts at no less length, casting the blame upon Mingo himself, i.e., the people. Much allegorical detail depends upon the fundamental idea of the sheepfold, — the four cardinal Virtues, for instance, becoming four dogs that have lost their pristine vigour, and the three scourges of Spain, famine, war, and pestilence becoming three ravenous wolves. The method of nomenclature is very precious and far-fetched, recalling such curious philology as Gloridoneo and other words in Alfonso de Palencia: characteristic are *Revulgo*, suggested by *vulgo*, the populace; *Azerilla* for Fortitude, a diminutive of *acero*, steel; *Esperilla* for Spain, a diminutive of *Hesperia*.

JUAN DE PADILLA

The only real attempt in Spain at an extended imitation of the *Divine Comedy* is made considerably later than our period in this Carthusian monk's *Twelve Triumphs of the Twelve Apostles* (1517) ; * but the very name at once indicates that even here the example of Petrarch is still a potent force. The supernatural peregrinations of Juan de Mena, who of the earlier poets was the most popular in the sixteenth century, also flitted before his imagination. The title of a lost work, the *Labyrinth of the Marquis of Cadiz,* doubtless another Panegyric, is likewise indicative of Padilla's admiration for his predecessor. The essential idea, the glorification of certain personages, is derived from the *Trionfi,* and with it is combined Dante's purpose of a journey to the threefold realm of the dead. Such a purpose, of course, as we have so often seen, is not necessarily Dantesque, but the many parallelisms reveal that the Spanish poet had the Italian constantly in mind.

Lost in the valley of sighs and hindered by the monster Idolatry from climbing Zion, the mount of salvation, the author is succoured by St. Paul and led forth on his journey. They visit in turn on one day of each month the signs of the zodiac, each of which is assigned to one of the twelve

Apostles according to the date upon which his feast falls; but since St. James the Less is commemorated by the church on the same day as St. Philip, and St. Jude on the same day as St. Simon, and since St. Thomas, like St. John, is honoured under Capricorn, these three have to be transferred to other constellations. He listens to the tale of each Apostle's pious achievements, and discusses also as separate stars in each constellation other saints whose feasts occur within the period. During the twelve nights they inspect purgatory and the twelve mouths of hell, in both of which places are punished the vices that are respectively the opposites of the several Apostles' virtues. Under the first ten signs the sins are violations of the Decalogue, under the eleventh it is the violation of Christ's injunction to love one's neighbour, and at the twelve mouth Padilla simply beholds Idolatry swallowed up together with the seven Vices. He encounters many ancients and contemporaries, and, like Dante, indulges in long historical digressions. For instance, in the sixth Triumph of St. James the Greater (Santiago), he causes Pelayo to recount the tale of Rodrigo, the last of the Goths, whom he here discovers undergoing the penalty for his crime. At sunset he is vouchsafed one of those geographical glimpses so dear to the mediaeval heart, in this case, of the different terrestrial regions where the Apostles have preached and wrought their works, and it is only in the last quarter of the night that he is permitted a brief respite of slumber.

The scheme may be illustrated by the typical example of St. Peter's Triumph in Cancer, where more subordinate incidents are introduced than anywhere else in the poem. Inasmuch as St. Paul is celebrated on June 29 together with St. Peter, he leaves the author for the nonce, unites himself to the beatitude of the Prince of the Apostles, and despatches as a guide in his stead his disciple Dionysius the Areopagite. After the celestial experience St. Paul returns, they both set forth in a ship, and are wrecked on the coasts of Italy, which, being the domain of St. Peter, are here properly described. St. Peter, curiously enough, has to be conceived as the exponent of obedience and humility for the sake of contrast with those transgressions of the fourth Commandment (according to the reckoning of the Roman Catholic Church) which they here find punished in purgatory and hell. In the former are those who failed to honour their parents; in the latter, in order to conform to the complicated system, the fourth Commandment has to be expanded to include traitors and rebels who have failed to honour God. This infernal mouth of Pride is, therefore, the deepest and contains

Lucifer himself. St. Paul engages in a battle with
the giants here confined and is victorious by means
of the cross on the hilt of the sword, his icono-
graphic attribute. On their return, at Padilla's request, his guide liberates a giant who had not joined
with his seditious brothers.

Finally, after witnessing the blessedness of St.
Matthias in Pisces and the death of the monster
Idolatry, Padilla mounts upon the chariot of the
Love of God. It is drawn by the three theological
Virtues, the four wheels are the cardinal Virtues,
and in it is seated Love upon a heart-shaped
throne. Thus he ascends into the heavens to con-
template supernal glory, but, as in the last canto
of the *Paradiso*, the wonder of the Beatific Vision
beggars his powers of memory and description, and
he brings the work to a conclusion.

The very summary of the poem reveals the
constant and rather close analogy to the *Divine
Comedy*, and additional similarities in such matters
as diction and patriotism have been so often indicated that I need not rehearse them.* Some of the
punishments are taken directly from the Italian
epic, although Juan de Padilla invents several
fantastic species of his own. As in earlier instances where even the general form remains unaffected, so here especially the figurative language
is largely modelled upon Dante's similes drawn

from atmospheric phenomena and from his own familiar experiences in every-day life. Padilla's artificially Latinized and Italianized style does not justify the title of the "Spanish Homer" that his editor of 1841, Miguel del Riego, applied to him, but, so far as anyone in the peninsula deserves the distinction, he may, in his small degree, be called by Riego's other epithet of the "Spanish Dante."

LATER ALLEGORY

The established forms still linger on through the waning Middle Ages and the dawning Renaissance. The nun, Doña Teresa de Cartagena, writing her *Grove of the Sick* at the end of the fifteenth century, almost reproduces the fiction of Berceo's *Milagros de Nuestra Señora*. Driven by the whirlwind of passion to a desert island, named the Opprobrium of Men and the Abjection of the People, she finds refreshment among the fruit trees, here symbolizing the pious books which afford relief to the spiritual invalids for whom the treatise is designed.* *The Dance of Death* appears in a new version published by Juan Valera de Salamanca at Seville in 1520, virtually identical with the older example for the first eighty-six stanzas and then adding a great number of new social classes to be visited by the gruesome personification. †

The overworked figures of the seven Vices are forced into service once more by Jerónimo de Artés in his *Gracia Dei*, with perhaps some dim recollection of the *Divine Comedy*.* Lost in a deep valley from which he can discover no issue, he is beset by the lion of Pride, the dog of Envy, the bear of Wrath, the ass of Sloth, the wolf of Avarice, the hog of Gluttony, and the parti-coloured lion (leopard?) of Lust, but he is succoured by an angel, led to a sage and absolved, and started upon the road of righteousness. The same moral content is endowed with a different allegorical dress, suggested perhaps by such compositions as Raoul de Houdan's *Voie d'Enfer et de Paradis* and Rutebeuf's *Voie de Paradis*, in some Castilian verses of the Portuguese Dom João Manoel.† Finding himself at the meeting of the two roads, the author chooses that which finally brings him to the mouth of hell, where converge also six other roads. Terror-stricken, he is consoled by the apparition of Divine Grace, who elucidates the roads as the seven Vices and names famous sinners who have travelled over each to their condemnation. She leads him back to an eminence, from which he views the pettiness of the world, and thence to the terrestrial paradise. In the midst stands the heavenly castle, upon the walls of which he beholds pictured the magnanimous deeds of the Portuguese

monarch John II, to whom the poem is dedicated.

In another allegorical sphere, Alfonso Álvarez
Guerrero, writing in 1520, imitates the *Laberinto*
of Juan de Mena with his two hundred, instead
of three hundred, stanzas on the *Castle of Fame*.*
Having climbed from the usual forest to the lofty
castle he meets the four cardinal Virtues, each
accompanied by her most renowned exemplars,
and he also beholds a kind of Hall of Fame with
the worthies of antiquity and his own time enthroned. The title of another work betrays the
sources of his inspiration, *Cincuenta del Laberinto
contra Fortuna*, which, as the numeral indicates,
depends for its quota of fifty stanzas upon Juan
de Mena's other production, the *Coronación*. The
substance is a tirade against the fickle goddess,
based upon Mena's idea that not she but Providence is the proper arbiter of the world, and the
scene is again laid in a wood, whither the author is
plunged by the revolutions of her wheel.

Political allegory still flourishes under Ferdinand and Isabella in the hands of the gallant monk,
Fray Iñigo de Mendoza. He reverts to Villasandino's figure of the ship of state † for a subject
that is often the burden of his verse, a petition to
the sovereigns to remedy the national ills. Justice,
holding Fortune captive, conducts the author to a

ruined vessel, the usurping commander of which is Avarice and the crew of which are pirates. When she has expelled these and herself taken possession, Mendoza concludes with a prayer to Ferdinand that the ship be repaired and that its sails be made of Faith and Prudence. In the better known *Pattern of the Rule of Princes,** addressed to Isabella, he imagines an ideal pattern or sampler (*dechado*) on which are to be embroidered in suitable materials and colours the symbols of good government, — the sword of Justice, the tower of Fortitude, with barricades against royal favourites and the lure of money, the bridle of Temperance, wrought by Timidity and Fear, and the harness of amorous restraint. Likewise addressed to the Queen, but without any specific political intent, a debate between Reason and Sensuality † is enshrined in the form of a tournament "in order that courtiers may read it more readily." The lady for whom they fight is the Will, Reason upon the steed of Understanding, with the Virtues as pages and God and the whole company of heaven as partisans, Sensuality upon the steed of the human body, with the Vices as pages and Lucifer and his host as partisans. Their arguments are the hard blows of the lances that they interchange, finally leaving Reason victorious despite infernal attempts to resuscitate Sensuality. Fray Iñigo meant to enliven his substance with flourishes of allegory, but the effect is exactly the reverse: the allegory seems perfunctory, and in its dullness may be endured only because of the real vigour and sincerity of the didactic and patriotic material that it accompanies.

The sixteenth century brings no relief from personifications and debates. The moral compositions of Juan de Narváez are typical examples.* The old forms, however, are likely to assume an amorous character. Thus Costana, prostrate upon a couch, the constituents of which are his woes, is visited by Affection, Desire, and Hope.† Rodrigo Cota imagines a dialogue in which an old man whose garden of pleasure has been laid waste by his mishaps in love is convinced by Cupid of the benefits that the god actually confers upon mankind and of the impropriety of passion at an advanced age.‡

All the erotic types of allegory, such as the ideal meeting embodied in the *pastourelle*, retain their popularity. The works of Jorge Manrique are especially rich in traditional and in fresh dressings of amorous motives. The idea of the Prison of Love bobs up everywhere in his poems and particularly in certain *coplas* to his lady.§ The combat with Love, at least as old in the peninsula as the Archpriest of Hita, appears in the *Escala de*

Amor,* which represents feminine charms as scaling the walls of his person and capturing his soul. Very similar are the verses of Juan de Tapia to Diego López de Ayala ;† and the *Guerra de Amor* of Luis de Vivero depicts Cupid as the same kind of besieger.‡ In the *Castillo de Amor*,§ which is more sincere and more chastely beautiful than the ordinary amorous fancies of the century, Jorge Manrique thinks of his loyalty as a fortress impregnable to other ladies but partly demolished by his mistress. In some *coplas* by a certain Barba,‖ the excellencies of the beloved become a castle that his own faculties unsuccessfully storm, leaving him severely wounded on the field. With a somewhat different turn, Juan de Tapia constructs a tower of his sorrows.¶ Juan Álvarez Gato, challenging his lady to a duel, adopts the idea of allegorical armour utilized by Imperial, endows himself with such weapons as the lance of constancy and the sword of faith in the scabbard of thought, and suggests for her such defence as the cuirass of modesty adorned with repose and such offence as disdain, anger, and haughty reply.**

The concept of an Order of Love, new in Spain, also finds expression in Jorge Manrique, when he makes his profession, vowing poverty of joy and pleasure, obedience to Cupid, and constancy instead of chastity.†† The Conde de Oliva combines this with the former fiction in imagining himself as counselled to build a metaphorical fortification against the lady by a hermit of the Order of Exile, founded by Brother Suspicion for the broken-hearted under the solitary vow of secrecy.* After a similar fashion, Francés Carroz y Pardo, in the *Consuelo d'Amor*, advises a company of elderly swains, whom, perhaps with the *Purgatorio* of Dante vaguely in mind, he encounters on a gruesome *sierra*, to abandon the thankless service of Love and to follow him in the pursuit of religion and virtue.†

The time-worn substance of amorous desperation is expressed in nautical terms by the Comendador Juan Escrivá, who constructs a Ship of Love out of his devotion and disappointment.‡ The fancy had already been treated more elaborately by Juan de Dueñas in the middle of the century. Putting out to sea with the vessel of his affection in the midst of fair weather, he meets with a storm and is wrecked by a ray of lightning (from his lady) upon a desert strand; with no opportunity for escape by land or sea, he ends the poem by supplicating Love to help him make another craft.§

Juan de Dueñas composed also an unpublished *Mass of Love.*‖ But an excellent example of these sacrilegious parodies of church services, with which Juan Rodríguez de la Cámara also demeaned him-

self, exists in the *Misa de Amor* by another rhyme-
ster at the Neapolitan court of Alfonso V, Suero
de Ribera.* The *Confession*, for instance, resolves
itself into a complaint against Love; the *Gloria in
Excelsis* is sung only by those who prosper in their
suit, and becomes in the latter part a supplication
for Cupid's mercy; the *Epistle* is inscribed *Lectio
libri sapientiae beati martyris amantis;* the *Gospel* is
an application to Love's subjects of Christ's pro-
phecies about the persecutions that would befall
His disciples, especially of the apposite passages
in the sermon on the mount; the *Creed* confesses
the deity's omnipotence; the *Sanctus* begins *Amores, amor, amores;* and the *Agnus* reaches the
height of blasphemy in *Lamb of God of Venus.*
Amador de los Ríos mentions a composition belonging to the same unsavoury type by the histo-
rian, Diego de Valera, the *Litany of Love,*† and
Juan del Encina's *Farsa de Plácida y Vitoriano* contains a requiem service for a dead sweetheart.‡

CHAPTER XVI

THE RELATION BETWEEN ALLEGORICAL ART
AND LITERATURE

A STUDY of Spanish art clarifies the evolution of Spanish allegory. History demonstrates that art and letters flow in a single course, and Spain of the Middle Ages and dawning Renaissance is no exception. Examples of this identity in the evolution of the world's culture stare one in the face. In Italy of the Quattrocento, classical ideals intrude themselves simultaneously into architecture, sculpture, painting, and literature. The Renaissance, transplanted to France in the sixteenth century, found expression, not only in the *Pléiade*, but also in the Louvre, the Tuileries and the carvings of Jean Goujon. Probability, therefore, would not admit disassociation of art and literature in Spain.

I have argued that the whole stream of Spanish letters, beginning with the twelfth century, feels strongly the vigourous impulse from the great flood of production across the Pyrenees. The arts afford one more channel for the communication of the current. Architecture and sculpture, the two most distinguished manifestations of art in mediaeval Spain, are even more Gallicized than literature. In the northeastern section of the peninsula, to be sure, a number of small churches, especially in the region of Oviedo and Leon, exhibit the embryonic stage of a peculiarly Spanish type of Romanesque architecture; but this indigenous outburst was stemmed and suppressed by the French influence, which, fostered by the powerful Order of Cluny, may be traced back as far as the eleventh century. If, according to the great Spanish architect, V. Lampérez y Romea, these churches could be accurately dated from the Visigothic period to the tenth century, the indigenous style would seem to have been superseded by the French.* If, on the other hand, with Enlart,† we assign their principal sections to a period not earlier than the twelfth century, we can only say that the more perfect type of Romanesque that had been evolved in France gradually acquired more popularity than the contemporaneous native manner and obtained the honour of employment for the most important ecclesiastical edifices of the country. In any case, the great Romanesque churches of Spain have a Gallic provenience, such as San Isidoro at Leon, San Vicente at Avila, and especially the cathedral of Santiago de Compostela, which is the twin-sister of St. Sernin at Toulouse. This indubitable relation is a cogent argument for believing that the Spanish epics of the period were deeply affected by the *chansons de geste*.

With the thirteenth century and with the introduction of the pointed style, the prevalence of French taste becomes even more marked. The transitional buildings, such as the old cathedral of Salamanca and the conventual church of Las Huelgas near Burgos, through the influence of the Cistercians, who now begin to supplant the Order of Cluny, reveal a close dependence upon the architecture of Burgundy and Aquitaine. Of the three great Spanish cathedrals in the fully developed pointed style, Burgos and Toledo imitate, and Leon reproduces, the Gothic of the Île de France.* In the fourteenth century the architectural centre is transferred to Catalonia, and the sources of inspiration are now the great aisleless churches of the *Midi*.

Sculpture naturally obeyed the same tradition as the ecclesiastical edifices that it was called into service to adorn. The lovely Romanesque carvings in the marvellous cloisters of Santo Domingo de Silos are even more French than the writings of the monastic poet who assumed the task of rhyming a biography of its patron saint. The generally Gallic character of sculpture in the twelfth century is best exemplified by the Pórtico de la Gloria at Santiago and the doors of San Vicente at Avila, in the thirteenth century by the portals of Burgos and Leon, and in the fourteenth by the portals of Pamplona, which seem to have been actually executed by French craftsmen.* What few tatters of frescoes from the twelfth and thirteenth centuries still hang upon the walls are likewise French or Franco-Byzantine.† As the allegorical loans from France receive an indigenous impress, so originality in the early history of the arts seems to have consisted, not in any innovation, but in the peculiarly national character imparted to borrowed elements, a certain heaviness and gloom to the ethereal lightness of French Gothic, a certain poignant realism to the sacred carvings.

If, then, unmistakable evidence of northern imitation did not exist in the literature itself, the strong current of influence in the arts would justify us in searching for it, or even, examples failing, in assuming that its traces were lost. The arts spring in their entirety from across the Pyrenees, and are a voucher for that French domination which we have already discovered in much of the epic, popular and cultured, in religious, lyric, and dramatic verse, in encyclopaedic, sententious, and narrative prose. Swept along thus in the midst of a great stream of art and literature arising in the north, the *genre* of allegory there finds one of its principal sources. On the grounds of antecedent probability, is it likely that the channel of French allegory will be suddenly obstructed and that the wells of Italy will wholly supply Spanish production?

During the fifteenth century, the attitude of art towards Italianism is the same as that of literature. In the previous century, the western peninsula had had little to do with the painting of Florence or Siena. Santillana mentions Giotto's name, but only in reminiscence of Dante's allusion in the *Paradiso* or Boccaccio's in the *Amorosa Visione.** Starnina and Dello Delli both laboured in Spain.† If from the scant knowledge that we have of the former, we may conjecture him to have been the master of Masolino and one of the transitional artists from the Giottesque or mediaeval to the new manner,‡ then he too would represent a cult in Spain rather for the precursors of the Renaissance than for the age of Dante. Dello Delli has now been proved to be identical with Master Nicholas the Florentine, who was responsible for the *retablo* of the old cathedral at Salamanca. As a follower or comrade of Gentile da Fabriano and Masolino, he imported in the fifteenth century a style that yet further inclined towards the emancipation of the Renaissance.§ In any case the remains of early Italian work in Castile are very slight, and it is Burgundian and Flemish pictures that exert the determinative influence. Like the literature, the painting of Italy does not become important for Spain until the days of Pedro Berruguete, Juan de Borgoña, and the fully evolved Renaissance; and it is then the matured *quattrocentisti* who obtain the vogue.

The currents of art and literature are now slightly disassociated. Although both are derived from northern prototypes, the former seeks inspiration chiefly in the Netherlands or Germany, the latter still in France. The description that I have given of fifteenth-century painting applies also to architecture and sculpture, the simpler styles of which now give way to the flamboyant. The artists who erect the towers, the *cimborio*, and the Chapel of the Constable at Burgos, who build the resplendent church of San Juan de los Reyes at Toledo, are Teutonic; the luxuriant façades of San Gregorio and San Pablo at Valladolid contain unmistakable Flemish elements. The extreme realism of Netherlandish sculpture is welcomed with open arms by the similarly inclined aesthetic temperament of Spain.* Despite the introduction of the Teutonic strain, however, no really significant alteration has been wrought in the artistic tradition of the peninsula, for flamboyant German and Flemish architecture and sculpture are only differentiated manifestations of that Gothic which in its French type has enjoyed so enthusiastic a

Spanish vogue during the earlier centuries, and which now assumes in France a florid form not essentially diverse from that of more northern countries. It is rather as if the continuous and single stream of Gothic artistic and literary tradition in the peninsula had broadened itself in one place to receive another rivulet, the Teutonic, derived from the same source. The predilection for Gothic is so firmly established in Spain that even in the sixteenth century, when the Renaissance is fast obliterating all vestiges of former movements, it yet is able to produce the new cathedrals of Salamanca and of Segovia.

Allegory remains Gothic throughout the fifteenth century, but fundamentally French, revealing little or no influence of Flemish and German literature. The comparative impotency of the Italian influences upon Spanish allegory of the time I have sought to demonstrate; and Italian models have no effect upon Castilian architecture and sculpture until they come as emissaries of the Renaissance, and, at that, later in the fifteenth century than is the case with literature. Italian mediaevalism in art as well as in letters leaves no appreciable impress upon the period under discussion. Even when Italian taste does make itself felt in the peninsula, it does not usurp the place of Gothic, but merely affects ornamentation, modifying the older manner to form that strange conglomeration known as the Plateresque style, the earliest example of which is found in the façade of San Pablo, Valladolid. Likewise in literature, Italianism is not yet organic but decorative.

The parallelism between art and literature extends beyond general tendencies to the subjects treated. The yearning towards the spiritual realms expressed itself not only in the literary visions but in the sculpture that almost overburdens the churches of Spain. The same temperament that told the tale of Oria's or Domingo's ecstasies, or encased the glories of the Apostles in a supernatural journey, fondly carved the scenes from the Apocalypse upon the choir stalls of the convent of Paular at Segovia, now in the Archaeological Museum at Madrid. The same hand that graphically described the infernal horrors in the *Alexandre* or in an Erotic Hell, if it had wielded a chisel instead of a pen, would have hewn with keen delight the punishments of the condemned in the Last Judgments upon the north portals of Avila and Burgos or upon the main portal of Leon. The coronations of the Virgin in the tympanums of arches combined with the written accounts to evolve the form of the Panegyric. The Virtues throng over the sepulchres as tediously as in the pages of mediaeval books. The struggle of Reason

with the Passions upon the façade of the great
church at Ripoll and the combat of Man with the
Beast of Sin upon a capital of San Pedro de la Rua
at Estella betoken the presence of the allegorical
battle and of the *débat* in the rich repertoire of
Romanesque sculpture. If the Gothic ivory of
French workmanship, mentioned by Koechlin as
existing in a private Spanish collection and representing an assault upon the Castle of Love,* was
imported into the peninsula at the time at which
it was made, it confirms what we should expect,
the entrance of the popular erotic allegory into
art, and it demonstrates strikingly the dependence
of the type upon France. Another startling analogue exists in the Capilla Dorada of the new
cathedral at Salamanca: into the midst of the
teeming splendour of its florid Gothic walls there
suddenly emerges from a high aperture the gaunt
figure of Death, hurling the same warning as she
has so often enunciated in the *danses macabres:*
" Memento mori."

It is the Gothic sarcophagi that furnish the most
interesting parallel. If their decoration consisted
of paintings instead of reliefs, they might serve as
illustrations to Panegyrics. A common sepulchral
motive, similar to that of Santillana's *Defunción* or
Gómez Manrique's lament for the Marquis, is the
representation of the deceased's burial in the midst

of mourners wailing and tearing their hair. Sometimes he is even translated to heaven, surrounded by groups of angels and saints. The fifteenth century treats sepulchral monuments in a fashion similar to the definite form that it now bestows upon the Panegyric. The figure of the deceased is accompanied, in order to set forth his glory, not only by grief-stricken mortals but also by the Virtues. The three theological and the four cardinal Virtues appear on the tomb of the bishop Alfonso Tostado de Madrigal in the ambulatory of the cathedral of Avila, and as a still further tribute to his achievements, at the sides of his chair are carved angels supporting books. A very common form for tombs is exemplified by the monument of Prince John, the only son of Ferdinand and Isabella, the white marble and noble lines of which are so impressive amidst the darkness of the monastic church of St. Thomas at Avila. The effigy of the young man lies upon an elevated base with the seven Virtues engraved at a lower level. The most pretentious sepulchre of this type, in the Cartuja of Miraflores, is that of the king, John II, who himself had played the patron to so many Eulogists of the age, — a sculptured apotheosis, with Virtues, old Testament worthies, prophets, apostles, and evangelists delighting to do him honour. It is hard to say whether such monuments suggested the written Panegyrics; probably the influence was mutual, both being products of the same mental attitude manifesting itself in art and in literature.

NOTES

NOTES

Page 4*. *Cancionero de Baena*, ed. P. J. Pidal, Madrid, 1851, no. 505.

Page 4†. *Baena*, no. 514.

Page 5. *Baena*, no. 248.

Page 6*. *Baena*, no. 234.

Page 6†. *Baena*, no. 238.

Page 6‡. *Baena*, no. 241.

Page 7. For the purposes of this discussion it is not necessary to distinguish between the ordinary dream and the vision vouchsafed by heaven. The events of the latter were doubtless conceived as existing on a plane of greater reality; but I use the terms as synonymous.

Page 13. *Historia crítica de la literatura española*, V, 190–219.

Page 14*. Théodore Joseph Boudet, Comte de Puymaigre, *La cour littéraire de Don Juan II*, I, 89–92.

Page 14†. G. Baist, *Geschichte der spanischen Litteratur*, in Gröber, *Grundriss der romanischen Philologie*, II, 2, 427–428.

Page 14‡. P. Savi-Lopez, *I precursori spagnuoli di Dante*, *Gior. dant.*, IV, 360–363, noticed in *Bull. della Soc. dant.*, n. s., IV, 25; *Un imitatore spagnuolo di Dante nel '400*, *Gior. dant.*, III, 465–469, noticed in *Bull. della Soc. dant.*, n. s., III, 61; *Dantes Einfluss auf span. Dichter des XV Jhs.*, Naples, 1901, noticed by Sanvisenti in *Gior. stor.*, XXXIX, 419.

Page 14§. B. Sanvisenti, *I primi influssi di Dante, del Petrarca, e del Boccaccio sulla letteratura spagnuola,* Milan, 1902.

Page 14‖. A. Farinelli, *Dante in Ispagna, Gior. stor.,* supplement, 1902–1905, no. 8.

Page 17. Cf. below, p. 112.

Page 20*. For a succinct and sensible discussion of early French influence, cf. J. Fitzmaurice-Kelly, *History of Spanish Literature,* 1908, pp. 34–42.

Page 20†. *Les vieux auteurs castillans,* Paris, 1888–1890.

Page 21*. *Antología de poetas líricos castellanos,* II, xviii–xx.

Page 21†. Baist, *op. cit.,* p. 392; for an account of the French original, cf. *Grundriss,* II, 1, 542–543.

Page 21‡. Baist, pp. 391–392.

Page 22*. Fitzmaurice-Kelly, p. 35.

Page 22†. J. Puyol y Alonso, *El arcipreste de Hita,* Madrid, 1906, pp. 21,191; for an account of the French poem, cf. *Grundriss,* II, 1, 571–572.

Page 22‡. P. 54.

Page 22§. For the sources of this poem we must consult the old but not antiquated article of Morel-Fatio, the wholly admirable *Recherches sur le texte et les sources du " Libro de Alexandre,"* *Rom.* IV, 7–90; cf. also Menéndez y Pelayo, *Ant.,* II, lxvii–lxviii.

Page 22‖. Baist, p. 404; Menéndez y Pelayo, *Ant.,* II, xxxiv.

Page 22¶. Puyol y Alonso, p. 191.

Page 23*. Fitzmaurice-Kelly, p. 54.

Page 23†. Fitzmaurice-Kelly, p. 65.

NOTES

aa

aaaaaaaaaaaaaaaaaaaaaaaaaaaaaaaaaaaaaaaaaaaaaaaaaaaaa

a

a

a

Page 23‡. E. Mérimée, *Précis d'histoire de la littérature espagnole*, Paris, 1908, p. 70.

Page 23§. Fitzmaurice-Kelly, p. 72; cf. also new French translation of this work, Paris, 1913, p. 45; Baist, p. 415; Puymaigre, *Les vieux auteurs castillans*, II, chap. vii; for the connection with the *Cansó d'Antiocha*, cf. G. Paris, *Rom.* XVII, 513; XIX, 562; XXII, 345; cf. also Menéndez y Pelayo, *Orígenes de la novela*, I, Madrid, 1905, cxxxv–cxxxvi and clv.

Page 24*. Menéndez y Pelayo, *Orígenes*, I, cxxxvi–vii and clviii–ix; Baist, p. 416; for a general discussion of the naturalization of the Carolingian and Breton matter in Spain, cf. Menéndez, I, pt. iv.

Page 24†. Baist, p. 416.

Page 24‡. Puymaigre, *Les vieux auteurs castillans*, II, 289. For the general French influence on Juan Ruiz, cf. pp. 261 and 277–278.

Page 24§. *Ant.*, III, xcvi.

Page 24‖. Menéndez y Pelayo, *Orígenes*, I, ci; *Ant.*, III, xcv; Puyol y Alonso, pp. 171, 180.

Page 24¶. *Nouveau recueil de fabliaux*, Méon, II, 173, 362.

Page 24**. Ed. Ducamin, *copla* 96.

Page 25*. Ticknor (*History of Spanish Literature*, Boston, 1863, I, 77) compares him to Chaucer in his borrowings from the French.

Page 25†. Fitzmaurice-Kelly, p. 103; Menéndez y Pelayo, *Orígenes*, I, clxxx.

Page 26. Menéndez y Pelayo, *Orígenes*, I, ccxxii.

Page 32. Outside the sphere of allegory, the sonnets were also popular, and were imitated, rather than

Dante's lyrics, by poets such as Juan de Mena, even before the full Renaissance of the sixteenth century; cf. C. R. Post, *The Sources of Juan de Mena, Romanic Review*, III, 273–277.

Page 34. For the Triumph form, which begins with the Roman military procession and is found in Ovid, cf. C. Ephrussi, *Étude sur le songe de Poliphile*, Paris, 1888, pp. 49 ff., and W. A. Neilson, *The Origin and Sources of the Court of Love*, Boston, 1899, pp. 11, 114.

Page 35. *Baena*, nos. 295 and 296, which, though separated in the *Cancionero*, are plainly parts of the same composition.

Page 36. Farinelli, *Dante in Ispagna*, p. 5; *Hist. litt. de la France*, XIX, 397 ff.

Page 37. W. A. Neilson, *op. cit.*

Page 38*. *Baena*, no. 239.

Page 38†. *Baena*, nos. 232–233.

Page 38‡. *Baena*, no. 234.

Page 38§. *Cancionero general de Hernando del Castillo*, Madrid, 1882, II, 429–442.

Page 39. Ed. A. M. Huntington, New York, 1902.

Page 40*. Pub. H. A. Rennert, *Der spanische Cancionero des Brit. Museums, Rom. Forsch.*, X, 1, no. 168; for the identity of Ludueña, cf. the introduction, p. 11.

Page 40†. *Canc. de D. Pedro Manuel de Urrea, Bibl. de escrit. arag.*, Saragossa, 1878, pp. 233–238.

Page 40‡. Farinelli (*Dante in Ispagna*, pp. 84–85) partially summarizes another unpublished treatment of the Court of Love, the *Decir sobre Amor* of Pedro Guillén de Segovia, who died about the time that Isabella began to reign. The author is conducted first by For-

tune through the usual forests and rocky wildernesses
into a smiling valley, and then by Solomon to the Cyp-
rian castle, which stands in the midst, ruled by Venus
and inhabited by such famous lovers as Leander, Per-
seus, Paris, Æneas, Jason, and Macías.

Page 41*. *Ephesians*, VI, 13–17.

Page 41†. *Baena*, no. 170.

Page 42. *Baena*, no. 34.

Page 45. *Baena*, no. 290.

Page 46*. *Baena*, no. 288.

Page 46†. *Baena*, the first composition numbered 289.

Page 48. *Obras de Don Íñigo López de Mendoza*, ed.
Amador de los Ríos, Madrid, 1852, pp. 343 ff.

Page 49. *Obras*, pp. 240 ff.

Page 50. *Obras de Juan Rodríguez de la Cámara*, Madrid,
1884, p. 48.

Page 51. The poem is quoted by Pidal, the editor of the
Cancionero de Baena, in his commentary upon Imperial
(p. 666), as drawn from the *Cancionero manuscrito de
S. M.*

Page 53*. Ed. J. D. Fitzgerald, Paris, 1904, stanzas
226–244.

Page 53†. *Cancionero de Ramon de Llabia*. This unpublished *Cancionero* at Vienna I was permitted to use
through the kindness of Dr. Rudolf Beer.

Page 54. *Baena*, no. 226.

Page 55. Ed. T. Wright, *Anglo-Latin Satirical Poets*, II,
268 ff.

Page 56. The great lady, who is unnamed, may, however, be a personification of Spain.

Page 58*. Cf. Suchier and Birch-Hirschfeld, *Gesch. der franz. Lit.*, pp. 74, 188, 234; on p. 235 is a reproduction of a miniature from a manuscript of the fifteenth century, representing one of these coronations.

Page 58†. *Obras*, pp. 332 ff.

Page 59*. Ed. Saint-Hilaire, II, 202, vv. 294 ff.

Page 59†. Ed. Scheler, I, 50, vv. 1654 ff.

Page 59‡. Ed. Scheler, II, 136, vv. 4602 ff.

Page 59§. Cf. the rubrics of the poem, published by G. Körting, *Altfranzösische Uebersetzung der Remedia Amoris des Ovid*, Leipzig, 1871, p. 78; Neilson (pp. 82–83) gives an analysis based upon these rubrics.

Page 59‖. Ed. Scheler, *op. cit.*, III, 3, vv. 64–112.

Page 60. Cf. above, p. 50.

Page 61*. Ed. Scheler, p. 43.

Page 61†. *Obras*, p. 258.

Page 61‡. *Obras*, p. 289.

Page 62*. No. XLI. Calixtus III, the Spanish pope whom he solicits. in this sonnet, actually canonized the Dominican friar in 1455.

Page 62†. *Canc. castellano del siglo XV, Nueva bibl. de aut. esp.*, 19, I, 208–214.

Page 64*. *Benvenuti de Rambaldis de Imola, Comentum super Dantis Aldigherij comoediam, Sumptibus Guilielmi Warren Vernon*, Florentiae, 1887, I, 13–14.

Page 64†. *Scelta di curiosità letterarie*, Bologna, 1874, CXXXVII.

Page 65. These may be read in the Seville edition of 1534.

Page 67*. For editions and discussions, cf. *Grundriss*, II, 1, 694.

Page 67†. *Grundriss*, II, 1, 749.

Page 67‡. Ed. Jubinal, II, 169 ff.

Page 67§. For a good summary of this poem, cf. the Abbé Claude Pierre Goujet, *Bibliothèque Françoise*, IX, 189 ff.; also *Grundriss*, II, 1, 1128. Farinelli (*Dante e la Francia*, Milan, 1908, I, 204–206) discerns Dantesque elements; but if they exist, they only show that Juan de Mena's conceptions are parallel rather to French adaptations of Dante than to the *Divine Comedy* itself.

Page 68. Published, with a prose preface to Pero González de Mendoza, Bishop of Calahorra, in the *Canc. de Gómez Manrique, Col. de escrit. cast.*, Madrid, 1885, II, 7–64.

Page 69. *Canc. gen.*, no. 91.

Page 71. Farinelli (*Dante in Ispagna*, p. 80) would find a reflection of the *Trionfi* in the general coronation form, but if it exists, it is very vague and merely coincides with the stronger influences that I have already mentioned. There is no definite imitation of Petrarch in this form until the *Triunfo del Marqués*.

Page 72. C. del Balzo, *Poesie di mille autori intorno a Dante Alighieri*, Rome, 1893, IV, 176 ff.

Page 73. The text as given by del Balzo is evidently not properly arranged. The passage about the celestial mansion of the Empyrean is suddenly interrupted by a continuation of the description of the embroidery upon Carrillo's garments and his enthronement (p. 211) and by a catalogue of the famous men around the goddess's throne. A second difficulty consists in the reference in this interpolated passage to the wood, which could not be supposed to exist in the Empyrean, and, as the place of Carrillo's throne, is plainly identical with that described as a part of the Elysian fields (p. 199). Another crux is offered by the reference in this same passage to the queen, Fame, who has no place in heaven. A final difficulty is, that in the prose argument which Diego Guillén prefixes to the poem he clearly states that the disappearance of Dante is preceded by the stories of the Romans and other famous persons, not, as in the text, succeeded by them. The necessary change is clear. The passage beginning with the continuation of the description of Carrillo's border and extending through the catalogue of famous Trojans (pp. 211–216) should be replaced in its proper order after the first description of the embroidery (p. 204). The structure of the poem thus assumes a harmonious aspect. The end of the first passage about the embroidery, dealing with the Bishop's religious activity in the construction of ecclesiastical edifices, is fittingly succeeded by the beginning of the interpolated passage, dealing with the religious activity as primate; his enthronement follows; next comes the catalogue of famous persons, beginning, as the argument states, with the Romans, and continuing in the interpolated passage with the Greeks and Trojans as of first import after the Romans, and after this passage, naturally as of less import, with the Asiatics, Africans, and Sicilians; as foretold in the Prologue, there ensues the excuse for not mentioning any more persons, and then the disappearance of his guide; and in heaven, the author's dazzled dismay at the sight of the Virtues' palace and his comfort by Divine Grace are brought into juxtaposition. Without the restoration of the proper order, the whole central division of the poem is unintelligible.

Page 74. Summary in Amador, *Hist.*, VII, 250–252; cf. also Menéndez y Pelayo, *Ant.*, VII, xliii–xlvi.

Page 76. Obras, pp. 373 ff.

Page 77. Ed. Saint-Hilaire, II, 182.

Page 78*. III, 373.

Page 78†. Cf. W. A. Neilson, *The Purgatory of Cruel Beauties, Rom.*, XXIX, 85 ff.

Page 79*. Ed. Trojel, p. 104.

Page 79†. Paul Heyse, *Romanische inedita*, Berlin, 1856, pp. 79 ff.; noticed by A. Piaget, *Martin le Franc*, Lausanne, 1888, p. 142.

Page 79‡. Ed. Scheler, I, 267 ff.

Page 79§. Les Oeuvres de Maistre Alain Chartier, André Du Chesne, Paris, 1617, p. 722.

This, one of the most original of French allegorical compositions, is probably not by Chartier, and may be due to a clerk, Achille Caulier (*Grundriss*, II, 1, 1105; A. Piaget, *Rom.* XIX, 403–404; Neilson, *Court of Love*, p. 88, n. 1). For our purpose the authorship is of no consequence; the Marquis ascribes it to Chartier, and at any rate the analogy to the *Inferno* would be as great, no matter who was its composer. M. Schiff (*La Bibliothèque du Marquis de Santillane*, Paris, 1905, p. 371) mentions certain other works of Chartier in Santillana's library, and he must also have possessed the *Hospital* and the *Débat des quatre dames*, which he mentions in the *Proemio* and which were probably lost in the fire of 1702 (Schiff, p. xc). An excellent and detailed summary of the *Hospital* is given by Neilson, pp. 87–89.

Page 79‖. Obras, p. 9.

Page 81*. Oeuvres complètes du roi René, M. le Comte de Quatrebarbes, Angers, 1846, vol. III. An elaborate summary is given in the introduction to this volume and a briefer one by Neilson, p. 90; cf. also *Grundriss*, II, 1, 1121.

Page 81†. Somewhat analogous conceptions under a more original form appear in the German *Das Kloster der Minne*, in which not unfortunate but offending lovers appear as penitents, with two of whom the author converses (Lassberg, *Lieder Saal*, no. 124, II, 205–264; for a good summary, cf. Neilson, pp. 126–127).

Page 84*. M. Schiff (*op. cit.*, p. 271) mentions this miniature.

Page 84†. *Cancionero de Lope de Stúñiga, Col. de lib. esp. raros ó cur.*, Madrid, 1872, pp. 71–79; there is a good biographical and literary notice of the poet in note xiv, p. 414.

Page 85*. The editors (p. 415) guess at Juan de Bardaxi, Chamberlain of Alfonso V of Aragon.

Page 85†. *Canc. gen.*, no. 964.

Page 88*. No. 963.

Page 88†. *Diego de San Pedro, Cárcel de amor, Bibl. hisp.*, 1904; ed. also by Menéndez y Pelayo, *Orígenes*, II, p. 1 ff.

Page 90. Ed. Scheler, vv. 321 ff.

Page 91. *Canc. gen.*, no. 223; for the identity of this poet, cf. H. C. Rennert, *Der spanische Cancionero des Brit. Museums, Rom. Forsch.*, X, 1, 8–11, and Amador de los Ríos, notes to edition of Santillana, p. 641.

Page 92*. *Canc. gen.*, no. 227.

Page 92†. *Canc. gen.*, nos. 219, 230.

Page 92‡. Nos. 150 and 151 of the Spanish *Cancionero* in the British Museum, published by Rennert, seem to me parts of the same composition.

Page 92§. *Canc. gen.*, no. 274; cf. also, E. Cotarelo y Mori, *Estudios de historia literaria de España*, Madrid, 1901, pp. 33–52.

Page 93*. Badajoz, when once embarked on the sea of allegorical unrealities, cares little for consistency of details: in another composition he listens to a nightingale recounting his own death and burial from love. (*Canc. gen.*, no. 273.)

Page 93†. *Canc. gen.*, no. 271.

Page 93‡. *Canc. gen.*, Appendix, no. 174.

Page 94. *Obras*, pp. 37 ff.

Page 96. P. xxi.

Page 97*. A. Paz y Mélia, *Opúsculos literarios*, Madrid, 1892, pp. 47–101.

Page 97†. Menéndez y Pelayo, *Orígenes*, I, cccxii–cccxv.

Page 99. *Canc. de D. Pedro Manuel de Urrea*, pp. 141–161.

Page 100. Pp. 196–212.

Page 101*. No. 950.

Page 101†. A convenient edition is found in the appendix to the second volume of the *Canc. gen.*, pp. 562–570.

Page 102. Cf. R. Schevill, *Ovid and the Renascence in Spain*, University of California, 1913, pp. 59–60.

Page 106*. Aimé Puech, *Prudence, Étude sur la poésie latine chrétienne au IVe siecle*, Paris, 1888, p. 246.

Page 106†. For the relation to Virgil, cf. Puech, pp. 251–252, and Franz Dexel, *Des Prudentius Verhältnis zu Vergil*, Landshut, 1907; for the relation to Claudian, Puech, pp. 240–242, and Otto Hoefer, *De Prudentii poetae Psychomachia*, 1895, pp. 7–45.

Page 107*. *Prudentius carmina*, ed. A. Dressel, Leipzig, 1860, *Psychomachia*, vv. 212 ff; and *Æneid*, ix, vv. 600 ff.

Page 107†. Ed. Dressel, vv. 393 ff.

Page 107‡. Puech, pp. 255–256.

Page 108. Ed. Migne, *Patrologiae cursus completus*, Second Series, LXXX, 118–122; also printed by Henrique Flórez, *España Sagrada*, XIII, 336–339.

Page 109. *Patrologia*, LXXXVII: life of St. Valerius, pp. 417–422; vision of Maximus, pp. 431–433. Cf. also *España Sagrada*, XVI: life of St. Valerius, pp. 324–349; works, pp. 366–416.

Page 110*. *Patrologia*, LXXXVII, 433–435.

Page 110†. *Patrologia*, LXXXVII, 435–436.

Page 111. B. Hauréau, *Singularités historiques et littéraires*, Paris, 1861, pp. 37 ff; B. von Simson, *Jahrb. des Fraenk. Reichs unter Ludwig dem Fr.*, I, 114; A. Ebert, *Theodulfs Geburtsland, Ber. über den Verhand. der könig. sächsichen Gesell.*, 1878, pt. II, pp. 95–97. This last article seems to me conclusive. Menéndez y Pelayo (*Ant.*, I, liii) appears to accept him as a compatriot without a question.

Page 112*. Cf. A. Ebert, *Hist. gén. de la litt. du moyen age en Oc.*, translation of Aymeric and Condamin, Paris, 1884, II, 85.

Page 112†. *Patrologia*, CV, 331; *Monumenta Germaniae historica, Poetae latini*, I, 543.

Page 115*. *Patrologia*, CV, 347; *Monu. Germ. hist., Poet. lat.*, I, 445.

Page 115†. For an analysis and discussion of the work, cf. Amador de los Ríos, *Hist.*, II, 244–249; cf. Menéndez y Pelayo, *Ant.*, I, lvi.

Page 116. Cf. C. Cañal, *San Isidoro*, Madrid, 1897, pp. 52–53.

Page 118*. *Hist.* III, 257.

Page 118†. T. A. Sánchez, *Col. de poes. cast. ant. al siglo XV.*, Madrid, 1780, Prologue to II, xx.

Page 118‡. Cf. ed. J. D. Fitzgerald, pp. xl–lx, and specifically for this extract, p. xlvi.

Page 119*. *Copla* 2.

Page 119†. Baist, *Grundriss*, II, 2, 402.

Page 120*. *Bibl. de aut. esp.*, Madrid, LVII (1898), 103 ff.

Page 120†. *Ibid.*, 137 ff.

Page 121. The actual figures are: total number of stanzas, 205; vision of the throne, 75; vision of the Virgin, 22; vision of the mountain, 12; vision of Don García, 5; vision of Oria, 14; total number of visionary stanzas, 128.

Page 122. An elaborate list of examples from French, Provençal, and English is given by C. G. Osgood in his edition of the Middle English poem, *The Pearl*, Boston, 1906, p. xvi, note 5; cf. also W. O. Sypherd, *Studies in Chaucer's Hous of Fame, Publications of the Chaucer Society*, 1907, for the issue of 1904, p. 51.

Page 123*. Cf. Beatrice's encouragement of Dante, *Purg.* XXXIII, 31–33.

Page 123†. *Par.* II, 22, etc.

Page 123‡. Cf. opening of the *Paradiso*; the preterition about the smile of Beatrice, *Par.* XXIII, 61–69; also *Par.* XXXIII, 106, *et passim*.

Page 124*. *Par.* XXVI, 67–69.

Page 124†. XXX, 124–148. This vacant throne and the tree, which he takes to symbolize faith, P. Savi-Lopez (*Gior. Dant.*, IV, 361) indicates as two analogies both to the *Vision of Tundale* and to the *Divine Comedy*.

Page 125*. A. Morel-Fatio, *El Libro de Alixandre*, Dresden, 1906, *coplas* 2302–2435 ; Baist, *Eine neue Handschrift des spanischen Alexandre*, *Rom. Forsch.*, VI, 292. Cf. for the whole discussion and bibliography of the question of authenticity, Morel-Fatio, *op. cit.*, pp. xx–xxii, and J. D. M. Ford, *Old Spanish Readings*, pp. 137–139.

Page 125†. *Æneid*, VI, 273–281.

Page 125‡. *Æn.*, VI, 282–289.

Page 126*. *Æn.*, VI, 426 ff.

Page 126†. *Æn.*, VI, 548 ff.

Page 126‡. *Æn.*, VII, 332 ff.

Page 126§. *Op. cit.*, p. 362.

Page 127*. *Inf.*, III, 9.

Page 127†. *Inf.*, III, 103–105.

Page 127‡. *Inf.*, IV, 10–12 and 34–36.

Page 127§. *Bibl. de aut. esp.*, LVII, 166, *coplas*, 612–613. Morel-Fatio (p. 81) omits the second *copla* from his edition, based upon the Paris manuscript.

Page 129. Published for the first time by P. J. Pidal, in the *Diario español*, 1856, no. 1239; for subsequent publications and a general discussion of later Spanish versions, cf. José M. Octavio de Toledo, *Visión de Filiberto*, *Zeit. für rom. Phil.*, II, 40 ff.; also C. M. de Vasconcellos, *Observações sobre alguns textos lyricos da antiga poesia peninsular*, *Rev. lusit.*, VII, 10; for a critical edition, see that of Menéndez Pidal, *Rev. de archivos*, 1900, pp. 450 ff.; for the Latin vision and German version, see K. Raab, *Ueber vier allegorische Motive in der lat. u. deut. Lit. des MA*, 1885, p. 22. An old French version, *De cors et d'ame*, is noted in the *Grundriss*, II, 1, 871; for a Middle English version, cf. E. Mätzner, *Altenglische Sprachproben*, I, 90. For a general study of the whole type, cf. G. Kleinert, *Ueber den Streit zwischen Leib und Seele*, Halle, 1880, and for the Anglo-Norman provenience of this fragment, pp. 58 ff. and J. D. M. Ford, *op. cit.*, pp. 130–131.

Page 130*. *Rom.*, XVI, 365 ff. The quotations are from this edition.

Page 130†. The participants in this controversy are: E. Monaci, *Testi basso-latini e volgari della Spagna*, Rome, 1891, col. 39–43; E. Gorra, *Lingua e letteratura spagnuola delle origini*, Milan, 1898, p. 217; G. Petraglione, *Il Romance de Lope de Moros*, *Stud. di fil. rom.*, VIII, 485–502, the first article to distinguish between the *Razón de amor* and the setting to the Debate; C. Michaëlis de Vasconcellos, *op. cit.*, pp. 1–32, the most comprehensive article; and Menéndez Pidal in his critical edition with introduction, *Rev. hisp.*, XIII, 602–618.

Page 131. *Ant.*, I, 1.

Page 132. This seems to be the general sense of a much corrupted passage:

> Mas una palomila ví,
> Tan blanca era como la nieve del puerto,
> Volando viene por medio del uerto.
> En la fuente quiso entrar
> Mas quando á mí vido estar,
> Entros en la del malgranar.

Un vaso avi' alí dorado
Tray al pie atado.
En la fuent quiso entrar
Quando á mí vido estar en el malgranar.
Quando en el vaso fué entrada,
E fué toda bien esfryada,
Ela que quiso exir festino,
Vertiós el agua sobrel vino.

The fact that I arrived at this conclusion before I had seen the editions of Mme. de Vasconcellos or Menéndez Pidal, which bear out my own reconstruction, has the force of concurrent testimony. The *mançanar* has become a *malgranar*, which would mean literally a pomegranate orchard or tree, but the change is probably due to a scribal error (cf. Pidal, p. 604). Morel-Fatio gives up, *Un vaso avi' alí dorado*; Mme. de Vasconcellos changes *vaso* to *lazo*; Menéndez Pidal prints *un cascauielo dorado*. Both Mme. de Vasconcellos and Menéndez Pidal rightly omit as a gloss one of the two almost identical sets of lines alluding to the dove's bath. In the second set, *en el malgranar* clearly should not follow *estar*, for the writer was not in the *malgranar* and the dove had sought a bathing place there just for that reason (cf. Vasconcellos, p. 16). Menéndez Pidal is thus right in correcting:

En la fuent quiso entra,
Mas quando a mi vido estar,
Entros en el vaso del malgranar.

The lines, important to our purpose, however, are perfectly plain: the dove overturns the water into the wine.

Page 133*. A. de Montaiglon, *Recueil des poésies françoises des XVe et XVIe siècles*, IV, 103.

Page 133†. It concludes with *Lupus me feçit de Moros*, but this is very likely only the name of a scribe.

Page 136. These collections are discussed by A. Mussa-fia in the *Sitzungsberichte der Wiener Akademie*, CXIII, the former on pp. 936 ff., the latter, which he abbre-viates as SG, on pp. 962 ff. Cf. also R. Becker, *Gonzalo de Berceos Milagros und ihre Grundlagen*, Strassburg, 1910.

Page 137*. *Coplas* 1929–1933.

Page 137†. *Op. cit.*, p. 366.

Page 137‡. A. Jubinal, *Nouveau recueil de contes, dits, fabliaux*, etc., Paris, 1839, I, 293–311.

Page 137§. J. D. M. Ford, *A Spanish Anthology*, 1901, p. 343; Menéndez y Pelayo, *Ant.*, II, xxviii; Vascon-cellos, *op. cit.*, p. 5, where the assertion of French in-fluence is very emphatic.

Page 138*. *Zeit. für rom. Phil.*, II, 42, 50–60.

Page 138†. Ed. M. E. du Méril, *Poésies populaires la-tines*, Paris, 1843, pp. 217–230; and T. Wright, *The Latin Poems Commonly Attributed to Walter Mapes*, London, 1841, p. 95.

Page 139. The references are to the edition of Jean Duc-amin, *Bibliothèque Méridionale*, I *Série, tome* VI, Tou-louse, 1901.

Page 140*. Venus is possibly derived from the *Pamphi-lus de amore*, which is closely imitated by Juan Ruiz in stanzas 580–891. The goddess plays a similar rôle in both works; cf. J. Puyol y Alonso, *op. cit.*, chap. xiii and R. Schevill, *Ovid and the Renascence in Spain*, pp. 30–31.

Page 140†. I translate *Carnal* as Flesh for want of a better term; the Spanish word really means the time of the year in which meat may be eaten as opposed to periods of abstinence.

Page 141*. In round numbers there are 750 stanzas with an allegorical basis out of the 1700 of the whole composition. These allegorical passages, of course, are often interspersed with illustrative fables, which are included in this estimate because they are either spoken by allegorical figures or connected with allegorical descriptions.

Page 141†. Puyol y Alonso, pp. 198–200; Puymaigre, *Les vieux auteurs castillans*, II, 297.

Page 141‡. Puyol y Alonso, p. 200.

Page 142. Cf. also the Biblical examples under the catalogues of the seven mortal sins, the seven works of mercy, and the five senses in López de Ayala's *Rimado de palacio*. Such lists, indeed, are broadly characteristic of mediaeval poetry, and in Petrarch and Boccaccio are typical rather of mediaeval than Renaissance tendencies.

Page 143. *Bibl. de aut. esp.*, LI, 89, cap. I: cf. Puyol y Alonso, pp. 164–165.

Page 144. A good instance is the bickering, allegorically unnecessary, over the question of a confession upon paper or by word of mouth.

Page 145. Puyol y Alonso, p. 197; the French poem may be found in *Barbazan et Méon, Fabliaux*, IV, 80. Personifications of Shrove Tuesday and Lent are very frequent.

Page 146*. Puymaigre, *Les vieux auteurs castillans*, II, 295. The *fabliau* is to be found in P. J. B. Legrand d'Aussy, I, 279–326.

Page 146†. Puyol y Alonso, pp. 165–166; *Roman de la Rose*, vv. 22009–22040. (The references to the *Ro-*

man are from the edition of Francisque-Michel, Paris, 1864.)

Page 146‡. F. B. Luquiens, in *The Roman de la Rose and Mediaeval Castilian Literature* (*Rom. Forsch.*, XX, 290–296), concludes that although the passage in Juan Ruiz presents some striking similarities to the *Roman*, yet because of the comprehensiveness of the *Roman*'s list and the dissimilarity of contexts, no relation can be assumed, especially since general considerations deny the possibility of the influence of the *Roman de la Rose* upon the *Libro de Buen Amor*. His reasons and his general considerations do not seem to me of sufficient weight. The wonderful popularity of the *Roman* in the Middle Ages throughout Europe is an argument for its influence in Spain, where the imitation of French letters was very general, and Luquiens himself (p. 315) admits a certain degree of influence in the fifteenth century. In any case, that this musical passage was suggested by French prototypes cannot be doubted, for in the elaborate form in which it occurs it is not a thing that develops of itself, and just such elaborate lists are commonplaces of French literature. Another occurs in the *Panthère d'Amours* of Nicole de Margival, ed. H. A. Todd, Paris, 1883, vv. 155–175; cf. B. de Roquefort, *De l'état de la poésie françoise dans les douzième et treizième siècles*, Paris, 1815, pp. 104–131.

Page 148*. *Hist.*, V, 194.

Page 148†. Quoted by the editor of the *Cancionero de Baena* in his commentary upon Imperial (p. 666) as drawn from the *Cancionero manuscrito de S. M.*

Page 150*. Vv. 1689 ff.

Page 150†. R. Schevill, *Ovid and the Renascence in Spain*, p. 58.

Page 151*. *Baena,* no. 239.

Page 151†. *Baena,* nos. 241–242.

Page 152. P. 665, n. cxxxi; p. 669, n. cxlii.

Page 153*. The end of the poem is ambiguous, and possibly the judgment is to be ascribed rather to Philosophy than to Imperial himself.

Page 153†. *Baena,* no. 231.

Page 153‡. For a detailed examination of these reminiscences, cf. C. R. Post, *Beginnings of the Influence of Dante,* etc., *Report of the Dante Society,* Cambridge, Mass., 1907, pp. 21–22.

Page 154*. Ed. Kaltenbacher, *Der altfranzösiche Roman Paris et Vienne, Rom. Forsch.,* XV, 393.

Page 154†. Kaltenbacher (pp. 362–363) and Luquiens (p. 298, n. 4) comment upon this borrowing.

Page 155*. The editor of the *Cancionero de Baena* for chronological reasons doubts this attribution, on insufficient grounds, it seems to me, since so little is accurately known of the dates of the versifiers in the first part of this century; cf. *Cancionero,* p. 658, n. lxxxi, and p. 668, n. cxxxvi.

Page 155†. *Baena,* no. 234.

Page 156. *Baena,* no. 248.

Page 157. *Baena,* nos. 235, 236, and 237.

Page 158. *Baena,* no. 238.

Page 159. *Baena,* no. 226.

Page 162*. *Hist. litt. de la France,* XXIII, 257; *Grundriss,* II, 1, 862.

Page 162†. Ed. Scheler, p. 246, vv. 1554–1707.

Page 163*. *Inf.,* VII, 67–96.

Page 163†. *Liber* IV, *prosa* vii.

Page 165. W. O. Sypherd (*Studies in Chaucer's Hous of Fame*, Publications of the Chaucer Society, 1907, for the issue of 1904, pp. 117–128) discusses these connections in the literature of other countries. I add to his references the early and important passage from the *Roman de la Poire*. His theory of the relation between these three personifications is confirmed by the strophe from Imperial; but like most students of English literature of the Middle Ages, he utterly neglects the important testimony of Spain, partly, I fear, because the critics of Spanish literature themselves have not stressed enough the close dependence upon the focus of literary inspiration, France.

Page 166*. *Baena*, no. 245.

Page 166†. *Baena*, no. 247.

Page 167*. *Baena*, no. 548.

Page 167†. VI, 1.

Page 167‡. F. B. Luquiens, *op. cit*, p. 299. The *verdes laureles*, *flores olientes*, *candidas rosas*, murmuring waters, and shade of a pine are commonplaces; the verbal parallelism is in no case strict enough; the streams of hot and cold water are not to be found in the *Roman*; and it seems to me far-fetched, indeed, to point to the *charboucle* in another passage as an analogy to the boiling spring for light. It is only the ordinary constituents of the garden that are paralleled in the *Roman*; and the presence of at least one extraordinary conception in both authors, such as the carbuncle or the two streams, would be necessary to confirm an interrelation.

Page 167§. This and the two other reminiscences of the *Paris et Vienne* are used by R. Kaltenbacher (*op. cit.*, pp. 362–363) to prove that the romance was known in Spain at least as early as the beginning of the fifteenth century. Whether or not the romance had its origin in Provence or Catalonia (cf. Kaltenbacher, pp. 362–364) is not germane to our purpose; it certainly obtained its greatest vogue in northern and southern France, and it is sufficient that we exemplify the connection of Imperial with these districts.

Page 168. *Par.* X, 64–81 ; XII, 1–21 ; XIII, 1–30.

Page 169. *Baena*, no. 250.

Page 170. The editor of the *Cancionero de Baena* explains these serpents, by a forced interpretation of the queer names, as seven heresies, but the analysis of their attributes and the contrast with the seven Virtues leave no doubt as to their real meaning; cf. Sanvisenti, p. 73, n. 22; Farinelli, pp. 4–5.

Page 171. *Il Tesoretto e il Favoletto di Ser Brunetto Latini*, Gio. Batista Zannoni, Florence, 1824, *cap.* XIII, 39–40 ; cf. also ed. *Bibliotheca romanica*, pp. 50–51.

Page 172*. P. Savi-Lopez, *Dantes Einfluss auf spanische Dichter des XV Jahrhunderts*, Naples, 1901, p. 5 ; Farinelli, *Dante in Ispagna*, p. 5; *Grundriss*, II, 1, 829.

Page 172†. Ed. Jubinal, II, 169 ff.

Page 172‡. *Grundriss*, II, 1, 870; *Hist. litt. de la France*, XXIII, 260.

Page 172§. *Grundriss*, II, 1, 1051 ; ed. Scheler, II, 162 ff.

Page 172‖. *The Works of John Gower*, ed. G. C. Macaulay, French works, Oxford, 1899, p. xlii ; for a brief and comprehensive summary, cf. pp. xlix–lii. Juan de la Cuenca in the fifteenth century translated the *Confessio amantis* into Spanish.

Page 173*. *Grundriss*, II, 1, 1152; Joseph Nève, *Antoine de la Salle, Sa vie et ses ouvrages*, Paris, 1903, p. 71 ; published by Nève, following the *Réconfort de Mme. du Fresne*, Brussels, 1881, pp. 45–63.

Page 173†. *Capitolo* III ; ed. Foligno, 1725, I, 261 ff.; for an analysis of the work, cf. Gaspary, *Gesch. der ital. Lit.*, Italian translation, II, 1, 88 ff.

Page 174. Cf. Sypherd, *op. cit.*, pp. 18, 77, where a list of invocations is given from mediaeval Latin writers, from French, and from Boccaccio.

Page 175. Cf. Scartazzini's note in the edition of 1903.

Page 177. Sypherd, *op. cit.*, p. 57.

Page 180. For a detailed discussion of these verbal imitations and of Dante's influence upon Imperial, cf. C. R. Post, *The Beginnings of the Influence of Dante*, etc., pp. 9 ff.

Page 182. For an extended examination of these topics, cf. C. R. Post, *op. cit.*

Page 183*. All that we know of him is comprised in the lines at the head of his pieces in the *Cancionero de Baena :* " Rruy Paes de Rrybera, vesino de Sevilla, el qual era omme muy sabio entendido." The editor of the *Cancionero* (p. 675, n. clxxii) collects hypotheses about him.

Page 183†. *Baena*, the first composition having the number 289.

Page 184*. Discussed and published by A. Piaget, *Rom.*, XXVII, 55 ff.; cf. *Grundriss*, II, 1, 831.

Page 184†. For bibliography, cf. *Grundriss*, II, 1, 1074.

Page 184‡. Ed. Scheler, pp. 163 ff. ; a good summary is given on page 460 of this edition ; cf. also *Grundriss*, II, 1, 851.

Page 185*. *Baena*, no. 288.

Page 185†. *Baena*, nos. 295 and 296, which, though separated in the *Cancionero*, are plainly parts of the same composition.

Page 187*. *Beginnings of the Influence of Dante*, etc., pp. 29–30.

Page 187†. *Baena*, no. 290.

Page 187‡. *Op. cit.*, pp. 320–320b.

Page 187§. V. 8928.

Page 187‖. *Baena*, no. 291.

Page 187¶. *Baena*, second of the compositions numbered 289.

Page 188*. Ribera's ideas about Poverty, as Puymaigre indicates (*La Cour*, I, 95), may have some connection with the thirteenth chapter of the apocryphal Book of *Ecclesiasticus*.

Page 188†. *Rime di M. Cino da Pistoia e d'altri del secolo xiv*, ed. G. Carducci, Florence, 1862, p. 303.

Page 189. For instance, Fray Diego de Valencia, cf. nos. 504–507 of the *Cancionero de Baena*.

Page 190*. *Baena*, no. 11; the poems to Doña Juana may very well have been written for the King himself to send to his mistress.

Page 190†. *Baena*, no. 42.

Page 191*. *Baena*, no. 12.

Page 191†. *Baena*, no. 15.

Page 191‡. *Baena*, no. 16.

Page 191§. *Baena*, no. 41.

Page 191‖. *Baena*, no. 40.

Page 192*. *Baena*, no. 25.

Page 192†. *Baena*, no. 199.

Page 192‡. *Baena*, no. 334.

Page 192§. Cf. above, p. 42.

Page 193*. Ed. Scheler, I, 288, vv. 2252 ff.

Page 193†. Cf. above, p. 191.

Page 193‡. *Baena*, no. 63.

Page 194*. *Baena*, no. 157.

Page 194†. *Baena*, no. 170.

Page 194‡. *Baena*, no. 94.

Page 195*. *Baena*, no. 258.

Page 195†. *Baena*, nos. 277–278.

Page 196*. *Baena*, no. 257.

Page 196†. *Baena*, no. 372.

Page 196‡. *Baena*, no. 255.

Page 197*. Cf. Luquiens, *op. cit.*, pp. 307–310.

Page 197†. *Baena*, no. 515.

Page 197‡. *Baena*, no. 338. The heading reads *Juana* by mistake (*Baena*, p. 682, n. ccvi).

Page 197§. *Baena*, no. 339.

Page 198*. His son, Bayezid, was the one really subjugated by Tamerlane (*Baena*, p. 683, n. ccvii).

Page 198†. III, 1.

Page 198‡. VI, 1.

Page 199*. Cf. Amador, *Hist.*, V, 298; Puymaigre, *La cour*, I, 51; *Canc. de Stúñiga*, p. 416, n. xvi.

Page 199†. *Canc. de Stúñiga*, pp. 86–93.

Page 199‡. *Canc. de Stúñiga*, pp. 180–184.

Page 200. *Bibl. de aut. esp.*, LVII, 379 ff.

Page 201*. *Bibl. de aut. esp.*, LVII, 387–388.

Page 201†. Although the vision takes place in 1382 (Spanish fashion, 1420), I consider it together with the present group because it belongs to the very end of the preceding century. With all probability it postdates the prose version, which was written after 1330 and which I have designated as the fourteenth-century link in the chain. (Cf. Octavio de Toledo, *op. cit.*, pp. 42 and 47.)

Page 201‡. Cf. *Purg.*, V, 103 ff.

Page 202. *Obras*, pp. 1 ff.

Page 205. The word *Ninfal* very probably refers to the *Ameto*, for Schiff (*op. cit.*, p. 333) notes a Castilian translation of it in Santillana's library under the title *Ninfal d'Admeto*; the point would be the same for the *Ninfale fiesolano*, which is an allegory in the mould of a classic myth.

Page 206*. Cf. Sanvisenti (p. 193, n. 112), who maintains emphatically that the piece is thoroughly French; also Luquiens (*op. cit.*, pp. 320 ff.), who unnecessarily traces the enmity between Venus and Diana to not very closely similar passages in the *Roman*. Santillana possessed at least three manuscripts of this poem (cf. Schiff, *op. cit.*, pp. 368–370).

Page 206†. Vv. 1689 ff.

Page 206‡. *Li Tornoiemenz Antecrit*, ed. G. Wimmer, *Ausg. und Abh.*, no. lxxvi, Marburg, 1888; ed. also P. Tarbé, Rheims, 1851.

Page 207*. Cf. the elaborate analysis of this encyclopaedic imitation of the *Roman de la Rose* by E. Sieper, *Les Echecs Amoureux*, Weimar, 1898, pp. 27 ff.

Page 207†. Cf. Gaspary, *Gesch. der ital. Litt.*, Italian translation, II, 1, 91.

Page 207‡. *Baena*, no. 309 ; *Macías*, ed. H. A. Rennert, Philadelphia, 1900, pp. 44–45.

Page 208. It is possible, also, that the unusual and recondite allusion in the twelfth *copla* of the *Defunción* is drawn from the eighth chapter of the *Fiammetta*.

Page 209. *Obras*, pp. 365 ff. By a strange error, Farinelli (p. 57) fails to recognize a fragmentary version of the poem which appears in the *Cancionero de Stúñiga* (p. 230) under the name of Juan de Mena, but which the editor, Fuensanta, (p. 447) rightly assigns to Santillana, to whom it is given by all the other manuscripts. Farinelli uses it as an example of Juan de Mena's mention of Dante's name.

Page 210. Ed. Trojel, pp. 91 ff.

Page 211.* The composition is published by Raynouard, *Lexique Roman*, I, 405 ff., and Mahn, *Werke*, I, 241 ff. It is not certain that the Peire in question is Peire Guilhem.

Page 211.† Ed. Saint Hilaire, II, 193 ff.

Page 211.‡ III, 31. In another reading of the Spanish strophe (*Obras*, p. 369, n. 21) Dante has not so much importance :

> Ví al sabio Salomon,
> Euclides, Séneca, Dante ;

and his name always furnishes a convenient rhyme in *ante*.

Page 211.§ Ed. Scheler, I, 30, vv. 971–1004.

Page 214.* Though in the manuscripts cited by Amador in his introduction (p. clvii ff.) these three poems do not appear in conjunction, the strong internal evidence still holds me to a belief in the trilogy. In both of the two principal codices, M. 59 of the Biblioteca Nacional and VII, Y, 4, of the royal Biblioteca Patrimonial (which according to Amador was certainly written during the poet's life and may be that which was given to Gómez Manrique), out of almost fifty separate compositions the three in question occur within the small space of eight numbers, and are interrupted only by five short pieces. In M. 28 of the Biblioteca Nacional the *Triunphete* follows directly upon the *Infierno*. It might be regarded as an objection to my order of arrangement that in the first two codices mentioned and also in VII, D, 4, of the Biblioteca Patrimonial the *Sueño* appears after the *Infierno*. But even though Santillana wrote it or published it after the other two, I contend that he meant it to be the introductory one of the series. I have pointed out how well such a position harmonizes with the opening lines of the *Triunphete;* and it is a process much more natural and more usual in other writers that one should fall under the dominion of Love, and then be freed, than that he should make so definite a renunciation as in the *Finida* of the *Infierno*, and then again be wounded. The *Infierno* also presents a more developed figurative style than the *Sueño*. Since the *Triunphete*, which precedes the *Infierno* even more logically than the *Sueño* does the other two, is placed, in the three codices mentioned, before the *Infierno*, but in M. 28 of the Biblioteca Nacional after it, inaccuracy in arranging the less closely related *Sueño* and *Triunphete* is more intelligible. Even if the final position for the *Sueño* could be proved, a certain relation between the three might still exist, and the order of the *Triunphete* and *Infierno*, which exemplifies an imitation of Petrarch, would be undisturbed. Foulché-Delbosc, in the recently published *Canc. cast. del siglo XV*, like Amador

de los Ríos in his edition, prints the three poems together in the order that I have suggested.

Page 214.† *Obras*, pp. 400 ff.

Page 215. *Obras*, pp. 405 ff.

Page 217.* *La Cour*, II, 39.

Page 217.† Ed. Du Chesne, pp. 594 ff.

Page 217.‡ Cf. *Grundriss*, II, 1, 1103.

Page 219. *Obras*, pp. 332 ff.

Page 220.* Santillana, like most others, read here *Titone*
and not *Titan*.

Page 220.† Santillana knew no Latin, at least in his early
life, but he seems to have acquired a smattering later,
although he read his classics chiefly in translation; cf.
J. Fitzmaurice-Kelly, *Chapters on Spanish Literature*,
London, 1908, p. 68.

Page 220.‡ *Obras*, pp. 240 ff.

Page 221.* V. 6815.

Page 221.† The phrase, *al pié de un collado*, is so ordinary
that its similarity to *al piè d'un colle* (*Inf.*, I, 13) implies
no relation.

Page 222. III, 29; IV, 69.

Page 223. *Obras*, pp. 93 ff.

Page 224. Ed. Lettenhove, VII, 75 ff.

Page 226.* This, Boccaccio's masterpiece, was not so
popular in early Spanish literature as his other works,
but it seems at least to have been known in the fifteenth
century: cf. C. B. Bourland, *Boccaccio and the Decameron in Castilian*, etc., pp. 24 ff.

Page 226.† *Fiammetta*, *cap.* V; Sanvisenti (p. 188, n. 14)
gives this as *cap.* III, in which is described only Fiammetta's grief at her lover's absence.

Page 227. *Obras*, pp. 299 ff.

Page 228. *Par.* VIII, 16–17. Farinelli (p. 55) would derive the similes of the eagle returning to its young and the lover to the beloved from the dove returning to its mate in the Francesca canto; but he is justified neither by similarity of context nor approximation of diction. In a Catholic country where the angelic salutation is so often said, the phrase *quien dixo : ave* might very naturally be applied to Gabriel without the interposition of extraneous influences; and in this phrase and others, critics are too ready to suppose a direct relation to Dante rather than to Imperial's treatment of Dante.

Page 229.* V. 29.

Page 229.† Employed only to give the *tiempo poético* in the beginning and to denominate the few symbolic animals.

Page 230.* *Obras*, pp. 145 ff.

Page 230.† P. 50.

Page 234.* I abbreviate this chapter, not because Juan de Mena is unimportant as an allegorist, but because I have already discussed him at length in a recent article to which I refer the reader, *Romanic Review*, III, 223–279.

Page 234.† *Canc. castellano del siglo XV, Nueva bibl. de aut. esp.*, 19, I, 152–182.

Page 236. Only 297 are usually ascribed to Juan de Mena, and the three others are thought to have been written by someone else.

Page 239. *Canc. castellano*, I, 208–214.

Page 240. *Canc. castellano*, I, 120 ff.

Page 241.* *Rev. hisp.*, IX, 252 ; now published in the *Canc. castellano*, I, 206–208.

Page 241.† Farinelli even questions the attribution to Juan de Mena. Cf. Farinelli, *Dante in Ispagna*, p. 58, n. 1 ; cf. also *Note sulla fortuna del Petrarca in Ispagna*, *Gior. stor.*, XLIV, 328, n. 1.

Page 242.* *Canc. Gom. Man.*, I, 103–115.

Page 242.† Of course, not the famous Garcilaso, who died in 1536.

Page 243.* *Canc. Gom. Man.*, I, 30–32.

Page 243.† *Canc. Gom. Man.*, II, 122–127.

Page 243.‡ *Canc. Gom. Man.*, I, 168–176.

Page 244. *Purg.*, XVI, 37–39 ; cf. also *Purg.*, III, 88 ff.

Page 246. If Sypherd (*op. cit.*, pp. 140 ff.) discerns some influence of Irish wattle houses in Chaucer's house of tidings, why may not Diego de Burgos have had in mind, at least indistinctly, bull-rings ? In connection with Chaucer's poem, it is interesting to note that the enclosure of the Spanish poem is also of wicker-work.

Page 249.* Cf. del Balzo, *op cit.*, p. 176.

Page 249.† Summarized by Menéndez y Pelayo, *Ant.*, VI, cclxviii.

Page 250. Menéndez y Pelayo, *Ant.*, II, 199 ff. On the question of this poet's identity, cf. *Canc. de Stúñiga*. p. 416, n. xv.

Page 251. Summary in Amador, *Hist.*, VII, 249, n. 2.

Page 252.* *Teatro completo*, ed. F. Asenjo Barbieri, Madrid, 1893, pp. 157 ff.

Page 252.† E. Cotarelo y Mori, *Don Enrique de Villena*, Madrid, 1896, pp. 36–37, especially 37, n. 3 ; also F. B. Navarro, Introduction to the *Arte Cisoria*, Madrid, 1879, p. xli; Menéndez y Pelayo, *Ant.*, V, xxxi, n. 1.

Page 254. *Obras*, Introduction, p. xxii.

Page 255. Cf. Farinelli, pp. 17–18 and 72; Menéndez y Pelayo, *Ant.*, V, p. ccxxxii.

Page 256. *Bibl. de aut. esp.*, XXXVI, 339 ff.

Page 261.* *Romanic Review*, IV, 1, 58–75. The same scholar has pointed out the sources of some of the didactic matter in *Publ. of Mod. Lang. Ass.*, XXVIII, 188–212.

Page 261.† *Dos tratados de Alfonso de Palencia*, *Libros de antaño*, Madrid, 1876.

Page 263.* *Ibid.*

Page 263.† F. R. Uhagón, *Un canc. del siglo XV*, Madrid, 1900, pp. 39–42.

Page 263.‡ For an account of this work, which I have not been able to read, cf. Menéndez y Pelayo, *Ant.*, VI, cclxxxiv ff.

Page 264. Ed. Menéndez y Pelayo, *Ant.*, III, 6–20.

Page 265. Ed. at London, 1842, *Col. de obras poéticas españolas*; now newly published in the *Canc. castellano del siglo XV*, I, 288–423.

Page 268. Cf. Amador, *Hist.*, VII, 266 ff.; Menéndez y Pelayo, *Ant.*, VI, ccxlviii ff.; Sanvisenti, pp. 226 ff.

Page 269.* Summary in Amado *Hist.*, VII, 176–177.

Page 269.† Published by Amador at the end of his *Hist.*, VII, 507–540.

Page 270.* *Canc. gen.*, no. 937.

Page 270.† *Cancioneiro de Resende*, ed. A. M. Huntington, New York, 1904, pp. lv–lvii; Menéndez y Pelayo, *Ant.*, IV, 102–118.

*Page 271.** For a summary of the two rare compositions of Guerrero, cf. Gallardo, *Ensayo*, I, 164–166; Farinelli (*Dante in Ispagna*, p. 66) is ignorant of the second's existence and confuses its material with that of the first.

Page 271.† *Canc. castellano del siglo XV*, I, 63–72.

*Page 272.** *Ibid.*, 72–78; Menéndez y Pelayo, *Ant.*, IV, 344–361.

Page 272.† *Canc. castellano*, 79–94.

*Page 273.** Cf. Menéndez y Pelayo, *Ant.*, VI, cclxxii ff.

Page 273.† *Canc. gen.*, no. 131.

Page 273.‡ *Canc. gen.*, no. 125.

Page 273.§ *Jorge Manrique, Poesías, Clas. cast.*, pp. 141–146.

*Page 274.** *Poesías*, pp. 59–61.

Page 274.† *Canc. gen.*, no. 832.

Page 274.‡ *Canc. gen.*, no. 109; Menéndez y Pelayo, *Ant.*, III, 189–193.

Page 274.§ *Poesías*, pp. 65–70.

Page 274.|| *Canc. gen.*, no. 818.

Page 274.¶ *Canc. de Stúñiga*, pp. 217–218.

*Page 274.*** *Canc. inédito de J. A. Gato*, Madrid, 1901, pp. 196–200; *Canc. castellano del siglo XV*, I, 261–263.

Page 274.†† *Poesías*, pp. 76–79.

*Page 275.** *Canc. gen.*, no. 890.

Page 275.† *Canc. gen.*, no. 908.

Page 275.‡ *Canc. gen.*, II, pp. 421–423.

Page 275.§ *Canc. de Stúñiga*, pp. 118–125.

Page 275.|| Amador, *Hist.*, VI, 180, n. 1.

Page 276.* E. de Ochoa, *Rimas inéditas*, Paris, 1844, pp. 389–391.

Page 276.† Amador, *Hist.*, VI, 180.

Page 276.‡ *Teatro completo*, pp. 326 ff.

Page 278.* For a thorough discussion of the character and date of these buildings, cf. Lampérez y Romea, *Historia de la arquitectura cristiana española en la Edad Media*, I, 119 ff., — perhaps the greatest work on architecture ever written.

Page 278.† C. Enlart, *L'architecture romane*, in A. Michel's *Histoire de l'art*, I, ii, 558 ff.

Page 279. Cf. Lampérez, II, especially pp. 16–18.

Page 280.* E. Bertaux in Michel's *Histoire de l'art*, II, i, 273 ff.; and ii, 654 ff.

Page 280.† E. Bertaux, *op. cit.*, II, i, 412 ff.

Page 281.* Cf. Farinelli, *Dante in Ispagna*, p. 56, n. 1.

Page 281.† G. Milanesi, edition of Vasari, Florence, 1878, II, 6–7, 151. The presence of Starnina in Spain has at last received documentary verification ; cf. A. Schmarsow, *Arte e storia*, XXX (1911), 205–206.

Page 281.‡ These surmises depend upon the untrustworthy assertions of Vasari. A. Schmarsow (*Masaccio-Studien*, V, Kassel, 1899, pp. 116–124) tends to consider him a transitional master ; A. Venturi (*Storia dell' arte italiana*, Milan, 1907, V, 835) confines himself to facts. Possibly the frescoes of the chapel of San Blas at Toledo are to be ascribed to Starnina.

Page 281.§ Cf. E. Bertaux, *op. cit.*, III, ii, 757 ff.

Page 282. P. Lafond, *La sculpture espagnole*, Paris, 1908, p. 60 ; E. Bertaux, *op. cit.*, IV, ii, 821.

Page 285. R. Koechlin in Michel, *op. cit.*, II, i, 502.

INDEX

INDEX

Alanus de Insulis, 55, 164, 221, 236, 261.
Alexandre, Libro de, 11, 22, 36, 44, 124, 137, 141, 284.
Alighieri, Pietro, 227.
Allegory: continuity, 13; definition, 3; delight in, 145; erotic, 34, 36, 40, 49, 252, 273, 285; handling of allegorical material, 42, 96; mythological allegory, 17, 204, 240, 253; political, 35, 261, 271; relation to vision, 7.
Amadís de Gaula, 25, 26.
Amador de los Ríos, J., 13, 20, 28.
Andreas Capellanus, 78, 210.
Andújar, Juan del, 26, 84.
Apocalypse, The, 229, 284.
Apologia Mulierum, 79.
Apolonio, Libro de, 22.
Architecture, Spanish: Flamboyant, 282; Gothic, 279; Plateresque, 283; Romanesque, 278.
Architrenius, The, 221.
Armour, Allegorical, 40, 143, 151, 155, 274.
Art, Allegorical, 277, 283.
Art, Its relation to literature, 277.
Artés, Jerónimo de, 36, 240, 270.
Arts, The Liberal, 52, 60, 64, 257, 260.
Aventura Amorosa, 131.

Baena, Alfonso de, 195, 196.
Baist, G., 13.
Barba, 274.
Bartolo, 255.
Bataille de Carême et de Charnage, 145.
Battle, The figurative, 40, 206, 273.
Benoît de Sainte-More, 24.
Benvenuto da Imola, 29, 60, 65, 227, 240.
Berceo, Gonzalo de, 16, 135, 145;

allegorical methods, 118; attitude towards the vision, 9; *Duelo de la Virgen*, 22; *Milagros*, 42, 118, 120, 136, 269; *Signos que Aparescerán*, 22, 128; *Vida de Santa Oria*, 52, 118, 120, 136, 228, 284; *Vide de Santo Domingo*, 53, 118, 136, 284.
Berruguete, Pedro, 282.
Biblical examples, 142.
Boccaccio, 31, 50, 81, 85, 98, 204, 212, 214, 255;
Ameto, 205, 255;
Amorosa Visione, 32, 60, 224, 236, 238;
Corbaccio, 32, 81, 208, 221;
Decameron, 226;
De Casibus, 32, 167, 197, 224;
De Claris Mulieribus, 142;
Fiammetta, 94, 208, 226;
Filocolo, 226, 240.
Boethius, 115, 165, 225, 261.
Borgoña, Juan de, 282.
Bornelh, Guiraut de, 192.
Botticelli, Sandro, 18.
Breton matter, 25.

Calderón, 107.
Cámara, Juan Rodríguez de la, 17, 47, 214;
Coronación de Macías, 256;
Erotic parodies of the liturgy, 254;
Siervo Libre de Amor, 50, 94, 204, 212;
Triunfo de las Donas and the *Cadira del Honor*, 254.
Capella, Martianus, 260.
Carrillo, Alonso, 72.
Carroz y Pardo, Francés, 275.
Castigos y Documentos, 23, 143.
Celestina, The, 26.
Chartier, Alain, 79, 203, 217, 223.
Chastellain, Georges, 224.